WALKING WITH THE POOR

WALKING WITH THE POOR

Principles and Practices of Transformational Development

Bryant L. Myers

ORBIS ✦ BOOKS

Maryknoll, New York 10545

World Vision

The Catholic Foreign Mission Society of America (Maryknoll) recruits and trains people for overseas missionary service. Through Orbis Books, Maryknoll aims to foster the international dialogue that is essential to mission. The books published, however, reflect the opinions of their authors and are not meant to represent the official position of the society.

To obtain more information about Maryknoll and Orbis Books, please visit our website at www.maryknoll.org.

ORBIS/ISBN 0-57075-275-3

To the triune God
who found this book in me and
helped let it emerge, and

To my wife and life-long
mentor and love, Lisa,
who encouraged me to believe
that God could do such a thing.

Contents

Development Theories

Figures

Foreword

Paul G. Hiebert

This book is a masterpiece of integration and application in thinking about Christian ministry. The author draws widely on the best Christian and scientific sources on introducing change in human societies and forms solid conclusions based on what we have learned from experience in development ministries around the world. He develops a solid, scripturally based framework, or theoretical structure, that challenges the spiritual/natural dualism which pervades our Western worldview and that offers a consistent biblical worldview in its place. He shows how this vision of Christian ministry can be implemented in transformational development that is truly *transformational* in the full sense of the word, and *development* in that the transformations are lasting and profound.

Myers's focus on relationships and stories is particularly helpful in developing a holistic view of ministry. This approach brings people together and builds bridges of understanding and communication, whereas abstract analytical categories often separate them. Relationships and stories also help us see that the kingdom of God is central to God's plan for the universe, for peoples, and for individuals.

Myers does more than give us a new vision of what Christian ministry might be like. He provides guidelines for implementing this vision in life and ministry in ways that are consistent with the vision, and he reminds us that the life and relationships of Christians are the most powerful testimonies to the transforming power of God. In this, Myers points out that those who serve and those who are served must both grow spiritually in encounters of ministry.

The book is written for those involved in Christian development programs and challenges them to move toward holistic ministries. It is of equal importance for those involved in evangelism and church planting. It is a "charter" for a new way of doing mission, and the implications of its vision are far-reaching for all who serve Christ in the world. Too often in church planting we have relegated God's transforming work to spiritual realities and assigned earthly matters to science and technology. The result is a schizophrenic Christianity that leaves the everyday problems of human life to secular specialists and limits God to matters of eternity. A truly holistic approach to mission rooted in biblical truth is as essential in planting vital churches that remain Christ-centered over the generations as it is in Christian ministries of compassion.

Probably the greatest reward to many readers will be the way the author challenges our own distorted worldviews that have blinded us from understanding what it means to be living witnesses and servants in a world in desperate need. Such challenges are often costly, for they call us to experience radical transformations in our own lives and ministries.

Acknowledgments

No book such as this one is the work of one author. A lifetime of relationships and a great deal of lived experience form the raw material from which an author tries to pull together an articulation of what he or she has learned and hopes that others will find worth reading. For me, this is even more the case, since I am a person who creates by synthesizing, by pulling things together and fitting them into larger frameworks. I learn in community, listening to others, reading widely, brainstorming with enthusiasm, knowing that in time I will tumble on a frame that fits the many and disparate pieces together. Yet few of the pieces are mine; they are the faithful and precious work of others. I may refine or even extend them, but I always begin with the offering of others. This is what makes thanking others an important place for me to start.

Generative ideas

This book draws and builds on two powerful sets of ideas: Paul Hiebert's description of the Western worldview and its excluded middle, and Jayakumar Christian's understanding of the nature of poverty as relationships that do not work and the cause of poverty as being spiritual. I am deeply indebted to the creative work of these two men and for their friendship and counsel over the years.

Drawing on his experience in India, Paul Hiebert has had two significant insights that have proved very helpful to me and others in Christian mission. The first is his formulation of the Western worldview in terms of two separated realms—material and spiritual—with a gap between the two, the "excluded middle." Linking this with the thinking of Lesslie Newbigin provides the explanation for many of the dichotomies with which Western Christians struggle: faith and reason, evangelism and development, church and state, and values and facts. These dichotomies are major hindrances to finding a genuinely holistic Christian approach to human transformation.

Hiebert's second important insight is that the Western worldview, with its separated spiritual and material realms, has a particular kind of impact when it encounters the holistic, spiritist worldview of traditional cultures. Those of us carrying a Western worldview take it for granted that the location of cause and effect is in the material world. In contrast, traditional cultures believe that the cause of things is located in the unseen world of spirits and gods. The absence of a "middle" in the Western worldview means that we have no way to make sense of or respond to the very active and important "middle" of traditional cultures. This framework has proved to have a great deal of explanatory power when one comes to the work of development promoters and their tool kit of technological interventions, as well as our thinking as to how Christian witness and development intersect.

Jayakumar Christian is a World Vision co-worker and a personal friend of almost twenty years. Jayakumar has offered a family of ideas about the nature and causes of poverty that break us free from the material language and definitions that tend to dominate conversations about poverty. In his Ph.D. work Jayakumar offered the idea that poverty is experienced most fundamentally by the poor as a marring of their identity and that this is caused both by the grind of being poor and also by being captive to the god-complexes of the non-poor. I found these ideas liberating and highly generative. They provide the platform on which I frame my understanding of transformational development done by Christians.

I employ Jayakumar's ideas liberally in this book and then build on them. To the idea that playing god in the lives of the poor results in a marring of the identity of the poor, I add that it also mars the identity of the non-poor. They cannot play god and be who they are in God's sight. To Jayakumar's proposal that transformation is the work of helping the poor recover their true identity as made in the image of God, I add the idea that vocation or calling is also part of true identity. Our identity in biblical terms is both who we are and what we do. The poor and the non-poor need God's redemptive help to recover their true identity as children of God made in God's image and their true vocation as productive stewards, given gifts by God to contribute to the well-being of all.

Formation

As a practitioner, I am indebted to many people. I began my journey in transformational development with Hal Barber and his relief and development innovation in World Vision in 1976. Our journey began with a stimulating three weeks with James Yen and Juan Javier at the International Institute of Rural Reconstruction in the Philippines. Over the years I have been influenced and enriched by a family of development professionals who have attended conferences, hosted me for field visits, and written papers that have influenced me. These include Mulegeta Abebe, Mulatu Belachew, Bruce Bradshaw, Rebecca Cherono, Ben Chitambar, Frank Cookingham, Helena Eversole, Judy Hutchinson, Bob Linthicum, Ken Luscombe, Eric Ram, Paul Peterson, Christina Lee Showalter, John Stewart, Morris Stuart, Bryan Truman, and Corina Villacorta.

In particular, I am deeply indebted to Ravi Jayakaran, Nora Avarientos, Sarone Ole Sena, and Jayakumar Christian, all of whom were willing to invest many hours in telephone interviews as a way of contributing to this book. Ravi Jayakaran is an expert in Participatory Rural Appraisals (PRAs) and has done pioneering work on enabling this method to allow the spiritual side of the traditional worldview to be heard. Nora Avarientos, together with Malcolm Bradshaw, developed the Scripture Search methodology for using the Bible in the context of community development in the Philippines. Sarone Ole Sena, a Masai anthropologist, along with Dirk Booy, a Canadian, is the World Vision pioneer in applying Appreciative Inquiry to development planning in Tanzania.

As a lay theologian, I am particularly thankful for those who shared in my theological formation, as ad hoc as it may have been. My introduction to thinking theologically about development began with Vinay Samuel and Chris Sugden and their workshops with World Vision in Asia in the early 1980s. I am also indebted to Dr. Sam Kameleson, who mentored me patiently over his years in World Vision. I also recall, with some chagrin, a challenging and stimulating evening at Wheaton '83, when a kindly and learned man spent four hours patiently answering my simple questions about missiology; his name was David Bosch. I learned to think biblically and to trust that the word of God always has something to say to the world from Tom Houston, when he was the international president of World Vision.

In addition, the International Network of Evangelical Mission Theologians (INFEMIT) has provided a family of friends who have nurtured my understanding of theology and development from the perspectives of cultures other than my own. These friends include Valdir Steuernagel, Tito Paredes, Rene Padilla, Kwame Bediako, and Miraslav Volf. In the United States I am indebted to Ron Sider and my co-workers in MARC, Saphir Athyal and Tom McAlpine.

For this book I must say a special thanks to my friend Bill Dyrness for his willingness to review, and then review again, my chapter on the biblical story. I am also appreciative of Saphir Athyal, who also reviewed the theology chapter. Of course, all the lousy theology that remains in the chapter is my responsibility.

Means

The chapter on Christian witness draws on research made possible by the Dellenback Initiative of World Vision US. Field research into Christian witness in the context of relief and development and several small consultations with practitioners and theologians were made possible through this initiative. I am very grateful to the leadership and commitment of Bob Seiple and Ron Vander Pol, whose vision made this possible.

Personal gratitude

In the Bible we are told that the last is really the first. And so it is with these acknowledgments. I am indebted to my mother, Patricia Myers, for setting aside her loft, enduring my bewildering pile of papers and books, and making my lunch during the months that I wrote this book in her home. She prayed for a lost and hopeless son for many years before God finally relented and dragged me into his kingdom at the age of 31. I am deeply grateful that she is alive to see the book that summarizes why she and God went to all that work.

I am also deeply grateful to Tom and Hazle Houston, who turned over their home in Oxford to the Myers clan for five weeks in the summer of 1997. This book was born in Tom's study, and our family became closer to each other and to God in Hazle's sitting room.

I must also thank Dean Hirsch, the international president of World Vision, and the International Board of World Vision for allowing me the time to complete the research and write this book. It took longer than I expected, and they were very patient. I can only hope that this book in some small way advances the mission of World Vision around the world.

Finally and most important, I must acknowledge the unpayable debt I owe my family. My children, Brooke and James, of whom I am exceedingly proud, have taught me more than I ever taught them. There is no better or harsher corrective to one's thinking about human transformation and development than one's children. There are not enough words to convey my appreciation, affection, and love for my wife, my long-time mentor, my friend and deepest love, Lisa. At great sacrifice to her own aspirations, she has encouraged, nurtured, and supported me. I can only pray that this all proves worthy of her sacrifice.

WALKING WITH THE POOR

1

Charting the Course

IN THE BEGINNING

The purpose of this book is to describe a proposal for understanding the principles and practice of transformational development (positive material, social, and spiritual change) from a Christian perspective. It is my intention to try to bring together three basic streams of thinking and experience. The best of the principles and practice of the international development community needs to be integrated with the thinking and experience of Christian relief and development nongovernmental organizations (NGOs). Then these two streams of experience need to be informed and shaped by a biblical framework for transformational development.

Throughout this book I will struggle to overcome problems presented by the persistent and insistent belief in the West that the spiritual and physical domains of life are separate and unrelated. This assumption has invaded and controlled almost every area of intellectual inquiry, including development theory and practice as well as much Christian theology. I will seek an understanding of development in which physical, social, and spiritual development are seamlessly interrelated.

Origins

The pilgrimage that this book represents had its origin in 1975, the year World Vision received a Development Program Grant from the Agency for International Development for the purpose of helping World Vision begin its relief and development ministry. I was part of the original team. We went to Washington, D.C., took a three-day course in development planning and were then released to help World Vision's seven offices in Asia begin planning their first development programs. God forgive us for our sins.

The 1970s and early 1980s were interesting times for Christian relief and development agencies. It was a time full of argument and sometimes divisive discussions among evangelicals as to whether or not Bible-believing Christians ought to do development. Some were deeply concerned that including social action in the Christian agenda blunted the church's commitment to evangelism. Evangelism must be primary, went the argument. The modern assumption that the spiritual and the material were unrelated areas of life had infected Christian mission thinking.

Throughout this pilgrimage, many of us in the World Vision family shared a deep-seated concern that development had to be holistic, by which we meant that development and Christian witness should be held together in a creative tension. In these early days we simplistically and incorrectly understood this to mean that Christian witness was something one added to the development mix to make it complete, just another sector, a wedge in the development pie.

In time we realized that this conceptualization was flawed. It implied that all the other development sectors had nothing to do with spiritual things and that we were treating spiritual work as a separate sector of life. This meant that, in the very communities where we wanted to be good models of the Christian faith, we were in fact witnessing that the material and the spiritual realms of life were separate and unrelated. Our struggle to escape this modern assumption led us to a great deal of inquiry concerning both the theology and the worldview of development.

The 1990s were a decade of seeking professionalism. Good intentions were no longer enough. The poor deserved better than gifted amateurs with their hearts in the right place. The world had learned a great deal about development and Christian organizations needed to take this on board. The social sciences were studied and our staff members were sent off to England, Canada, and the United States to learn from centers of development learning in the West.

It is now 1998 and a lot has happened in the intervening twenty-three years. Much has been learned. As a cadre of long-time friends, we have shared our successes and wept over our failures. Hundreds of workshops have been celebrated or endured. Hundreds of papers have been pored over, and many books have been read. Thousands of hours of discussion, anguish, and discovery have taken place in long rides on dusty roads and over the dinner tables in featureless hotels. The outworking of all of this is the source of the thinking in this book.

Definitions

I will use two phrases over and over in this book: *transformational development* and *Christian witness*. It may help the reader if I define them here in the beginning.

Transformational development is the term I use as an alternative to the more traditional *development*. There are two reasons for this. First, the term *development* is heavily loaded with past meaning, not all of which is positive. When most people think of development, they think of material change or social change in the material world. Second, *development* is a term that many understand as a synonym for Westernization or modernization. Too often this understanding of development is associated with having more things. Many in the development business, including many of us in the West, are not sure that this is the kind of development that is good for people or for this planet.

I use the term *transformational development* to reflect my concern for seeking positive change in the whole of human life materially, socially, and spiritually. The adjective *transformational* is used to remind us that human progress is not inevitable; it takes hard work, and there is an adversary who works against our desire to enhance life. True human development involves choices, setting aside that which is not for life in us and our community while actively seeking and supporting all that is for life. This requires that we say no to some things in order to say yes to what really matters. Transformation implies changing our choices.

Transformational development is a lifelong journey. It never ends. There is always more before us. Everyone is on this journey: the poor, the non-poor, and the staff of the development agency. The transformational journey is about finding and enjoying life as it should be, as it was intended to be. In this book I suggest that the goals for this journey of transformation are to recover our true identity as human beings created in the image of God and to discover our true vocation as productive stewards, faithfully caring for the world and all the people in it.

Christian witness is the second phrase that I use frequently. Understanding what I mean by this requires a short introduction. Everyone believes in something, and what we believe in shapes what we do and how we do it. This is no less true for those who are concerned for the poor and wish to help the poor on their development journey. This ideological center is a matter of faith, whether we are Christian, Muslim, Buddhist, agnostic, or atheist. These core values and beliefs are where we get our understanding of who we are and what we are for. These guiding principles shape our understanding of what a better human future is and how we should get there.

I am a Christian, and I have been working among Christians in the development business for over twenty years. My Christian identity and my understanding of my faith shape my view of what development is for and how it should be done. Part of that understanding is my conviction that the best news I have is the knowledge that God has, through his Son, made it possible for every human being to be in a covenant relationship with God. We need only say yes to this offer. To not share this news, to not yearn that everyone might share what was given to me through no merit of my own, would be wrong in the deepest and most profound sense. *Christian witness* is the term that I use to describe this news that Christians are compelled by love to share.

I deliberately chose the phrase *Christian witness* over the word *evangelism* for several reasons. First, like the term *development*, *evangelism* is also a loaded phrase. Images of street evangelists yelling through megaphones and of crusade evangelists exhorting stadiums full of people come to mind, neither of which fits the idea of transformational development very well. Second, and more important, evangelism tends to be used in the limited sense of referring to the verbal proclamation of the truth of the gospel of Jesus Christ. I need a phrase that includes proclamation, but that is not limited to it.

I understand Christian witness to include the declaration of the gospel by *life*, word, and deed. By *life* I refer to the fact that Christians are the message. We are the sixty-seventh book of the Bible. People read our lives, our actions and our words and believe they know what being a Christian means. By *word* I refer to the need to say what the gospel story is and to invite others to make it their story. By *deed* I refer to the fact that the Christian faith, at its best, is an active faith, engaged with the world and seeking to make it more for life and for the enjoyment of life.

There is an important nuance here. There is no such thing as not witnessing. Christian development promoters are witnessing all the time. The only question is to whom or to what? Their deeds, both what they do and how they do it, declare in whom or in what they place their faith and also demonstrate the moral content of that faith. The way they live their lives declares whom they love and on whom they depend. And, if they are truly living lives that demonstrate their love of God and their neighbor, then questions will come to which the gospel is the answer and they will witness with the words that provide this answer.

THE MODERN BLIND SPOT

I have already mentioned that one of the primary characteristics of the twentieth century has been the belief in the West that the spiritual and physical domains of life are separate and unrelated. This dominating assumption controls almost every area of intellectual inquiry, including development theory and practice. The result is a tragic pair of reductions. First, poverty is reduced to a merely material condition having to do with the absence of things like money, water, food, housing and the lack of just social systems, also materially defined and understood. Second, development is reduced correspondingly to a material series of responses designed to overcome these needs.

Since the search for a genuinely biblical and holistic understanding of poverty and transformational development is the focus of this book, I believe it may be helpful to explore the nature of this modern blind spot more fully before going on. Why do we need the word *holistic* in the first place? What is the nature of the problem we are trying to solve by using such a term? There must be something that is not holistic.

The great divorce: Separating the spiritual and physical realms

The place to begin is the way we understand and interpret the world in which we live, something anthropologists call our worldview. Our modern worldview is like a pair of glasses through which we see and make sense out of our world. Unlike glasses, however, our worldview also includes our assumptions about how the world works. Our need for holism has its roots in our modern worldview.

As the foundational paradigm shift of the Enlightenment has worked itself out in Western culture, one of its most enduring features has been the assumption that we can consider the physical and spiritual realms as separate and distinct from one another. On the one hand, there is the spiritual or supernatural world where God lives and acts, along with other cosmic Gods like Allah. This is the world of religion. On the other hand, there is the real world: the material world where we hear, see, feel, touch, and smell. This is the world of science.

Sadly, this is not just a problem for Western folk. This dichotomy, or absolute separation, between the spiritual and the physical is a central tenet of what some call modernity, and modernity is rapidly becoming a dominant overlay on the world's cultures. Modernity is deeply embedded in the modern economic system and in contemporary information technology, both of which are being extended wherever Coca Cola is sold. This same culture of dichotomies is taught in every classroom where the curriculum is based on Western educational models. Thus, every third-world professional has imbibed this worldview as an unspoken part of his or her professional training.

This framework of separated areas of life is also deeply embedded in the Western part of the Christian church, in its theology, and in the daily life of its people. On Sunday morning or during our devotional or prayer life, we operate in the spiritual realm. The rest of the week, and in our professional lives, we operate in the physical realm and, hence, unwittingly act like functional atheists. Simply being Christian does not heal our dichotomous understanding of our world.

The dichotomies of the modern worldview

Lesslie Newbigin (1989) has shown how the modern separation of the physical and spiritual realms explains a wide range of the modern dichotomies that are prevalent in the modern worldview. For example, the spiritual world is the arena of sacred revelation, in which we know by believing. The real world where we hear, see, feel, and touch is where scientific observation allows us to know things with certainty. Faith and religion are part of the spiritual world, while reason and science provide the explanations in the real world. The spiritual world is an interior, private place; the real world is an exterior, public place. This means that values are a private matter of personal choice, having no relevance in the public square where politics and economics reign. Publicly, we only need to agree on the facts. Sadly, the church has also succumbed to this modern worldview and has allowed itself to be relegated to the spiritual world, while the state and other human institutions assume responsibility for what happens in everyday life.

Spiritual	**Material**
Revelation and believing	Observation and knowing
Faith	Reason
Religion	Science
Private and personal	Public
Values	Facts
Church	State

Figure 1-1: The dichotomies of the modern worldview.

Separating Christian witness and social action

Modernity's separation of the physical and spiritual realms is part of the explanation for how we have come to understand Christian witness, and specifically evangelism, as being unrelated to community development. Loving God is spiritual work, and loving neighbors takes place in the material world. So evangelism (restoring people's relationship with God) is spiritual work, while social action (restoring just economic, social, and political relationships among people) is not. In the final analysis this false dichotomy leads Christians to believe that God's redemptive work takes place only in the spiritual realm, while the world is left, seemingly, to the devil.

This two-tiered understanding of the world explains another curious phenomenon. Western governments, as carriers of modernity, separate religion from development because they accept modernity's dictate that church and state be separate because they deal with separate realms. Because the church understands evangelism as an activity appropriate to the spiritual world, while social action—if it is an appropriate activity for the church at all—is the appropriate response in the physical world, the church goes along with this imposed separation of what the gospel suggests is inseparable.

The Christian development agency is not immune to the phenomenon. We express our captivity to a modern worldview when we say that holistic ministry means combining evangelism (meeting spiritual need) with relief and development (meeting physical need) as if these were divisible realms and activities. Then we make it worse by insisting that the church or the evangelism part of our organization do the former, while the development agency does the latter. By so doing we declare development independent of religion, something most of us do not really believe.

Separating word, deed, and sign

Paul Hiebert has developed a very helpful framework that compares the worldviews of modern and traditional cultures. He portrays the modern worldview as two-tiered, with the physical and spiritual worlds completely separated. The traditional worldview is holistic, with the spiritual and material worlds interrelated in a seamless whole. The world of high religion is occupied by the great gods that should not be bothered or disturbed. The interrelationship between the seen and unseen worlds is mediated by shamans, sacred books, spirits, and others who have access to both worlds. This is the world of curses, amulets, charms, and other attempts to bargain with or "handle" the unseen world.

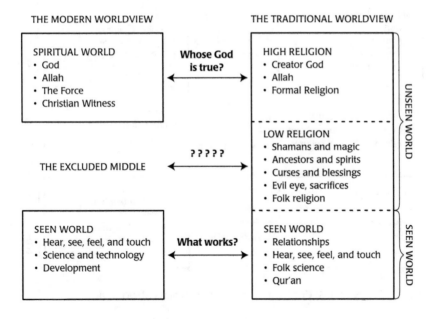

Figure 1-2: Modern and traditional worldviews.
(Adapted from Hiebert 1982)

While the modern world has something to say about high religion and about the physical world, we have nothing to say to the world of folk religion. We suffer from what Hiebert calls "the excluded middle."

We no longer believe in ancestors, spirits, the demonic, and the unseen. That's all superstition and ignorance, after all. Yet, most traditional cultures spend a lot of time being concerned about this world and locate cause and effect there. The impact of this excluded middle from a development perspective is a blind spot. We fail to hear the community's story about the unseen world, and we fail to have answers that, in their minds, adequately take this world into account.

For Christians, it should be humbling to note that, while in no way the same, the biblical worldview is closer to the worldview of traditional cultures than it is to the modern worldview.[1] The biblical worldview is holistic in the sense that the physical world is never understood as being disconnected or separate from the spiritual world and the rule of the God who created it. Moreover, Christ—the creator, sustainer, and redeemer of the creation—is both in us and interceding for us at the right hand of God the Father. The fact that the Word became flesh explodes the claim that the spiritual and physical can be separated meaningfully.

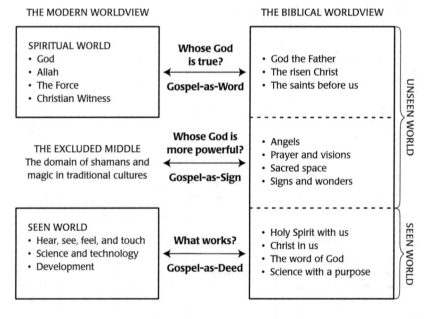

Figure 1-3: Contrasting modern and biblical worldviews.

This comparison also calls attention to the fact that the critical questions change depending on the level at which one is functioning. The gospel addresses the question of truth with gospel-as-word, the truth of God. The gospel addresses questions of power with the gospel-as-sign; the power of God. At the material level of empiricism, the biblical worldview answers the question What works? with good deeds that express the love of God.

This reveals another level of the problem modernity poses to Christian mission. When we separate the spiritual from the physical, not only do we separate evangelism from development, but we separate gospel-as-word from the gospel-as-deed, and provide no home for gospel-as-sign. In the spiritual realm, the critical question is, Whose God is the true God?, and the answer is an idea. This frame allows us to reduce the gospel message to truth in the form of propositions, even a set of "spiritual laws." Christian witness is reduced to words and speaking.

At the level of the physical world, the question is, What works? The answer comes in the form of effective methods and good technology. Deeds and doing are the real thing. We then reduce the gospel message and evangelism to working for justice or saving God's creation.

Separating gospel-as-word, gospel-as-deed, and gospel-as-sign has serious consequences. In cultures in which words have lost their meaning, as is often the case of the West, deeds are necessary to verify what the words mean. Saying we are Christian is ambiguous, since almost everyone claims to be Christian. If we want to know what people mean when they say they are Christian, we look at the quality of their lives. The way we live and act declares to others what we mean when we say we are Christians.

In other cultures deeds can be ambiguous. Whether we speak or not, people receive a message. Discovering water in the desert is a miracle, and animist cultures often interpret the technology that brings it as magic and witchcraft. Research done by Bruce Bradshaw (1993) has discovered this repeatedly in World Vision's development work. In the view of local villagers World Vision has outstanding diviners and powerful shamans on its staff. Development technology, without accompanying words to interpret its good deeds, can result in glory being given to clever or "magical" soil scientists and hydrologists, rather than to God.

We should also note the inadequate way the modern worldview deals with signs. Because there is no place for the appearance of the supernatural in the physical world, there is no home for signs and miracles. For most animists, the existential question has little to do with truth; it has to do with power. Since cause is located in the unseen or spiritual world, the critical question is, Whose god is more powerful? The fact that charismatic and Pentecostal folk have an answer for this question is a major part of the reason they are the fastest growing expression of the church today. The inability of the modern to deal with signs and miracles makes it very difficult for carriers of modernity, such as development practitioners, to carry out meaningful conversations with people who hold a traditional or animist worldview. The development practitioner thinks people are sick because of germs and dirty water, while the people believe they are sick because of curses and witchcraft.

Therefore, in dealing with the gospel message, we cannot separate word, deed, and sign without truncating our message. Words clarify the meaning of deeds. Deeds verify the meaning of words. Most critically, signs announce the presence and power of One who is radically other and who is both the true source of all good deeds and the author of the only words that bring life in its fullest.

Limiting the scope of sin and the gospel

Because we have tended to accept the dichotomy between the spiritual and the physical, we sometimes inadvertently limit the scope of both sin and the gospel. If God's concern is only for the spiritual, then we reduce our understanding of sin to something personal that separates people from God. This in turn tempts us to reduce the scope of redemption to the spiritual or personal realm alone. This makes it hard to understand the impact of sin in the material world of economics, politics, culture, and the church as an institution, and even harder to believe that God's salvific and redemptive work extends to this messy, sinful world. Yet this is the world in which the Christian development agency works.

By limiting the domain of sin to a person's soul, we inadvertently limit the scope of the gospel as well. We need to transform this way of thinking. God's rule extends to both the spiritual and material; the redemptive work of Jesus Christ is needed wherever sin has penetrated. This means we must redefine our understanding of salvation to be more inclusive or holistic without losing its meaning in terms of restoring our relationship with God.

Revelation and observation

Revelation is the way we know in the spiritual realm, while observation and reason are the accepted ways of knowing in the physical realm. This modern dichotomy between revelation and observation conceals some interesting things.

First, the source of knowing is different. Revelation comes from God to us; observation and reason we do for ourselves and, if we are not Christian, without any reference to God. Christians who separate the physical and spiritual realms tend to be God-centered in their spiritual lives and human-centered when they think and act in the physical world. For our spiritual work, we turn to the church and our bibles; for development work, we turn to the social sciences. This goes a long way in explaining why development practices of Christian development agencies often feel "secular."

Second, prayer, fasting, meditation, and other forms of spirituality become spiritual activities relegated to knowing things about the spiritual world. We then fail to see spirituality as a tool for knowing or working in the real world. Few development workers understand prayer and fasting as tools for human transformation or for working for justice. At best, prayer is either a personal, inner communion with God or a request to God for an extracurricular, "hit-and-run" intervention in the real world. On the other side, God and God's revelation are banished from our social analysis, and we are left to interpret our world for ourselves.

Having explored the problem that modernity presents for the Christian practitioner who seeks to promote transformational development, it should be easier to understand why this book follows the path that it does. In every chapter, from the biblical account to principles and practice, I have attempted to overcome this blind spot and either suggest answers or point to further work that needs to be done.

THE PATH OF THIS BOOK

The biblical story

I begin with a chapter on theology. If transformational development is to be biblical, then we need to develop a biblical framework that informs the following discussions on development theory and practice.

Traditional approaches to theology of development have tended to be propositional in nature, drawing on the Exodus account for an understanding of oppression and liberation, the psalms for evidence of God's concern for the poor, and the gospels for examples of how Jesus responded to the poor and taught his disciples. All of this is very helpful and is still important.

In this book, however, I attempt to shift the perspective to a narrative account of the biblical story. I have done this because this perspective better fits and supports what I believe is a very helpful framework for setting the context in which development takes place: the convergence of stories.

The poor already have a story before the development agency arrives. It is both their immediate story and the story of their people. And God has been active in this story since its very beginning, whether or not God's involvement is recognized or not. When development promoters arrive, they bring their story, both their personal story and the story of their development agency. And, for the life of the program, the community and the promoters share a story. The implication is that the community's story is the story that must have the final say and that both the community and the development promoters should anticipate that both of their respective stories will change as a part of the transformational development process.

Viewing the transformational development process as a shared story invites us to question what our stories are for, where they are going, and whose story is the true story. The biblical story provides a very helpful framework for seeking answers to this complex question. The biblical story explains how every community's story began and why its story is full of pain, injustice, and struggle at the same time that it is full of joy, loving relationships, and hope. The biblical story provides the answer to how the stories of the community and the promoter may reorient themselves to that intended by their Creator and describes, in the metaphor of the kingdom of God, what the best human story is like. The biblical story also tells us how all our stories will end. Most important, we can learn what our stories are for: the worship of the one true God.

Poverty

The way we understand the nature of poverty and what causes poverty is very important, because it tends to determine how we respond to poverty. Articulating what poverty is and what causes it helps us determine the source of much of our understanding of what transformational development is and how it should be practiced. The purpose of Chapter 3 is to try and integrate the best of what people have been thinking about the nature of poverty and its cause.

We must begin with ourselves. We need to work hard to discover our assumptions and our preconditioning regarding poverty. This is particularly true for Christians, because there has been a variety of views of the poor, depending on one's Christian tradition.

Chapter 3 then reviews the changing views of poverty as a way of showing that understanding poverty is a never-ending task. In the early days of development many assumed that poverty could be explained by the absence of things. This was followed by adding the absence of ideas or knowledge to the mix, and then, as the systemic nature of poverty was explored, the absence of access to power, resources, and choices became part of our understanding of poverty. In the 1980s a systems view of poverty emerged with Robert Chambers's proposal that poverty is a system of entanglement. In the early 1990s John Friedman added to the discussion by describing poverty as the lack of access to social power, with an emphasis on adding political participation. Weighing in from a Christian perspective, Jayakumar Christian built on Chambers and Friedman by describing poverty as a system of disempowerment that creates oppressive relationships and whose fundamental causes are spiritual. Finally, I introduce Ravi Jayakaran's holistic framework of poverty as a lack of freedom to grow.

The chapter then explores the causes of poverty. I look at the interplay between the physical and social causes of poverty as causes largely external to the poor. I then explore the largely internal contribution to poverty resulting from mental and spiritual causes. Drawing heavily on Jayakumar Christian, I propose that the nature of poverty is fundamentally relational and that its cause is fundamentally spiritual.

The poor are poor largely because they live in networks of relationships that do not work for their well-being. Their relationships with others are often oppressive and disempowering as a result of the non-poor playing god in the lives of the poor. Their relationship within themselves is diminished and debilitated as a result of the grind of poverty and the feeling of permanent powerlessness. Their relationship with those they call "other" is experienced as exclusion. Their relation with their environment is increasingly less productive because poverty leaves no room for caring for the environment. Their relationship with the God who created them and sustains their life is distorted by an inadequate knowledge of who God is and what God wishes for all humankind. Poverty is the whole family of our relationships that are not all they can be.

The relationships of the poor don't work for the well-being of the poor because of spiritual values held by others and by the poor that do not enhance and support life. Selfishness, love of power, and feelings of ordained privilege express themselves in god-complexes. Loss of hope, opportunity, and recognition mar the identity of the poor. Racism, ethnocentrism, and ostracism erode the intended blessing of having many cultures. Fear of spirits and belief in gods that cannot save obscure the offer of the God who desires to save. At the end of the day, the causes of poverty are spiritual.

Perspectives on development

Having developed a holistic framework for thinking about poverty, Chapter 4 surveys a number of ways of thinking about what development is and what it does.

I begin by exploring where our ideas of development come from. The central question is, Who will save us? This is important because there are competing stories in this century, all of which offer salvation. Some believe we will be saved by science and technology. Others rest their faith on free markets and a global economic system. Still others put their faith in human ingenuity and the idea of inevitable human progress. The Christian view of salvation points to the cross and the resurrection as the only framework that can truly bring us home.

I explore a range of proposals for thinking about development. For evangelicals, the conversation started at a Lausanne consultation, Wheaton '83, at which theologians and practitioners moved beyond the debate as to whether evangelism and social action were both legitimate Christian activities and began the search for a biblical framework for understanding development. Of particular note was a paper by Wayne Bragg, then of the Wheaton Hunger Center, in which he proposed the phrase "transformational development" as a holistic biblical alternative to Western modern-ization.

I describe the "people-centered development" proposal of David Korten, in which he calls into question economic growth as an engine for sustain-able development and insists that the environment and the limitations of "spaceship earth" become more central to development conversations. I explore John Friedman's view of an "alternative development" that focuses on expanding the political and social power of poor families by supporting grassroots democratic practices and building civil society. I summarize Robert Chambers's recent proposal of development as responsible well-being, built on the principles of equity and sustainability and pursued by means of in-creasing the livelihood, security, and capabilities of the poor. I close the chapter with a summary of Jayakumar Christian's idea of development as a kingdom response to the powerlessness of the poor that exposes the web of lies about the identity and worth of the poor and the god-complexes of the non-poor to the transforming truth and demands of the kingdom of God.

Toward a Christian understanding of transformational development

With these three pieces in place—a biblical framework, a holistic under-standing of poverty, and a survey of development thinking—Chapter 5 at-tempts a synthesis that pulls many of the pieces together into a proposal for a Christian understanding of transformational development. My proposal begins by stating the obvious: the transformational development journey belongs to God and to those who are on it, not to experts, donor agencies, or development facilitators. Whatever our framework or our methods, we must be willing to set them aside and let the poor discover their own way, just as we have done.

The first question is, What better future? The biblical narrative pro-vides the answer. The best of human futures lies in the direction of the kingdom of God and Jesus Christ as the person who offers the way to be-come part of God's kingdom. Because poverty is fundamentally relational, I then articulate the twin goals of transformational development as changed people and just and peaceful relationships. By "changed people" I mean people who have discovered their true identity as children of God and who have recovered their true vocation as faithful and productive stewards of gifts from God for the well-being of all.

These twin goals of development transformation apply to the poor, the non-poor, and development facilitators as well. The human search for mean-ing and purpose is a universal and never-ending quest. It is only the nature of the struggle that is different. The poor suffer from marred identities and the belief that they have no meaningful vocation other than serving the powerful. The non-poor, and sometimes development facilitators, suffer from the temptation to play god in the lives of the poor, and believe that what they have in terms of money, knowledge, and position is the result of their own cleverness or the right of their group. Both the poor and the non-poor need to recover their true identity and their true vocation.

I then explore the implications of these twin goals for transformational development in terms framing the process of change. Neither revolution nor accepting the status quo is acceptable. I speak of a process of change that affirms the joint roles of God and human beings, the need to focus on restoring relationships in all dimensions, the need to keep the end in mind and to recognize that there is an adversary who actively works to defeat any genuine transformation, and the importance of seeking truth, justice, and righteousness. I address the importance of Christian agents of transformation, the need to take care to do no harm while expressing a bias toward peace, and finally to affirm the critical role of the church in the process of seeking sustainable change.

The chapter closes with a brief exploration of the four dimensions of sustainability—physical, mental, social, and spiritual—and some reflections on the different ways in which we need to think holistically about transformational development.

Principles and practitioners

Chapter 6 moves to the practice of transformational development with a focus on the kinds of principles and people that will be needed to pursue the Christian understanding of transformational development proposed in the foregoing chapter.

I begin by reiterating the basic affirmation that the ownership of the development process lies with the people themselves. They have a history that we need to hear and respect, while still affirming that God has also given us something to offer them. We need to overcome our modern blind spot in terms of the spiritual world so that we can hear their whole story, including the fact that they believe that many of the causes of their current situation and the dominant influence in terms of their future lie in the unseen world of spirits, gods, and ancestors. I also remind us that they already know a great deal and that this indigenous knowledge needs to be allowed to surface and to be respected. The poor already know how to survive. Any journey of transformational development needs to begin with this significant fact.

The chapter then moves to an aside on development planning in which I suggest that the traditional management-by-objectives approach to planning is not well suited to planning for social systems. Social systems are counter-intuitive and dynamical (a technical term meaning non-repeating and nonlinear). They will self-organize, but they are not particularly amenable to management and control. This means that rather than "planning our way to transformation" we and the people with whom we work will be better served by "learning our way toward transformation." And so the emphasis is less on goals and milestones (except in the short term) and more on vision, values, and evaluation.

The chapter continues with a discussion about moving from participation to empowerment. Participation is not an end in itself and hence the quality of participation matters. When people change by becoming less passive and more the primary actors in their own development, participation has become empowerment. And it is changed people who change people. Finally, participation that fails to build community is also flawed.

The chapter then moves from the principles to the practitioners of transformational development. Development is mediated through people and relationships. The attitude, knowledge, and behavior of the holistic practitioner are all critical to any chance of seeing any genuine transformation. The mindset of the practitioner must be holistic for the program to be holistic. If the holistic practitioner treats people as if they were made in the image of God, then the people can come to believe that they are truly children of God and are not God-forsaken. If the holistic practitioner believes people have gifts and a contribution to make, then people will make this discovery, too.

A profile for holistic practitioners is offered. Holistic practitioners must be Christians with a truly biblical worldview. They must have Christian character, acting, thinking, and working as holistic disciples. Holistic practitioners must be development professionals who are able to take advantage of the best the profession has to offer. Holistic practitioners must know the whole of their Bible and be lay theologians who understand that there is only a fine line between doing development and doing theology. Finally, holistic practitioners must themselves be part of an ongoing process of professional and spiritual formation.

The tool kit

Chapter 7 provides a survey of the tools that are available to help the holistic practitioner work with communities in transformational development processes that are consistent with the framework of this book. The chapter begins with some thoughts on what happens to our development response when we move from needs analysis to social analysis. It describes the way this is done using the vulnerabilities and capabilities analysis of Mary Anderson and Peter Woodrow. It then moves to one of the major development research and planning tools of the 1980s and 1990s, Participatory Learning and Action (PLA), which "puts the stick in the hands of the community" so that the research and planning method itself becomes potentially transformational. The chapter then introduces Appreciative Inquiry, a recent development in participatory research and planning based on the work of David Cooperrider of Case Western Reserve University. Appreciative Inquiry's assumption of health, vitality, and life-giving social organization in even the poorest communities holds particular promise for helping the poor recover their identity and discover their true vocation.

The chapter moves to the important topic of evaluation or how we learn our way toward transformation. It addresses a series of questions: Who is the evaluation for? What is it for? What changed? Who changed? What do we assess? Will it last? Are we doing the right thing? And, because the most fundamental cause of poverty is spiritual, there is a section on holistic evaluation.

The chapter concludes with a brief discussion of other critical issues related to development research and learning. There are critical voices that sometimes are not heard. Ignoring the voice of women is now known to work against positive social change as well as sustainability. I go on to suggest that children are not only not heard but are also invisible and that this is also a mistake. The chapter goes on to talk about getting the pace of the process right. What is too fast? What is too slow? To whose understanding of time do we give most attention? I also return to one of the dominant themes in this book: letting the spiritual come through. I cite several examples in which development methodologies, which were successful in allowing the spiritual worldview of the community to come through, made an important difference to the development process.

This chapter closes with three appendices that may be helpful to the practitioner: standards and indicators for the Isaiah 65 vision of transformation, a framework for the evaluation of holistic area development programs in India, and a set of twelve impact measures for holistic area development programming.

Christian witness

The book closes with a chapter on Christian witness as it is seamlessly expressed in the context of doing transformational development. It begins by exploring both the necessity and the problem of Christian witness for the Christian relief and development agency. We must witness because witnessing is a central feature of our faith commitment; it is not an option. Yet how we witness raises a difficulty and a challenge. The difficulty is that everyone—Christian or non-Christian—is witnessing all the time anyway. The only question is to what or to whom are they witnessing? There are no "value-free" development promoters. The challenge is to discover a framework for thinking about Christian witness in a way that is consistent with the principles of transformational development.

The chapter then presents a framework derived from the work of Lesslie Newbigin. Doing development and living our lives in ways that result in the community or some of its members asking questions of us to which the gospel is the answer unites gospel-as-life and gospel-as-deed with gospel-as-word. This approach places the initiative for inviting witness with the people and the onus of responsibility for effective witness where it belongs—on the Christian. Our witness depends on our living lives so that the Holy Spirit may evoke questions to which our faith is the answer.

Using this framework of provoking the question, the chapter then discusses issues relating to holistic witness, including the need to tell the whole biblical story; the interrelationship of life, word, deed and sign; and the need to avoid making a dichotomy between evangelism and discipleship.

The chapter goes on to explore issues relating to ensuring that our understanding of Christian witness is consistent with our framework for transformational development. It begins by pointing out that the goals of Christian witness are the same as the goals for transformational development: changed people and changed relationships. The only difference is that primary emphasis of Christian witness is on people's relationship with God. This convergence of goals is evidence that we have overcome the dichotomy between the physical and the spiritual.

This section goes on to present an organic or integrated understanding of the gospel as *being with* Jesus so that we may *witness by deed, word, and sign.* The Christian message is an embodied message, carried by living witnesses. The clarity and attractiveness of this message is dependent on the quality of our life with Jesus and our willingness to give expression to that life through word, deed, and sign. A warning is then presented that we must avoid separating evangelism and discipleship. This is a false dichotomy, and overcoming it is critical to overcoming our concern for the kind of Christians that are resulting for our witness. The section concludes with a call to be sure that, when we witness, we do so in a way that sooner or later shares the whole biblical story. It is the whole biblical story that carries the account of who we are and what we are for, that declares the lordship of Christ over all of creation and all our relationships.

The chapter moves to the issue of how we must witness. It begins with a call for Christians to live eloquent lives, the key to provoking questions to which the gospel is the answer. It goes on to remind us of the importance of carrying out our Christian witness with a crucified mind, not a crusading mind. I take note of the importance of helping the community—and ourselves—discover the fingerprints of God in our history, in creation, and in development interventions. I point out that questions about meaning and purpose hold the most promise for changing worldview and changing the view the poor have of themselves and their future. This section includes a brief discussion of how we can interpret technology so that it points not to its own efficiency but to the activity and character of the God who made it possible. This section concludes with a reminder that we need to avoid being apologetic for being Christian and thus be willing to say what we believe.

At this point the chapter shifts to the importance of the Bible to the process of transformational development. The argument is made that the Bible, as the living word of God, must be released from its spiritual captivity to Sunday morning and personal devotion and be allowed to be active in the development process. The chapter challenges us to find ways to let the Bible speak for itself. I then share the examples of Scripture Search and the Seven Steps in which the Bible is being used in development programming. I also briefly describe the New Tribes Mission innovation of Storying the Bible and make a suggestion as to how it could be made more holistic and thus more applicable for use in the development process.

The chapter on Christian witness closes with discussion of the focus of Christian witness. The central focus for Christian witness must be on the twin goals of transformation: changed people and changed relationships. The poor, non-poor, and the development practitioner (and his or her agency) must work together in seeking their true identity and recovering their true vocation within the context of just and peaceful relationships. The section then discusses how this can happen as a result of Christian witness and worldview change. The section closes with the question, Who changes? The answer is that everyone must change. Transformational development is a journey that everyone is on and that everyone must seek.

2

The Biblical Story

WHY DO WE NEED TO DO THEOLOGY?

Why does a book on transformational development need a chapter on theology? First, some people think that development is an activity of the material world, something done in the real world of human life. They think that theology is different, assuming that theology is about God, about other-worldly and spiritual things. These very assumptions are part of the problem this book is addressing. To solve the problem the practitioner must take time to do some theology. By the end of this chapter I hope the reader will under-stand that because God is working even now in the concrete world of space and time, doing transformational development is a form of doing theology.

Second, I understand the Bible to say that God is the creator of this world. Furthermore, the Bible asserts that in Christ all things hold together through the work of the Holy Spirit. This suggests that God is actively at work in the world, working for God's purposes. If this is so, then God has a stake in what we are making in the world. God is very interested in our work of transformational development, since it either supports or works against what God is doing.

Finally, the development process is a convergence of stories. The story of the development practitioner is converging with the story of the com-munity and together they will share a new story for a while. Because the development promoter is a Christian and because God has been active in the community since the beginning of time, the biblical story is the third story in this confluence of stories. This brings the development practitioner back to theology and the biblical account.

Every community needs a big story, a story that frames our lives and our understanding of the world. Everyone must have some kind of transcen-dent narrative that gives answers to questions of meaning and provides moral direction and social purpose. We need to know who we are (identity and purpose), where we are (location in the world and the universe), what went wrong (making sense of the poverty, pain, and injustice we see), what we must do (what must change and how it can be changed), and what time it is (how our past, present, and future fit into this picture).

Development practitioners need a big story too. At its heart, transformational development is about seeking a better human future. Any vision of a better human future must have its roots in the story that makes sense of our lives. Sadly, there is more than one story competing for the allegiance of most development workers. First, we all live within the story of our culture. Second, all of us who have been educated in Western schools or schools using Western curriculum also carry the story of modernity. Finally, if we are Christian, we carry the Christian story as well. These three stories shape our view of the better future and how to get there. Therefore, before we set out to accompany the transformation of others, we need to be sure we are clear on the biblical story that has the final say on our individual stories.

COMPETING STORIES

The modern world has a number of competing stories. Some are age-old stories rooted in the great religions of the world. Others are the products of the Western Enlightenment. Communism is a comprehensive narrative about what the world is like, how it got that way, and a seductive promise of a better human future. It lasted almost a century and its idolatry claimed the lives of millions of people. Science, technology, and capitalism continue to demand our faith and allegiance, claiming to be the only remaining story. They are gods that we are often too quick to worship. Koyama tells us that these gods "are fascinating because they claim to give us our identity and security more directly and quickly than our crucified Lord. . . . The selling point of these gods is directness and security. . . . They give us instant service" (Koyama 1985, 259). Yet at the end of the twentieth century the authority of these modern stories is fraying in the face of broken promises.

Science claims to understand how the universe works and promises the power to master nature, but it does not provide the answers most of us require: How did the world begin? By accident. How will it end? By accident? Why are we here and what moral guidance do you offer? Science is silent. (Postman 1997, 31).

Technology speaks only of power, offering mastery of nature to all. Technology offers convenience, efficiency, and prosperity here and now with its benefits available to rich and poor, or so it claims. Technology is a jealous god; those who follow must "shape their needs and aspirations to the possibilities of technology" (ibid., 31). Worshiping any other god or good means slowing down or frustrating the benefit of technology. Yet the technological god is a false god: "It is a god that speaks to us of power, not limits;

speaks to us of ownership, not stewardship; speaks to us only of rights, not responsibilities; speaks to us of self-aggrandizement, not humility" (ibid., 31).

Capitalism asks for faith in a god called "the hidden hand" and seems to have forgotten the goal of the original story. Adam Smith, the original story-teller, "wrote that the ultimate goal of business is not to make a profit. Profit is just the means. The goal is general welfare" (Wink 1992, 68). Instead, capitalism reduces people to economic beings driven by utilitarian self-interest toward the goal of accumulating wealth. What is wealth for? What are we for if we do not have wealth? Who are we if we do not have wealth? No answer.

Finally, even the human story (history) is not a big enough story. The human story can explain the story of my people and even my personal story. The human story also contains the stories of science, technology, and capitalism. It fails, however, to provide the answers to the questions of identity and meaning for which we search. Only God's story, the story that is outside human history but containing human history, can do this. Yet you can't get there from here. Beginning from the human story only leads to the smaller stories, the story of my people, my story, and the story of my atoms and molecules. You cannot get from the smaller stories to God's story. The only point of departure that works is to begin with God's story.

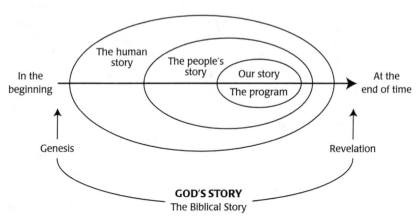

Figure 2-1: The constellation of stories.

In the latter years of the twentieth century, it is becoming clear that the modern world is discovering that it has lost its story. Part of the malaise in the West is the sense of loss and confusion that the absence of a true story brings. There is no widely shared story that makes sense of our lives, nor is there any promise of a better human future that compels belief. Modernity has failed to create a story line, and it has failed because it has no storyteller. "If God does not invent the world's story, then it has none" (Jenson 1993, 21).

Christians do have a story, however. The Bible is the narrative of God's creative and redemptive work in the world; thus it also contains the story of the Christian community. It is God's story about what God is doing. This Christian story was received; we did not make it up. It is not our story about God. Nor is it the sum of our individual stories, even though God holds these stories in high regard.[1] It is this story of what God wants and is doing that compels us to care for the poor and to work for human transformation. God's story is the source of our motivation, our vision, and our values of mission.

The biblical story also puts our stories in their place. We learn that it is not my story, or your story, or our story, that is the main story, the story that gives meaning. Meaning only comes from God's story. To pursue human transformation as Christians means understanding where humanity is coming from, where it is going, and how it can get there. To do the work for transformation, we have to embrace the whole of the biblical story, the story that makes sense and gives direction to the stories of the communities where we work, as well as to our own stories.

God's story is at heart a simple one. In a nutshell, it is the story of creation and redemption by the God of Israel and Father of the risen Christ working through the Holy Spirit. God's story tells us how things started, lost their way, can be redirected, and how the human story comes out in the end.

But the biblical story is also a very unusual story. We are told the beginning, the middle, and the final chapter of the story. But the piece between Jesus and his work on the cross and the final chapter is still being written. God's story is not just about what God has done, but also about what God, through his church, is doing now. God is still writing the story, and incredibly, God has invited us to participate in that writing.

Because God is still doing things in our world, we must begin our theology with the storyteller. The storyteller of the biblical story is a unique storyteller, because the storyteller is also the main actor in the story. Before there was any story, there is God. And now, in the chapters just before the end of the story, this same God is working in this world through the church, doing what God has been doing since the fall: working for the redemption and transformation of human beings, their relationships, and the creation which God made and in which they live.

THE STORYTELLER

We have to begin with God because he is the storyteller and the author of the story as well. The question Who is God? must be the first question. This is the question "that frames and anticipates all other questions" (Leupp 1996, 89). We must know who God is before we can answer the question about who we are and what we are supposed to be doing.

The Christian response is that God is three in one, Father, Son, and Holy Spirit. While we affirm this in worship, we don't use this Trinitarian formulation very much in thinking about issues of daily life. In the last decade a lot of work has been done to help us recover and make use of the

Trinitarian understanding of God. Some of this thinking is important to developing a framework for human transformation.

Who is God? The question must be carefully put. One of the recent developments in philosophy is that being must not be separated from doing when addressing the question of identity. The better question is, Who is God and what is God doing? (LaCugna 1991, 1-3). If we focus solely on who God is, God's being and character, then we struggle when pressed with hard questions: Can we believe in a God who seems to allow the poor to be poor in an unjust world? Can we believe in a God in the face of the genocides in Cambodia in the 1970s and in Rwanda and Bosnia in the late 1990s? Does belief in God hinder human development? To answer that God is all-powerful, all-knowing, and all-caring fails to provide a believable answer to these questions. If there isn't more to God, then there isn't enough.

To respond effectively, we have to go beyond who God is to talk about what God is doing. What God is doing is also expressed in a Trinitarian formulation: God is saving the world through Christ in the power of the Holy Spirit. The question of who God is in an unjust and violent world can only be answered adequately by talking about what God is doing: saving a fallen and failed world in a particular way. Thus, God is not the God who permitted the Holocaust; rather, God is the God who is hard at work trying to prevent future ones.

Jesus provides another example of the importance of keeping who God is and what God is doing together in our thinking. Knowing that Jesus is God is not enough to know fully who Jesus is. We also need to know that Jesus emptied himself of his prerogatives as God and, in obedience to the Father, died for the sins of all humankind and provided for our forgiveness by his resurrection. Jesus is God (being) and Jesus became like us, died, and in so doing saved us (doing). This provides a more complete account as who Jesus is.

Why does this Trinitarian formulation of being and doing matter to the development worker?[2] There are at least two reasons. First, it frames our mission response as Christians. We must both be Christians and do Christian work. Doing transformational development is acting out who we truly are. If there is no dichotomy between being and doing in God, then there can be none in us.

Second, this Trinitarian view leads to another helpful conclusion: we need to think of God as a loving, self-giving community; three, yet one. "Three persons in a single communion and a single trinitarian community: this is the best formula to represent the Christian God. Speaking of God must always mean the Father, Son and Holy Spirit in the presence of one another, in total reciprocity, in immediacy of loving relationship, being one for another, by another, in another, and with another" (Boff 1988, 133). The Christian God is a relational God and this defines God's character: self-giving love. "Trinitarian theology could be described as *par excellence* a theology of relationship, which explores the mysteries of love, relationship, personhood and communion within the framework of God's self-revelation in the person of Christ and the activity of the Holy Spirit" (LaCugna 1991, 1).

A lot follows from this for the development worker. First, if human beings are made in the image of this triune community, then our understanding of the individual must be very different from the autonomous, self-determining individual of Western culture. Development cannot be reduced to simply empowering individuals with new choices. Second, if God is in God's very essence relational, then our understanding of the impact of sin must also be relational and this will shape how we understand poverty (more on this in the next chapter). Third, if this triune God is saving the world by inviting people to join the movement toward the best of human futures in God's kingdom, then our view of the better future of transformational development must be fundamentally relational too. Finally, as Leupp points out, "Christian ethics that hope to be triunely grounded must be an ethics of relationality" (1996, 159). Thinking in Trinitarian terms "is practical because it is *the* theological criterion to measure the fidelity of ethics, doctrine, spirituality and worship to the self-revelation of God and the action of God in the economy of salvation" (LaCugna 1991, 410).

THE BEGINNING OF THE STORY

Creation

In the beginning was God, the triune God. The story begins by God making something out of nothing. This relational God created the earth and everything in it. Genesis tells us that the triune God spoke the creation into being (Gn 1:1). God's first action was to create a material world that could be seen, heard, felt, and touched. John tells us that Christ was God's Word in the beginning (Jn 1:1-2) and that through Christ all things were made (Jn 1:3). The Holy Spirit hovered over the deep (Gn 1:2). Thomas Aquinas said, "God the Father wrought the creation through his Word, the Son, and through his love, the Holy Ghost" (quoted in Boff 1988, 222). The whole person of God, creating and active, from the beginning of time. The world was God's act, not God's thought or dream. And the result was very good, according to the one who created it.

God created male and female in God's own image and told them to "be fruitful and increase in number, to fill the earth and subdue it" (Gn 1:27). Human beings are more than simply alive (being). Our purpose as human beings is to tend the earth and make it productive (doing). In addition to establishing that we are to be and to do in a particular way, this story also establishes the requirement for a Christian ecology. We are to be stewards. Everything belongs to God—humankind, the creatures of the earth, and the earth itself. The call to and promise of productivity and fruitfulness find their ground in the intent of the God who created them.

The Trinitarian formulation helps us understand the doctrine of creation more fully. God is God and the world is the world, distinctly separate and yet personally related. Creator and creation are in continuing relationship, distinct yet inseparably linked together in a relationship of love. God transcends creation, yet through Christ is actively involved in sustaining it (Heb 1:2-3). The creation account is neither an example of the distant high God of traditional religion nor the blind clockmaker of the modern West.

There is an important two-part observation that needs to be made. Having been made in the image of the triune God, we are meant to be in loving, self-giving relationships with one another and to be caring stewards, participating in the continuing process of creation. So, first, we need to understand that human beings, as bearers of the image of God, are intentionally placed in a system of relationships: with God, with self, with community, with those perceived as "other," and with our environment. This is our identity. Second, the calling or vocation of human beings (individually and in relationship) is to be fruitful, productive stewards of God's creation. We are to make a contribution that adds value. The creation account gives every human being an identity and a vocation. Just as I have already explained that we better understand God when we acknowledge who God is and what God is doing, we understand ourselves more fully when we acknowledge who we are and what we were created to do.

The Trinitarian understanding of creation also allows us to understand that the rich diversity of creation and the human family is a gift of God, a reflection of who God is. "The plurality in unity of the triune revelation enables us to do justice to the diversity, richness and openness of the world without denying its unity in relativist versions of plurality. It is this vision that trinitarian theology has to offer to the fragmented modern world" (Gunton 1997, 103).

Going back to the story of creation, Gerhard Von Rad reminds us that the account of creation in Genesis ends with the creation of the nations in chapter 10. Human institutions are also part of creation. The story of creation does more than explain how and why humankind was created, it also "provides a common foundation for all human enterprises we call culture—not just theology, but science, politics, ethics and art as well" (Gunton 1997, 98). This raises an important idea that will keep coming back to us in this book. We cannot separate people from the social systems in which they live.

An interesting set of implications for the development worker can be derived from the creation account. Since God owns the earth but has entrusted it to humankind, the critical metaphor for us is that of the steward and the principle of stewardship. From this, Wright develops four ethical principles (Wright 1983, 69-70):

Sharing resources: The land and natural resources are gifts to all humankind, not to only a few. While this does not mean there can be no private ownership, Wright argues that "the right of all to *use* is prior to the right to *own.*"

Responsibility to work: Work is part of being fruitful. God is productive, and thus it is in our nature to be productive. Work then is a responsibility. It also follows that we have a responsibility to enable or allow others to work so that they can fulfill their purpose.

Expectation of growth: "Be fruitful and increase" applies to the number of human beings and to the means of supporting them. God has provided abundantly in creation so that this can be done, and God has given humankind the ingenuity and adaptability necessary to create this necessary increase.[3]

Shared produce: Being productive is also accompanied by the idea of being able to consume or enjoy the end-product of one's work. This is part of the biblical image of the better human future (Is 65:21-22). "We are as responsible to God for what we do with what *we* produce as we are for what *he* has given us" (Wright 1983, 70).

The fall

Sadly, the big story did not end with the fruitful garden where human beings are obedient stewards and God walks in the afternoon. Yielding to temptation from an adversary working against God, humankind, man and woman together, decided to disobey God. They acted as if they knew better than God (Gn 3). Being like God was apparently more attractive than listening to God and doing as God asked. The effect of this disobedience ensured that human identity and all dimensions of human relationships would be marred. The scope of sin proved very broad—very holistic, if you will. It led to widespread deception, distortion, and domination in all forms of human relationships—with God, within one's self (and family), within the community and between others, and with the environment.

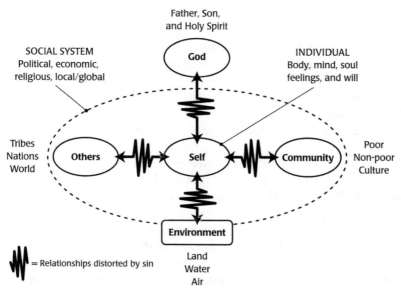

Figure 2-2: Impact of sin on all relationships.

I do not want to move past the issue of an adversary too quickly. Someone other than human beings created the temptation that resulted in the fall. Too often we dismiss the idea of a form of personal evil that actively works against God and God's intentions for human beings and creation. Yet, without Satan's role in the first part of the biblical story, there would be no need for the rest of the biblical story. We cannot read Satan out of the story and have it make any sense.

Each of Wright's ethical domains in creation was affected negatively by the fall. Instead of shared resources, land and natural resources have become a universal cause of strife and violence. They are hoarded by some and squandered and abused by others. Land and natural resources have become the counters in games of domination and oppression (Wright 1983, 71-74).

Instead of a way of using our gifts for ourselves and others, work has been corrupted. It can be toilsome and frustrating (Gn 3:17). Work has become a commodity, something we sell and buy with the temptation to reduce the human being to an economic asset, a living machine. Work has become a tool for greed, and even an idolatry whereby one makes a name for oneself. For the poor, this distorted work is often not available and the poor are vilified as "not productive."

Production and growth have become pathologically obsessive in many parts of the world. Covetousness has replaced contentment. "I saw that all labor and achievement spring from man's envy of his neighbor" (Eccl 5:4). There is never enough. "The effect of the fall was that the desire for growth became excessive for some at the expense of others, and the means of growth became filled with greed, exploitation and injustice" (Wright 1983, 81). The result of this pathology is the systems of poverty that keep some people poor.

Finally, the product of work is seen as human property, no longer belonging to God. Claims of ownership are privatized and made an absolute, ignoring the claim of God on all things in creation or the transcendent responsibility each has for the well-being of the larger community. Worse, those who create wealth use that wealth to influence the laws and the economic, political, and cultural system to protect their advantage. "A poor man's field may produce abundant food, but injustice sweeps it away" (Prv 12:23).

The bottom line of the fall is that the good creation of God became bent and no longer points at the purpose for which it was created. "The narrative of the Fall portrays the personal force of evil approaching man by means of the material creation and using the same material creation as a means of enticement to unbelief, disobedience and rebellion" (Wright 1983, 73).

Sometimes, evangelicals get so focused on the impact of the fall on the individual that they forget that the impact of the fall was on the whole of human society as well. Remember that the nations and their corresponding social institutions were part of the creation narrative. Linthicum does an excellent job of outlining the impact of the fall on these institutions (1991, 106-7):

The *economic system* was created by God to steward responsibly and justly the natural and human resources of the nation and to encourage men and women to be productive, using the gifts God has given to create wealth. Distorted by the fall, people occupying positions of influence within the economic system now act more often as owners and less as stewards. They skew the system to enhance and protect their own self-interest and insulate themselves from the impact of these distortions on the less fortunate.

The *political system* was created by God to encourage kingdom ethics and to bring a creation order into the management of human affairs, an order based on justice and peace. Yet, as a result of the fall, the political system becomes captive to the economic order and begins to serve the powerful; its ministries of justice cease being either ministries or just.

Finally, the *religious system*, which was created by God to bring the nations and their institutions into relationship with God, too often colludes with the fallen political and economic systems. The prophets of accountability are gradually seduced by money, power, and prestige, gradually becoming silent (Ezek 22:28).

The net result of the fall on the economic, political and religious systems is that they become the places where people learn to play god in the lives of the poor and the marginalized. When fallen human beings play god in the lives of others, the results are patterns of domination and oppression that mar the image and potential productivity of the poor while alienating the non-poor from their true identity and vocation as well.

We need to return to our observation that human beings cannot be separated from the human institutions of which they are a part. As Linthicum points out, both the institutions and the person experience an interrelated weakening when we examine Ezekiel's account of Jerusalem's sins (1991, 106). The spiritual nature of the nation and its human institutions, business, church, family, and government, all created for good, become increasingly anti-life, anti-kingdom, and evil (Ezek 22:1-13). The people, embedded in these distorting, deceiving, and dominating systems, themselves become exploiters of each other (Ezek 22:29). Wink says, "Human misery is caused by institutions, but these institutions are maintained by human beings. We are made evil by our institutions, yes; but our institutions are also made evil by us" (1992, 75).[4]

Because economic, political, and religious systems are so important to our understanding of poverty and therefore to the work of transformation, we need to look a little more closely at the underlying spirituality of these institutions. Walter Wink (1992, 65-85) has a significant contribution to make in this regard. Wink proposes that Paul's "principalities and powers" are the "interiority of earthly institutions or structures or systems." Wink points out that Paul says that the powers are said to be created in, through, and for Christ (Col 1:16-17), thus supporting the claim that social institutions are God's creations and not simply human artifacts. They were created by God because they are necessary to a full human life in community.

However, these powers—these social systems and structures—were profoundly distorted by the fall. They became idolatrous, along with the people who inhabit them. "An institution becomes demonic when it abandons its divine vocation—that of a ministry of justice or a ministry of social welfare—for the pursuit of its own idolatrous goals" (Wink 1992, 72), usually by serving the powerful in the name of self-preservation.

Wink goes on to argue that the doctrine of the fall is essential to understanding ourselves in relationship to these principalities and powers. The doctrine of the fall affirms the radical nature of evil and frees us from any illusion that we or our social institutions are perfectible apart from the redeeming work of Jesus Christ and the full coming of the kingdom of God. This should save us from any temptation toward optimistic belief in the ability of government or the free market or our own efforts at human transformation to change the reality of the poor in and of themselves. The relationship between this understanding of the fall and why people are poor will be developed in the next chapter.

The liberation story

To get from the fall to Jesus, God called a man, whom we know as Abraham, and made a promise to him: God would make through him a great nation that would be a blessing to all the nations (Gn 12:2-3). God kept his promise, and the Old Testament is the story of Abraham's nation, of its greatness and its flaws, of its loyalty and its betrayal of the God who called it into being. It is also the story of a promise-keeping God, who would not be diverted from completing the story God began at creation.

For the development professional, the Exodus story is instructive because it is the defining narrative for the people of Israel. It is a story of their liberation and of their formation. The liberation was from the oppression of Egypt and its pharaoh, and the formation was God transforming them from a group of slaves into a people. This was hard work. It took a day to get Israel out of Egypt and forty years in the wilderness to get Egypt out of Israel.

The Exodus narrative highlights the holistic and relational nature of God's redemptive work. Spiritually, Exodus is the story of the one God revealing himself and demonstrating his power so that Israel would believe and be faithful. Israel was freed from Egypt's gods and invited into a covenant with an ethical God who did not belong to any one place and who was too terrible to see face to face.

Sociopolitically, Exodus is the story of moving from slavery to freedom, from injustice toward a just society (at least that was the intent of God's instructions for pre-monarchy Israel [Wright 1983]) and from dependence to independence. Economically, the Exodus story is about moving from oppression in someone else's land to freedom in their own land, a land fairly distributed to all so that everyone could enjoy the fruit of his or her own labor. Psychologically, the Exodus story is about losing self-understanding as a slave people and discovering the inner understanding that, with God's help, they could be a people and become a nation.

What is sometimes overlooked is the other intention of God in the Exodus account. Throughout, there was a twofold agenda. The one we all know is the one just described—liberating Israel from its slavery and taking it to the Promised Land. The second was so that "the Egyptians might know that I am the Lord" (Ex 7:5). God was not being capricious in hardening Pharaoh's heart. Pharaoh believed that he was God and thus fully justified in playing god in the lives of "his" people. This could not be ignored. "I have raised you up for this very purpose," God said through Moses to Pharaoh, "that I might show you my power and that my name might be proclaimed in all the earth" (Ex 9:16). The non-poor are also the subjects of the good news, although I am sure it was very hard for Pharaoh to see liberation from his god-complex as such. The cost of discipleship is very high for those with wealth and power (see also Acts 16: 16-21). Jesus pointed out that the rich have a particularly hard time getting into the kingdom; this is part of the reason why.

The prophets

The history of Israel was not always consistent with the story God was attempting to create. Though they were God's chosen people and the instrument through which Jesus came into the world, Israel was also a source of pain for God. Hosea 11:8 reveals the "agitated mind" of God, whose emotions were always "jumbled up within him" (Koyama 1985, 220): loving Israel as a husband loves his wife and yet hating her idolatry and injustice.

Deuteronomy tells us that the prophet was "raised up" by God and set up over and against the priest and the king, taking on the character of God's own voice: "I will put my words in his mouth" (18:15, 17). The stories of the prophets tell us a great deal about how God views sin and its impact and serve to remind us of what God wants in creation as well as what God intends to do.

In the prophets we learn a great deal about how idolatry and injustice are related. When God, speaking through Isaiah, deplores "meaningless offerings" and "evil assemblies," Jerusalem is told, not to improve its worship in the temple, but to "stop doing wrong, learn to do right, to seek justice and encourage the oppressed, to defend the cause of the fatherless and plead the case of the widow" (Is 1:17). Loving God and loving neighbor are a seamless whole.

In Isaiah, we also see a strong message as to how God feels when the non-poor play God in the lives of the poor.

> Woe to those who make unjust laws,
> to those who issue oppressive decrees,
> to deprive the poor of their rights
> and withhold justice from the oppressed of my people,
> Making widows their prey and robbing the father-
>   less (Is 10:1-2).

Echoing Mary's Song (Lk 1:46-55), God will show the bankruptcy of power, privilege, and wealth (Is 5:8-10, 15-16). In front of a holy God it is made clear that there is no salvation in riches or power:

> What will you do on the day of reckoning,
> when disaster comes from afar?
> To whom will you run for help? (Is 10:3).

The prophets also alert us to the fact that idolatry, personal sin, and social sin are a seamless package. We all associate Sodom with sins of sexual impurity. Ezekiel speaks of their "detestable practices," when declaring Israel an "adulterous wife" who has become "more depraved than they" (Ezek 17:48). Then he surprises us when he describes Sodom's sin: "She and her daughters were arrogant, overfed and unconcerned; they did not help the poor and needy" (Ezek 17:49).

Ezekiel, interpreting the exile as God's punishment, condemns Jerusalem for a political system that "has eaten the people" and seized their wealth (Ezek 22:23), for an economic system that "bribes for shedding blood" and "robs your neighbor by extortion" (Ezek 22:27) and a religious system that draws no distinction between the sacred and profane and does not "teach the people the difference between clean and unclean" (Ezek 22:26).

Finally, the prophets keep reminding us of what God's story is all about, where God is going, what God is doing, and what God expects of us:

> He has showed you, O Man, what is good
> And what does the Lord require of you?
> To act justly and to love mercy
> and to walk humbly with your God (Mic 6:8).

The wisdom of the people

The wisdom literature is the accumulated wisdom of the people who have lived under and within the Old Testament part of the biblical story. This literature summarizes the learnings of the community of faith concerning right and just relationships and testifies to people's experience that God's rule is the only rule at the end of the day. The rich are warned, as are the poor. God's concern for just social relationships surfaces throughout Psalms and Proverbs. This part of the biblical story illustrates God's interest in the everyday things of life—eating, drinking, playing, and laughing.

Our inability to see God active in and interested in daily life is a serious weakness.[5] It is as if we believe that God is absent from or disinterested in this part of life. This view results in serious blind spots. Our practice and interpretation of development technology is an example of this. More on this later.

THE CENTER OF THE STORY

The center of the biblical story is the birth, ministry, death, and resurrection of Jesus Christ, a Jew who lived in Palestine almost two thousand years ago. This part of the story begins in Nazareth in Galilee, a place far from the center of political, economic, and religious power. "Can anything good come from Nazareth?" (Jn 1:46). It was understood by those in religious authority that neither the messiah nor a prophet could come from Galilee (Jn 7:41,52). A son of ordinary people, living in an unremarkable place, Jesus "grew in wisdom and stature, and in favor with God and men" (Lk 2:52).[6]

The Christ of the periphery

The Christ of God was very much the Christ of the powerless and despised geographical and social margins of Israel. The news that the Messiah finally had come came from a lonely prophet preaching in the desert of Judea. Jesus learned his true identity at his baptism in the Jordan River, far from Jerusalem and the Temple. Jesus then came to understand the fullness of his true vocation in the desert wilderness. By struggling with the temptations and deceptions of the Evil One, the one who is against life and against God, Christ determined that he was called to be the Son of God and the Suffering Servant, both at the same time.

Much of Christ's ministry took place in Galilee, on the edge of Israel. His work was done among the common people, those whom society labeled "publicans and sinners" or "unclean." Christ chose to do his work of preaching, healing, and casting out of demons in this backwater of the Roman Empire, without any political or religious position. An itinerant preacher, Jesus was supported by some faithful women (Lk 8:3). In a sense, the political and economic power of Jerusalem had only one benefit to Jesus. By acting out its role as the center of power, it would put him to death.

This strange location for the work of the Messiah of the whole world has implications. Koyama reminds us that since Jesus is the true center of the kingdom of God, where he is becomes the center (1985, 251-52). This means that Galilee becomes the weak center, outside the powerful center of Jerusalem. The powerful go to the periphery to see this person, this one who teaches with authority and who does things only God can do (Lk 5:17), who takes the center with him wherever he goes. Development workers must search their heart to see where they believe the center is that can transform the poor, where they believe Jesus will be found, where the "foolishness of God is wiser than man's wisdom, and the weakness of God is stronger than man's strength" (1 Cor 1:25). Perhaps the periphery is not God-forsaken at all.

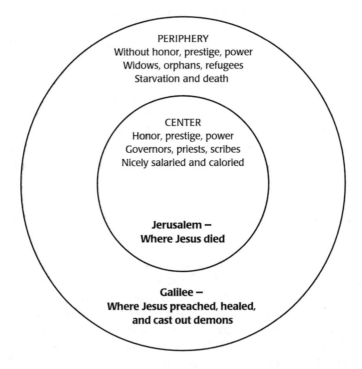

Figure 2-3: Center and periphery as the location of transformation.
(After Koyama 1985, 251-53)

This poses some interesting questions for the development practitioner, especially when involved in advocacy work. Where is the periphery today, and what does it mean to say that Jesus can make it the center? What is the proper location for advocacy work? What result is likely if we go to the centers of power on behalf of the periphery? Are we willing to pay the price? Where are the real transformational frontiers? The ones that make foolishness into wisdom and weakness into power? Where are the places where the false wisdom of the world is unmasked and declared a lie?

The mission of Jesus

At the synagogue in Nazareth, Jesus said that the Holy Spirit had anointed him "to preach good news to the poor. He has sent me to proclaim freedom for the prisoners and recovery of sight for the blind, to release the oppressed, to proclaim the year of the Lord's favor" (Lk 4:18-19). Jesus' mission is a holistic mission to the poor.

Jesus preached the good news of the kingdom because this is what he was sent to do (Lk 4:43). While we can see no pattern of activity, no "model" for transformation, the gospel story is full of stories of preaching, teaching, healing, and casting out of demons—word, deed, and sign. Surely, Christian transformation should aspire to the same—word, deed, and sign. As for the kingdom, we will come back to this defining theme.

Jesus did not fulfill his mission alone

The triune God would not be expected to become an individual savior. He chose twelve fairly ordinary people "to be with him" in order that he could send them to do what he had been doing—preaching, casting out demons, and healing the sick (Mk 3:13-15, 6:12). A company of women helped support him "out of their own means" (Lk 8:3). Transformation is the work of a community; it is not served well by lonely "cowboys." The gospel message is a way of living with Christ and each other that then enables the ministry of word, deed, and sign.

The greatest commandment

When asked what must be done to inherit eternal life, Jesus said that the greatest commandment was a twin affirmation: "Love God with all your heart and with all your soul and with all your strength and with all your mind and love your neighbor as yourself" (Mt 23:36). This is a commandment about relationships, not law; about who we must love, not simply what we must believe or do. This commandment must frame our approach to transformational development. It is both our motive for helping the poor and a point of departure for what a biblical understanding of transformation means: right and just relationships.

Jesus died alone on a cross

Outside the city gates, in the company of criminals, Jesus died on a cross, abandoned by everyone, even God. The physical pain of death was insignificant compared to the pain of being wholly alone. "My God, my God, why have you forsaken me?" (Mk 15:33). There is no greater loss, no greater pain for the three-in-one God than abandonment. This must shape our view of poverty. Poverty is about relationships that don't work, that isolate, that abandon or devalue. Transformation must be about restoring relationships, just and right relationships with God, with self, with community, with the "other," and with the environment.

The cross, Leupp tells us, is a great clarifier. The cross is the vantage point of the triune God, God's point of view. From its perspective, Jesus revealed "not tarnished human possibility, but divine forgiveness" (Leupp 1996, 89). We are good, fallen, and redeemable all at once. The downward spiral of the fall meets the radical possibility of redirection toward the kingdom in the cross and resurrection of Christ.

The cross clarified something else. On the cross, in addition to canceling our sin, Paul tells us that Christ disarmed the powers and authorities, making a public spectacle of them (Col 2:20). In Christ, we no longer have to accept the rule of oppressive structures or of deceiving and dominating social systems. Their transformation is also included in Christ's finished work. Wink says, "The final subjugation of the Powers under Christ's feet will happen (1 Cor 15:24-25), but it is already, in anticipation, experienced now (Eph 1:19-23) in the new reality of resurrection experience" (Wink 1992, 70). Like us, the powers are good, fallen, and redeemable all at the same time. Transformational development that does not declare the good news of the possibility of both personal and corporate liberation and redirection toward God is a truncated gospel, unworthy of the biblical text.

Finally, there is an important paradox in the cross. From the epistles we learn that Christ has the power "that enables him to bring everything under his control" (Phil 3:21) and that "God has placed all things under his feet" (Eph 1:22). Yet, Wink points out that this Jesus who subjects all things to himself also "did not consider equality with God something to be grasped" (Phil 2:6). Jesus emptied himself of all desire to dominate, and taking the form of a human, identified himself with the poor and suffered a criminal's death. "Subjection to such a ruler means the end of all subjugation. The rulership (of Christ) thus constituted is not a domination hierarchy but an enabling and actualizing hierarchy. It is not pyramidal, but organic, not imposed but restorative" (Wink 1992, 83). This non-coercive, upside-down turning, healing, releasing Christ has implications in terms of who must own the development process and how we must run our development institutions.

Christ is risen

This is the transformation that begets all other transformations. Death to life. Something only God can do. Any work of human transformation that does not announce this incredibly good news is fatally impoverished. The cross and the resurrection are the very best news that we have.

The Jesus story does not end with an empty tomb outside the gates of Jerusalem, the center of power. Jesus, risen in power and glory, returns to the periphery, to Galilee. The center has nothing more to offer him. Also, Jesus is concrete again: "Touch me and see" (Lk 24:39). He eats in the presence of his disciples. He appears to them for forty days, speaking about the kingdom of God (Acts 1:3). His last reported instructions were to go, to make disciples, to baptize in the name of the triune God, and to "teach them to obey everything I have commanded you" (Mt 28:20). Teaching about the kingdom of God seems to be something important to the risen Jesus, and so it must be to those of us who follow him.

THE CONTINUING STORY

One of the many peculiar elements of the biblical story is that, after his resurrection, Jesus did not stay on earth to see his mission through, at least not in the way that anyone would have expected. After forty days of speaking about the kingdom of God, Jesus announced that the disciples would be his witnesses to the ends of the earth, once they received the power of the Holy Spirit (Acts 1:8). At Pentecost, the Holy Spirit reversed the story of Babel and those present heard them "declaring the wonders of God in our own tongues" (Acts 2:11). The biblical story was now a story for every language, for every person to hear in their mother tongue.

The church

From that point until now, you and I are the ongoing work of Christ in the world, his body here on earth. Surely this is hard to understand: handing over the work of saving the world to people who, while redeemed, are yet flawed and struggling with sin. Yet, this is what Jesus chose to do. The church, the community of faith, is the bearer of the biblical story, the "cracked pot" that is to continue announcing the good news of the unchanging person and the unshakable person until Christ comes again.

E. Stanley Jones helps us a great deal by describing the church in relationship to the triune God. Jones says that the kingdom is the Father's, while Jesus is the embodiment of the kingdom. The Holy Spirit is the first fruit of the kingdom, the assurance that there is more to come, and the one who helps us discover the truth and fullness of the kingdom. When it is at its best, the church is the sign, a witness, to the kingdom of God breaking into the world.

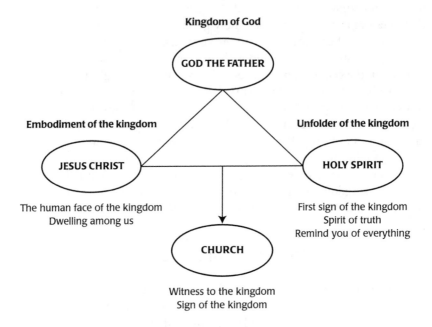

Figure 2-4: The triune God and the church.
(After Jones 1972, 26-29)

This has two important things to say to development workers. First, God brings the kingdom; it is neither our task nor that of our transformational development. We must not put the weight of building the kingdom on our shoulders; we cannot carry it, nor are we expected to. Second, the sign of the kingdom is the church, the community of faith, not the development worker or the development agency. Somehow development workers must become a part of the church. As Christians, their local community of faith is the local church. Their work needs to be seen as the sign of that church and not as some personal beacon.

The body of Christ is a community. This seems obvious enough, but sometimes we forget it. If our life with Christ is our first call (Mk 3:14), then our church is our family in which this life is nurtured. Our worship and our experience of the sacraments are the sole sources of the drive to take the whole message of Jesus and the kingdom of God into the world. The church is also our hermeneutical community, a community of and around the word of God. Believers are to study and interpret the Scriptures, doing so within a community as a correction against error. Every Christian community has the responsibility to read the biblical story in light of its own story for the purpose of shaping its vision of mission and repenting of its errors. Where else does the vision of human transformation come from?

Most of us in the development business have deeply ambiguous feelings about this church of which we are a part. David Bosch reminds us that "the church is both a theological and a sociological entity, an inseparable union of the divine and the dusty" (1991, 389). Bosch continues with an eloquent description of our contradictory feelings about the church:

> We can be utterly disgusted, at times, with the earthliness of the church, yet we can also be transformed, at times, with the awareness of the divine in the church. It is *this* church, ambiguous in the extreme, which is "missionary by its very nature," the pilgrim people of God, "in the nature of" a sacrament, sign, and instrument, and "a most sure seed of unity, hope and salvation for the whole human race" (Bosch 1991, 389).

We must remember that the church, while it is to be sign of the kingdom, is not the kingdom itself. The kingdom judges and redeems the church. The church is successful in being a sign to the extent that the Spirit makes it so. The church is a true sign only to the degree that it lives up to the spirit and life of the kingdom. "The church is not the end of mission, the kingdom is the end" (Jones 1972, 35).

This has two implications for the development worker. First, it is a counter-balance to the earlier claim I made that the church is to be the sign of the kingdom, not the development worker. While true, the church is as fallible as we are and sometimes fails to be this sign. Our greatest pain comes when we wish our work to be part of the sign of the kingdom, expressed through the local church, and yet find ourselves with a church that is unwilling or unable to be this sign with us. Such is the ambiguity of being in development work, especially if one works for a so-called parachurch organization.

Second, this means that church planting cannot be the final objective of mission, only the beginning. A church full of life and love, working for the good of the community in which God has placed it, is the proper end of mission. Transformational development that does not work toward such a church is neither sustainable nor Christian.

The church represents a special challenge to many involved in Christian development, since much of the work in the last quarter-century has been done by the so-called parachurch agencies. Made up of Christians, these agencies go directly to Christians in the pew to solicit funds and then directly to poor communities to help the poor. The local church on both ends is too frequently ignored, or worse, seen as part of the problem. This is a seriously flawed view. I will address the role of the local church in the chapter on transformational development.

To summarize, the church is the bearer of the biblical story because it is Christ's body in the world. As Christians, we are part of this body, and that's the way it is. With all our warts and pimples, witnessing about Christ and doing his work within the context of the church is our mission. Fortunately, to carry out our role as the body of Christ in the world, the church has some additional help. We have been given a person and a book.

The Holy Spirit

The Holy Spirit is the third person of the Trinity. The Holy Spirit is the experience of God that accompanies the church on its fallible journey of witnessing to Christ and the kingdom. God's Spirit of truth reminds us of everything Jesus taught us (Jn 14:16,26) and unfolds the meaning of the kingdom to us (Jones 1972, 38).[7] The Holy Spirit is the actor of mission who convicts the world, including the prince of this world, of its sin (Jn 16:8-10).

The Holy Spirit is the source of power (Lk 24:49) that transformed a fairly ordinary group of disciples, who had abandoned their Lord, into a fearless group of witnesses who would not surrender their mission even under threat of death (Acts 4:19). This Spirit is the source of our mission: "The same Spirit in whose power Jesus went to Galilee also thrusts the disciples into mission" (Bosch 1991, 113). The Holy Spirit initiates mission (Acts 13:2), guides mission (Acts 8:28, 16:9), and creates the response to mission (Acts 16:14). The signs and wonders of the Holy Spirit demonstrate the power of God in a way that demands an explanation so that credit is given to whom credit is due (Acts 14:8-18). Any transformational development that is not guided, empowered, and made effective by the Holy Spirit will not prove sustainable. Furthermore, expecting and praying for supernatural interventions by the Spirit must be part of the spirituality of Christian development workers.

The Bible

We were also given a book, the Bible. This book is the received story of what the author of the story has done, is doing, and plans to do. In this living word we have the whole story that makes sense of our stories. This book tells the only story that answers the questions that really matter: Who am I? Where am I? What's wrong? How can it be changed? What time is it?

We are to be the living illustrations of the truth of this story. Newbigin says, "We live in the biblical story as part of the community whose story it is, find in the story the clues to knowing God as his character becomes manifest in the story, and from within that indwelling try to understand and cope with the events of our time and the world about us and so carry the story forward" (1989, 99).

We also received the story in another way. The story of the church is the story of how the biblical story has been lived out in the two thousand years since Christ created his church and set it on its mission. The history of the church—its thinking and its actions in the world—is the lived-out story that we inherit. The flaws and failings we see in this history should remind us how fallible we are, create in us a deep-seated suspicion of our own righteousness, and lead us to humility. At the same time, this story of Christ's body also reveals many who have tried to live out God's story by caring for the poor and working to transform society. We need to know that, with all its imperfections, the church has been in the transformational development business since its beginning.

We must also take note of the fact that the Bible is more than a book. It is the living word of God, "sharper than any double-edged sword, it penetrates even to dividing soul and spirit, . . . judges the thoughts and attitudes of the heart. Nothing in all creation is hidden from God's sight" (Heb 4:12-13). The Bible is unique among books, it is "the only book that reads me" (Weber 1995, ix). Because it is the living word of the living God, it always has something to say to every situation, and it always has more to say than we can ever know.

For too long evangelicals have treated the Bible as a book for the spiritual world[8] and have failed to give it the freedom to inform the material world of everyday life and everyday "non-spiritual" decisions. One of the challenges of Christian holism in development will be to release the Bible and the biblical narrative to speak to all phases of the process of human transformation. One of the best gifts that we have for the poor and the non-poor is the living word of God. We need to share it with them and let the living word speak for itself. More about this in the chapter on Christian witness.

THE END OF THE STORY

The end of the biblical story is the end of history. John tells us that Jesus will come again in power and glory. This leads to the judgment of judgments, the one and true judgment, the one that ends in the eternal destruction of the Evil One and of those whose names are not written in the book of life (Rv 20:15). Then the first earth and first heaven pass away and a new earth and new heaven, in the form of the new Jerusalem, descend from heaven. The story that began in a garden ends in a city.

Once again the dwelling place of God is with men and women (Rv 21:3). There are no more tears, or death, or crying, or pain, nor is there famine or drought (Rv 7:16, 21:4). Everything is made new—the people and their city. There is no church in this new Jerusalem because it is no longer needed; God and the Lamb live among the people (Rv 21:22). The mission of the church as a "history-making force" (Newbigin 1989, 129) is completed. The kingdom of God stands alone at the end of time. It is the final reality; all other kingdoms have passed away.

The nations now walk by the light of the glory of God shone forth by the Son. The honor and glory of the nations, all their "artistic, cultural, political, scientific and spiritual contributions" (Wink 1992, 83), transformed and no longer a seduction away from the worship of God, are brought into the city (Rv 21:24,26). The gates never shut.

The measures of value are turned upside down. Gold, the most valuable commodity in this world, the commodity of greed and violence, is so common that it is used to pave the streets. The foundations of the city are made with precious stones (Rv 21:20-21), because we have a new understanding of what is valuable. These gemstones are simply beautiful, no longer objects of greed in the eyes of humankind.

Finally and most important, this new Jerusalem is a city of life (Rv 22:1-3). The earth itself is redeemed and once again produces the fruit and the healing that humans and their nations need. Our true vocation is once more within our grasp as "his servants will serve him" (Rv 22:3).

It is important for those concerned for human transformation to keep the end of the story in mind. This is where the triune God is going. This is the best human future. While this triumphant vision should guide us, it should also instill a sense of awe and humility in us. This end comes only at great cost. Christ died and the saints suffered. There is a cross on the way to this triumphal end.

THE POINT OF THE STORY

By now, the point of the story should be clear. From the day our first parents walked out of the garden, estranged from God, each other, and the earth itself, God has been at work redeeming the fallen creation, its people, and its social systems. God's goal is to restore us to our original identity, as children reflecting God's image, and to our original vocation as productive stewards, living together in just and peaceful relationships.

This restoration project has required hard work, very costly work; work that could only have been motivated by the most profound, self-giving love. "The center of the New Testament lies in the narrative of the death and resurrection of Jesus Christ understood as an act of obedience toward God and an expression of self-giving love for his followers as well as a model for his followers to imitate" (Volf 1996, 30).

The goal of the biblical story, then, is the reconciliation of all things, on earth and in heaven (Col 1:19) with Christ as the head (Eph 1:10). Relationships are restored in all the dimensions distorted by sin. "The gospel is the news that distorted patterns of power have been broken; the reception of the gospel is the embrace of radically transformed patterns of social relationships" (Brueggemann 1993a, 34). This is the story into which every human being has been invited by God to be a participant. This goal must inform our understanding of transformational development.

REFLECTIONS

Who are we?

This seems a simple question. Sometimes we move too quickly past it, assuming everyone knows the answer. We need to pause a moment and be sure that the Western understanding of the autonomous, self-directed individual has not distorted our Christian understanding of who we really are.

We are human beings made in the image of God. We all know this. What we forget sometimes is that the God in whose image we are made is the three-in-one God, the God who is communion, the relational God. This means that our individual self can never be itself apart from our being-in-communion with God and with other human beings. The Trinitarian nature of God means that we are self-in-community when we are fully human. Our human selves are embedded in relationships, finding their fullest meaning in just and harmonious relationships or losing meaning and worth when these relationships do not work. This view of the human being is radically contrary to that of modern times, at least in the West.

This Trinitarian view of the self does not mean that the self is submerged in the group. As Leupp clarifies, "Egocentricity is different from ego awareness" (1996, 100). Every person is unique and should be aware of his or her uniqueness, just as the Father, Son, and Holy Spirit are aware of their respective uniqueness. This uniqueness, however, does not lead to egocentricity but rather finds full expression in self-giving love. "The triune premise is that love is completed when it is invested in the other. Love that is given away does not impoverish, but enriches and perfects the giver" (ibid., 101). Thus the thrust for mission—for loving God and loving neighbor—is found first in God and then in us because we are made in his triune image.

This has practical implications. As Christians, we can no longer simply view the world as a collection of individuals. Instead, we need to view each individual is an encumbered self, embedded in families and communities as well as being participants in the whole gamut of social institutions—economic, political, cultural, and religious. All of this is what it means to be human, to be made in the image of God.

This view of the self is also helpful in terms of what the self is not. While no one can deny the importance of an assured and centered self, a Trinitarian view of self will not validate metaphors like the lonesome, self-contained, "I don't need help from nobody" cowboy; the entertainer who "does it my way"; or the entrepreneur who gambles with corporations without regard for the people who work in them and contribute to their true value. Self-actualization in any form will not create the full human self of the Bible.

Finally, just as we cannot understand who God is without reference to what God is doing, the same applies to human beings. We are made in the image of a God who is and who is acting. Thus, we must be who we are—bearers of the image of a relational God—and do what we were made by God to do—be fruitful in self-giving relationships.[9] To be true to our identity as Christians, we must be in Christ and be doing mission, loving God and loving our neighbor. We are not who we truly are unless we are doing both.

One final observation as to who we are. Human beings are located in a concrete place and at a particular point in time. We are material as well as spiritual. Our self breathes, eats, laughs, and walks through the bush. We are located in God's creation and are sustained by it. We are not disembodied ideas, thoughts, or spirits. We do not float above history or time. Our story and nature's story are inseparable.

What are we to be and do?

We are first of all to be with Christ. Being is the beginning. We cannot do what we are not. Furthermore, life in Christ means life in his Body; we are with Christ when we are in his church. As Christians, the church is our community because our being is being-in-community. There is no transformational development apart from people who themselves are being transformed and who live in the community that is the home of their transformation.

We are then to live the life that God gave us through Christ. We are to live the biblical story. We are to live from and for God, from and for others; we are to live a life of being and doing. We do transformational development because this is what the biblical story tells us that God is doing.

> Living the trinitarian faith means living as Jesus Christ lived: preaching the gospel; relying totally on God; offering healing and reconciliation; rejecting laws, customs and conventions that place persons beneath rules; resisting temptation; praying constantly; eating with modern day lepers and other outcasts; embracing the enemy and the sinner; dying for the sake of the gospel if it is God's will (LaCugna 1991, 401).

We are to do transformation in the Spirit since the mission is God's. The Holy Spirit empowers us for mission, leads us into mission, and is responsible for the results of mission. If there is to be any human transformation that is sustainable, it will be because of the action of the Holy Spirit, not the effectiveness of our development technology or the cleverness of our participatory processes (see Chapter 6). Because our role is to be faithful and obedient, in contrast to being successful, we must modify our ambitions and redirect our praise.

> The chief actor in the historic mission of the Christian church is the Holy Spirit. He is the director of the whole enterprise. The mission consists of the things that he is doing in the world (Taylor 1972, 3).

We are to embrace the "other," and this must include the non-poor as well as the poor. This is the heart of the gospel and the beginning of transformation. The open arms of the father embracing the son who had made himself wholly other and the healing embrace of the Jew by the Samaritan are the images that must shape our mission of transformation to the poor and non-poor alike. God has no enemies whom he does not love, and hence neither can we. The embrace is the necessary first step toward reconciliation and justice (Volf 1996, 29).

We must fulfill our mission by accepting the paradoxical location of every Christian (Walls 1996, 53). The gospel is infinitely translatable, available to everyone in every language. Therefore, as bearers of the gospel story, the Christian agent of transformation can and should be thoroughly local, at home everywhere, just as the gospel is. At the same time, however, the kingdom is not yet fully here and will not be until the second coming of Christ. Thus, we are also pilgrims, at home nowhere, because our real home is the transcendent Christian community moving toward a kingdom not yet here. This means we are in the world and not of it. This also means that we accept people where they are without judgment, while also knowing that the Spirit of God celebrates the good, unmasks the evil, and calls for the most fundamental change in everyone.

We are to see the world as created, fallen, and being redeemed, all at the same time. We must not separate creation and fall from redemption. As a story, the parts are inseparable, each giving meaning to the other. Wink reminds us,

> God at one and the same time *upholds* a given political or economic system, since some such system is required to support human life; *condemns* that system insofar as it is destructive to full human actualization; and *presses for its transformation* into a more human order. Conservatives stress the first, revolutionaries the second, reformers the third. The Christian is expected to hold together all three (1992, 67).

Our practice of transformational development must be informed by these three lenses for making sense of the human story. Understanding creation helps us understand what was meant to be. Understanding the fall helps us recognize what is working against life in poor communities and why. Understanding the redemption story helps us know what can be and who and what can help us get there.

Three important theological ideas

There are three theological ideas that seem useful for Christians working for transformational development.

Incarnation

One of the most incredible parts of this biblical account is the idea that the triune God would stoop to becoming flesh and make his dwelling place among us (Jn 1:14). For many inside and outside the faith, this is a stumbling block of major proportions. The Incarnation is a powerful theological metaphor for those who practice transformational development for several reasons.

First, the Incarnation is the best evidence we have for how seriously God takes the material world. The Incarnation smashes any argument that God is only concerned for the spiritual realm and that the material is somehow evil or unworthy of the church's attention. God embodied himself. God became concrete and real. It was possible to touch God's wounds and hear God's voice. Real people were healed; a dead man lived again.

This suggests that doing transformational development is what God does. We are only following after God. This is the bottom line of the biblical story. This is why "Christians cannot, indeed they must not, simply believe the gospel; they must practice it so that by God's grace they might embody its reality—what the Christian scripture calls the down payment of God's future glory" (Dyrness 1997, 3). To declare that the mission of the church is solely about spiritual things ignores the Incarnation.

Second, the Incarnation provides a highly instructive model for how we must be willing to practice transformational development. God emptied himself of his prerogatives. Are we willing to empty ourselves of ours? Jesus did not come as a conquering, problem-solving Christ. Jesus is not the quick-answer god Koyama warned us against (1985, 241). Jesus was the God who was not able to save himself, and so he was able to save others. There are lessons here for development professionals, full of technical skill and confident of their "good news" for the poor. Any practice of transformational development must be framed by the cross and the broken Christ.

Finally, we must always remember that Jesus chose freely to empty himself of his prerogatives as God, making himself nothing (Phil 2:7), so that every tongue might confess that "Jesus Christ is Lord" (Phil 2:11). The entire purpose of the exercise was to invite people to redirect their lives and to provide the means by which they could do so. Transformational development must have the same end in mind.

Redemption

The point of the biblical story is to redeem and thus redirect the trajectory of the human story after the fall. This was made possible by the finished work of Jesus Christ. We need to remember, however, that this act
took place in the concrete world of Israel, at a particular point in real human history with the real death of a real man. Redemption is material as
well as spiritual. Both our bodies and our souls are redeemed. The new
heaven comes down to earth. The glory of all nations will enter the city at
the end of the day, our cultures, our science, our poetry, our art, even our
transformational development—all are redeemed and part of the end of the
story.

For this reason we must remind ourselves constantly that the work of
transformational development is part of God's redemptive work (Bradshaw
1993, 43). Don't misunderstand me. Transformational development, by itself, will not save. The charitable and transforming acts of Christians will
never mediate salvation. But, having said this, it is also wrong to act as if
God's redemptive work takes place only inside one's spirit or in heaven in
the sweet by-and-by. This disembodied, wholly spiritualized view of redemption is not biblical. God is working to redeem and restore the whole
of creation, human beings, all living things, and the creation itself. "For the
creation was subjected to frustration, not by its own choice, but by the will
of the one who subjected it, in hope that creation itself will be liberated
from its bondage to decay and brought into the glorious freedom of the
children of God" (Rom 8:20-21). It is in this sense that transformational
development is part of God's redemptive work in the world.

Finally, because God is working out God's redemptive purposes in spiritual, physical, and social realms, this also means that we are God's agents of
redemption, however flawed and unsatisfactory we may be in this incredible role. When we work for transformational development, we are working as God's hands and feet.

The kingdom of God

Finally, a word about Jesus and the kingdom of God. The kingdom of
God is something Jesus talked about a great deal. It has been recovered as
an important biblical concept, beginning with the social gospel movement in the United States early in the twentieth century. The kingdom of
God was the subject of Christ's first sermon (Mk 1:14), was the only thing
he called the gospel (Mt 4:23), and was the topic on which he focused his
teaching to the disciples during his last forty days on earth (Acts 1:3).
Jesus said that the kingdom is the key to understanding his teaching (Lk
8:10). In the Sermon on the Mount, Jesus said that the kingdom of God
was the first thing we should seek and that everything else will follow (Mt
6:33). The coming of the kingdom is the first petition in the prayer Jesus

taught us to pray (Mt 6:10). Luke closes the book of Acts by telling us that Paul "boldly and without hindrance preached the kingdom of God and taught about the Lord Jesus Christ" (Acts 28:31). Jesus even said that "the gospel of the kingdom will be preached to the whole world as a testimony to all nations, and then the end will come" (Mt 24:14). The idea of the kingdom of God is an important idea for those who work for human transformation.

Recalling the importance of the interrelationship of people and the social systems within which they live, E. Stanley Jones, long-time missionary to India, makes an important contribution to kingdom theology when he presents the biblical metaphors of the "unshakable kingdom" and the "unchanging person" (Jones 1972). The kingdom of God is unshakable (Heb 12:28) because it is the true reality, the way things really are. Christ is the unchanging person (Heb 13:8), the reality of the kingdom in human form, the only way to enter God's kingdom.

The kingdom of God, Jones says, is both radical and conservative at the same time. It is radical in that no one or anything is beyond the claim of God's kingdom. It is conservative in the sense that it "gathers up everything that is good [God's good creation peeking through the results of the fall] and fulfills the good, cleanses the evil and goes beyond anything ever thought of or dreamed anywhere. This is the desire of the ages—if men only knew it" (1972, 27). Jones continues, the kingdom of God simply "is and you must come to terms with it" (ibid., 46).

Jones also rejects the reduction that limits the gospel to the individual alone. People and social systems are interrelated. While people create the political, religious, and economic institutions of their society, at the same time these institutions shape (create) the people who live in them. The impact of sin, and hence the scope of the gospel, includes both the personal and the social.

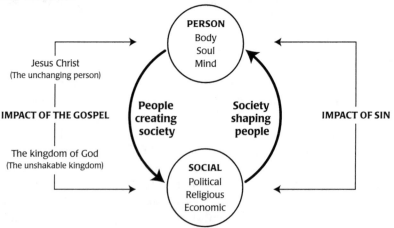

Figure 2-5: The inseparability of the person and the social order.
(After Jones 1972, 32-35)

If we reduce the gospel solely to naming the name of Christ, persons are saved but the social order is ignored. This is a "crippled Christianity with a crippled result" (Jones 1972, 30). If we act as if individuals are saved now and the kingdom is only in heaven when Jesus comes, then we in effect leave the social order to the devil. "Vast areas of human life are left out, unredeemed—the economic, the social and the political" (ibid., 31). Into this vacuum other ideologies and kingdoms move with their seductive and deceptive claims of a new humanity and a better tomorrow—socialism, capitalism, nationalism, ethnic identity, and denominationalism—shakable kingdoms all.

Therefore, the scope of the gospel of the unshakable kingdom and the unchanging person is the individual, the social systems in which we live, and the earth on which we depend for life. Jones's argument anticipates Wink's analysis to a remarkable degree. The impact of the fall is on both the individual and the social system, and so the impact of the gospel of the kingdom must be on both. Wink makes this provocative claim, "The gospel is not a message of personal salvation *from* the world, but a message of *a world transfigured, right down to its basic structures*" (Wink 1992, 83). Even the creation itself has "been groaning as in the pains of childbirth" waiting "in eager expectations for the sons of God to be revealed" (Rom 8:22, 19). To work for human transformation as a Christian means working for the redemption of people, their social systems, and the environment that sustains their life—a whole gospel for all of life. This is the kingdom of God.

We must never separate the person and the kingdom, Jones warns us (1972, 37). Jesus, the unchanging person, is the embodiment of God's kingdom. The best news is that God's kingdom is not a theological phrase, but "is now a name with a human face" (Newbigin 1981, 32-33). Better yet, this person came and dwelt among us, "tempted in every way just as we are" (Heb 4:15). The kingdom of God has indeed drawn near in the form of the unchanging person. "Jesus is the kingdom of God taking sandals and walking" (Jones 1972, 34). Any Christian understanding of transformational development must keep the person of Jesus and the claims and promise of the kingdom central to the defining of what better future we are working for and for choosing the means of getting there.

Like the cross, there is something paradoxical about the kingdom that is worth noting. Jayakumar Christian, a development practitioner and colleague in India, has explored the reversal of power in Revelation (1994, 11-12). The lamb of God that was slain is the one worthy to open the scroll. The lamb, convicted by Pilate and sentenced to death as a criminal, sits on the only throne that matters at the end of time. The slain lamb, not the British lion, the Indian tiger, or the American eagle, is the symbol of power when history ends. In the kingdom of God, what we believe to be the natural order of things is reversed (Kraybill 1978). Further, because Jesus promised it, this kingdom is peopled by those we think of today as powerless: the poor (Lk 6:20), the meek and the persecuted (Mt 5:5,10). Finally, all expressions of human power, every tribe and language and people and nation, will stand in front of the lamb and acknowledge who he is and what he has done (Rv 7:9-10). The kingdom of the broken and humiliated Christ is the only kingdom standing at the end of time.

This creates some challenging questions for development practitioners. Where do we believe the power is that can help the poor? In whom or in what do we trust? What does the image of the slain lamb say to the development practitioner? Or, even more provocatively, to the development agency?

The biblical story and transformational development

Evangelistic intent

This biblical story, of which the Jesus story is the center, is a transformative story. The story of Jesus can heal our story and can heal the story of any community or society by giving it hope and life, if we will accept God's offer of redemption. Failure to share this story is to withhold the only story that Christians believe brings real hope. No other story leads to life. This is the only story that has good news, transformative news, for human sin and for dominating human systems. There can be no better human future apart from this story. For this reason, transformational development done by Christians must include sharing the biblical story in a way that people can understand and that calls for a response.

Restoring relationships

The point of the biblical story is ultimately about relationships, restored relationships. "Living as persons in communion, in right relationship, is the meaning of salvation and the ideal of Christian faith" (LaCugna 1991, 292). Relationships must be restored in all their dimensions. First and foremost, in an intimate and serving relationship with God, through Jesus Christ. Second, in healthy, righteous, and just relationships with ourselves and our communities. Third, in loving, respectful, "neighboring" relationships with all who are "other" to us. Finally, in an earth-keeping, making-fruitful relationship with the earth.[10]

The integrating and focusing importance of relationships in the kingdom is a consistent biblical theme. The creation account, including the fall, is a relational account. The Ten Commandments are about relationships with God and each other, with a bias in favor of the well-being of the community. The covenant with Israel was about a relationship between God and God's people. Melba Maggay, a Filipina theologian and practitioner, reminds us that "Israel was sent into exile because of idolatry and oppression, prophetic themes resulting from the laws of love of God and love of neighbor" (Maggay 1994, 69). Loving God and loving neighbor must be the foundational theme for a Christian understanding of transformational development.

Jesus made a radical extension to loving neighbor when he told us to love our enemies (Mt 5:44). This is not like us, but it is like God. God has no enemies who lie beyond the love of God, even the most vicious, grasping, greedy landlord. Therefore, we must love the poor and non-poor alike. This is not, however, a call to a smarmy, uncritical, "I'm OK you're OK" kind of love. God's love is often a very tough love. Egypt suffered greatly so that Pharaoh might know "that I am God" (Ex 7:5, 14:4). God sent his beloved Israel into exile, even to Babylon, and then did not speak to her for almost six hundred years. God's love of us and our neighbor can be a tough, truth-telling, there-are-consequences, your-soul-is-in-danger kind of love. But, there is never hate; the enemy is never demonized or declared hopeless. The offer of grace is always there.

We need to spend a moment exploring the nature of these relationships. What do we mean? How should such relationships be assessed? The biblical image of shalom is particularly helpful here. Nicholas Wolterstorff points out that *shalom* is usually translated by the word "peace," but that it means more than the absence of strife. First, shalom is a relational concept, "dwelling at peace with God, with self, with fellows, with nature." Then, Wolterstorff suggests, we must add the ideas of justice, harmony, and enjoyment to capture the full biblical meaning of the word. Shalom means just relationship (living justly and experiencing justice), harmonious relationships and enjoyable relationships. Shalom means belonging to an authentic and nurturing community in which one can be one's true self and give one's self away without becoming poor. Justice, harmony, and enjoyment of God, self, others, and nature; this is the shalom that Jesus brings, the peace that passes all understanding (Wolterstorff 1983, 69-72).

The idea of shalom is related to one of the interesting ways Jesus described his mission: "I have come that they may have life, and have it in the full" (Jn 10:10). Life in its fullness is the purpose; this is what we are for and what Christ has come to make possible. To live fully in the present in relationships that are just, harmonious, and enjoyable, that allow everyone to contribute. And to live fully for all time. A life of joy in being that goes beyond having. While shalom and abundant life are ideals that we will not see this side of the second coming, the vision of a shalom that leads to life in its fullness is a powerful image that must inform and shape our understanding of any better human future.

A holistic story

Holism is an important word for Christian thinking about development. There are a variety of ways in which we must think holistically.

First, we need to remember the whole story from beginning to end. Sometimes we are tempted to shorten the biblical story and limit it to the birth, death, and resurrection of Jesus. While this is the center of the story, it is not the whole story. To think properly about human transformation, we must see the world of the poor and the non-poor in light of the whole story. We must be clear on what was intended, how things got as they are, what God is offering to do to change them, and what we can and cannot do as participants in the story. We must have a holistic view of time, of biblical time.

The whole story is also important because it helps those who have not heard the story to understand the gospel. It is hard to make sense out of any story if the storyteller insists on starting in the middle. For example, telling people that Christ died to forgive their sins can be hard to understand if people do not know which God you are talking about or understand the idea of sin. We need a holistic view of the narrative to create a complete framework of meaning for all the gospels have for us.

Second, we need a holistic view of persons. This brings us back to an earlier theme: God's redeeming work does not separate individuals from social systems of which they are a part. People come first, of course. Changed people, transformed by the gospel and reconciled to God, are the beginning of any transformation. Transforming social systems cannot accomplish this: "No arrangement of social cooperation, in which power controls power and anarchy is tamed, will produce human beings free from the lust for power" (Wink 1992, 77). Therefore, transformational development that is Christian cannot avoid giving the invitation to say Yes to the person of Jesus and the invitation to enter the kingdom. At the same time, however, this individual response does not fully express the scope of God's redemptive work.

Social systems are made up of persons, but they are also more than the sum of the persons involved in them. Corporations, government ministries, and even church structures have a character or ethos that is greater than the sum of the individuals who work in them. Wink explains this ethos or spirit in terms of the biblical concepts of principalities and powers: "The principalities and powers of the Bible refer to the inner and outer manifestations of the political, economic, religious and cultural institutions" (Wink 1992, 78). As I have said, this social dimension of human life is also fallen and is thus a target of God's redemptive work.

The Great Commission calls for making the nations into disciples, not just people. This commission of the living Christ instructs us to baptize the nations in the name of the triune God, "teaching them to obey everything I have commanded you" (Mt 28:20). What did Jesus command? To love God and your neighbor as yourself. Kwame Bediako, the Ghanaian theologian, articulates the full meaning of the Great Commission nicely:

The Great Commission, therefore, is about the discipline of the nations, the conversion of the things that make people into nations—the shared and common processes of thinking; attitudes; world views; perspectives; languages; and the cultural, social and economic habits of thought, behavior and practice. These things and the lives of the people in whom such things find expression—all of this is meant to be within the call of discipleship (Bediako 1996b, 184).

Recalling Hiebert's three-tiered worldview scheme in Figure 1-2 in Chapter 1, God's redemptive work addresses all three levels. God is the only true God, the God of power and the God who loves and works in the real world of sight, sound, and touch. His redemptive agenda works in truth (upper level), in power (the excluded middle of the West) and in love (the concrete world of science and the earth). A whole gospel for all levels of our worldview.

Finally, one other aspect of holism needs mentioning. The gospel of Jesus and his kingdom is a message of life, deed, word, and sign, an inseparable whole, all expressions of a single gospel message. Mark's account of the calling of the disciples says that Christ "appointed twelve—designating them apostles—that they might be with him and that he might send them out to preach and to have authority to drive out demons" (Mk 3:14-15). When the apostles are sent on their first solo ministry outing, Mark reports that "they went out and preached that people should repent. They drove out many demons and anointed many sick people with oil and healed them" (Mk 6:12-13).

Activists are quick to pick up on the preaching, the healing, and the casting out stuff. They too often overlook that Christ's call was first and foremost "to be with" Christ. Being must precede doing.

I find it helpful to picture the gospel message in the form of a pyramid. The top of the pyramid is being with Jesus, life in and with the living Lord. This relationship frames all that lies below it. Each of the corners of the pyramid are one aspect or dimension of the gospel: preaching—the gospel-as-word; healing—the gospel-as-deed; casting out—the gospel-as-sign.

Each of these can be developed in turn. Gospel-as-word includes teaching, preaching, and the doing of theology. Gospel-as-deed means working for the physical, social, and psychological well-being of the world that belongs to God. This is the sole location of transformation for too many Christians. Gospel-as-sign means signs and wonders, those things that only God can do, as well as the things the church does as a living sign of a kingdom that is and has not yet fully come.

The metaphor of a pyramid is helpful because one cannot break off a corner and still claim to have a pyramid. This reminds us that for the gospel to be the gospel all four aspects—life, deed, word, and sign—have to be present. They are inseparable, and so is the holism of the Christian gospel.

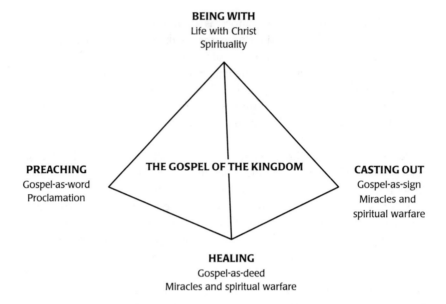

Figure 2-6: The gospel of the kingdom: Being, preaching, healing, and casting out.

Technology and science have a place in the story

One of the increasingly clear features of the modern era is that science has lost its story (Postman 1997, 29-32). Science and technology do not, indeed cannot, provide the answers we need. Science helps us figure out how things work, but not why they work or what they are for.

> Science cannot create. Because science is assumed to be value free, it did not operate within a vision of what ought to be. It could relentlessly and efficiently disassemble; it could not construct an alternative whole (Shenk 1993, 67).

It was not always this way; science was once part of a larger story. Postman reminds us that the "first science storytellers, Descartes, Bacon, Galileo, Kepler and Newton for example—did not think of their story as a replacement for the great Judeo-Christian narrative, but as an extension of it" (1997, 31). Yet in the intervening centuries science and technology increasingly seemed to be able to explain themselves without need to include God as part of the explanation. God became increasingly marginal to their story and was ultimately dismissed as no longer needed. Today science and technology explain themselves: "We work, don't we? Nothing else matters." Relationships, ethics, and justice are pushed to the sidelines.

Yet technology and science are an inseparable part of working for human transformation. Immunizations, water drilling, improved agricultural practices, indigenous or folk science make positive impact in the lives of the poor. Any Christian understanding of transformational development must have space for the good that science and technology offer. Yet, to be Christian, this science and technology cannot be its own story, cannot stand apart from the biblical story that is the real story. We need a modern account of divine action in the natural order (Murphy 1995, 325). If we fail to recover a fully Christian narrative for science and technology, one that recognizes God at work through science in the natural order, and one that places science at the service of life and enhancing relationships, we will bring the poor the same story-less science that is impoverishing the West. This would not be good news. I will develop this more fully in the chapter on Christian witness.

The biblical story is for everyone

In our eagerness to be with and for the poor, we must not forget the biblical story is everyone's story, poor and non-poor alike. Both are made in the image of God, both experienced the consequences of the fall, and both are the focus of God's redemptive work. The hope of the gospel and the transformative promise of the kingdom are for both. The only difference is social location. The poor are on the periphery of the social system while the non-poor, even when living in poor communities, occupy places of preference, prestige, and power.

While God's story is for everyone, there are two ways in which human response to the story creates a bias that favors the poor. First, it is apparently very hard for the non-poor to accept the biblical story as their story (Lk 18:18-30). Wealth and power seem to make people hard of hearing and poor at understanding (Lk 8:14). Even Christians who are not poor have a problem living out the story. There is a strong temptation to domesticate the story in a way that uses it to validate their wealth or position. For the Christian non-poor, there is a need to appropriate the whole biblical story as stewards, not owners. The church has lost its way in this regard from time to time.

Second, it is the poor who most consistently seem to recognize God's story as their story. The church has a long history of growing on its margins and declining at its center (Walls 1987). Furthermore, God has always insisted that caring for the widow, orphan, and alien is a measure of the fidelity with which we live out our faith. No story in which the poor are forgotten, ignored, or left to their own devices is consistent with the biblical story. If the poor are forgotten, God will be forgotten too. Loving God and loving neighbor are twin injunctions of a single command.

If the biblical story is for both poor and non-poor, then we must work to understand the poverties of both as seen from God's perspective. Furthermore, we must see how the poverty of both interact, reinforcing each other. Any theory or practice of transformational development must be predicated on an understanding of the whole of the social systems and those—both poor and non-poor—who inhabit them.

This leads us to explore the meaning and expression of poverty. We need to understand who the poor are and why they are poor, as well as who the non-poor are and how their poverty contributes to the poverty of the poor.

3

Poverty and the Poor

Poverty is an important word for a relief and development agency. After all, we exist in response to the material poverty of our time. Helping the poor is what we do. *Poverty* is a word, however, whose meaning we tend to take for granted. Everyone knows what poverty is. When we see its images on television or hear its stories, we recognize poverty with ease. So, why define it?

Like so many of our ideas, the meanings we ascribe to an abstract noun reflect our way of looking at, thinking about, and making sense of our world. Therefore, we need to examine how we understand poverty as well as how we think and feel about the poor. We need to identify our assumptions and look for blind spots. In addition, sociologists have been studying poverty for a long time. Development academics have been doing field research and codifying what they have found.

This chapter attempts an overview and presents a series of different but related ways of understanding who the poor are and why they are poor.

WHERE DO WE BEGIN?

We need to begin by reminding ourselves that poverty is the condition of people whom we describe abstractly as "the poor." Referring to people by a label is always dangerous. We may forget that the poor are not an abstraction but rather a group of human beings who have names, who are made in the image of God, whose hairs are numbered, and for whom Jesus died. The people who live in poverty are as valued, as important, as loved as those who do not.

Why is this reminder important? The world tends to view the poor as a group that is helpless; thus we give ourselves permission to play god in the lives of the poor. The poor become nameless, and this invites us to treat them as objects of our compassion, as a thing to which we can do what we believe is best. We, the non-poor, take it upon ourselves to name them—homeless, destitute, indigenous, working poor, and so on. Talking about the poor as an abstract noun invites well-intentioned people of compassion to speak for the poor and to practice the latest fads in social engineering. The poor become the custodians of the state, objects of professional study, or a social group to be organized. Whenever we reduce poor people from names to abstractions we add to their poverty and impoverish ourselves.

Our point of departure for a Christian understanding of poverty is to remember that the poor are people with names, people to whom God has given gifts, and people with whom and among whom God has been working before we even know they are there.

Who do you say that they are?

When Jesus asked his disciples, "Who do you say I am?" (Mk 8:29), he received a variety of answers. Most saw who they expected to see—Elijah or another of the prophets. Only Peter saw the Messiah, and we are told it was only because the Holy Spirit helped him to see truly. Seeing what we expect to see is a common human weakness. Therefore, before we begin the work of exploring the world of the poor, we need to begin with ourselves.

We view the poor from a point of view—as Christians, as development professionals, as urban folk, in terms of our personality, and in terms of the culture from which we come. We have a lot of different lenses through which we gather information and by which we try to make sense out of what we observe. We need to make our assumptions explicit and to ask God's help to see the poor and the circumstances of the poor more truly.

One useful exercise is to make a list of all the adjectives used to describe poor people. This usually results in a list of negative labels: dirty, uneducated, lazy, hopeless, superstitious, ineffective, and so on. Then we can ask ourselves if these labels describe the poor people we actually know, and of course they do not. One simple bias is exposed. We can do a similar exercise by making lists of why we think people are poor, what our agency advertising reveals about why people are poor, and what the culture from which we come believes are the reasons people are poor. Uncovering our biases is an important exercise. Only when we do this are we able to deconstruct the lenses we use to work for transformation. We need to remove the log in our own eye so that we have eyes to see and ears to hear.

Who are you?

This is especially important for development workers. We come with a full array of information and perspectives that affect how we view the poor and understand poverty. As Vinay Samuel has pointed out:

The development worker is shaped by a particular understanding of progress, health, modern education, family life, democracy, partici- pation, decision making, market reality, economic principles and per- spectives (1995, 153).

As professionals, we can bring another level of bias that can be quite destructive, if it is unseen and unnamed. Robert Chambers (1997, 78-83) identifies four particular areas of concern:

Conditioning: Every development worker is a conditioned human being. The temptation to transfer our view of how things work and what will make things better is very powerful. After all, we've studied hard and have a lot of field experience, all done so that we could pass it on to others.

Dominance: All of us have within us the desire to feel superior or domi- nant over others. This can be part of personality as well as culture. The fact that we can read, express ourselves clearly and effectively when we speak, write things down, reduce complex problems to diagrams, come in a car or a motorcycle, ask for a meeting with important people and get it, all com- municate a position of power and privilege that we can unwittingly assume as part of who we are.

Distance: Development professionals often work at a distance, geographi- cally and psychologically. When we are with the poor we are "in the field"; our office is in the city where we have access to email, fax, and telephone, where we can "get things done." In addition, the differences in language, food, customs, and ways of problem solving all serve to create distance. We know the poor only at a distance.

Denial: When the real world of the poor conflicts with who we are or how we are trained or what we believe, the reaction can too often be denial. We simply reframe or recompose the discordant experience. This all-too- human reaction allows us to remain untroubled and unchanged, leaving the poor to adapt to us.

So we must begin where we are, with ourselves. "Know thyself" is a use- ful reminder for any development worker. Work spent articulating one's worldview, one's assumptions about how the world works, why it is as it is, and what might improve it is work worth doing. It will make life easier for the poor, and should make us more effective.

CHRISTIAN VIEWS OF THE POOR

Since this book addresses poverty and human transformation from a Christian perspective, the process of uncovering our views of the poor should begin with the ways Christians think about the poor at the end of the twen- tieth century. Richard Mouw (1989, 20-34) has outlined a simple typology or classification that is helpful.

View of the poor	Theological frame	Key biblical texts	Expressions	Why the poor are poor	Christian response
Poor made in the image of God	Creation	Genesis 1-2	Poor as creative. Poor as a work of art. See God's hidden glory.	The poor lack skills, knowledge, and opportunity.	Enable the poor to be fruitful and productive.
Poor as people in rebellion	Fall	Genesis 3 Proverbs	Poor as lazy. Poor make bad choices. God helps those who help themselves.	The poor are in rebellion and their culture keeps them poor.	Challenge the poor with the gospel and encourage them to make better choices.
Poor as Christ incarnate	Incarnation	Gospels	Christ in the distressing guise of the poor. What you did for the least of these...	The poor lack love.	Accompany the poor and relieve suffering as possible.
Poor as God's favorites	Prophetic Eschatological	Exodus Prophets	Blessed are the poor for theirs will be the kingdom. Liberation theology	The poor are oppressed by the non-poor. Poverty is structural.	Work for justice. Help the poor find their voice and place in socio-political-economic system.
Poor as lost souls	Salvation Soteriological	Matthew 28 Acts	The better future lies in eternity. Save as many as we can. The poor will always be with you.	The poor are lost from God, and the kingdom is coming soon.	Proclaim the gospel and encourage the poor to respond.

Figure 3-1: Christian views of the poor. (Developed from Mouw 1989, 20-34)

Poor as made in the image of God: This view draws on the creation narrative and tends toward a romantic view of the poor. Their poverty is the result of lack of skills and opportunity. What they need is a "leg up."

Poor as people in rebellion: This view draws on the fall as the defining reason why the poor are poor. They are lazy and make bad choices. The poor need to accept the gospel, go to work, and make better choices.

Poor as Christ incarnate: Drawing on Matthew 25, this view of the poor centers on the Incarnation and, with Mother Teresa, "sees Christ in the distressing guise of the poor." The poor lack love and relationships; they do not belong. The poor need accompaniment; we should relieve as much suffering as we can.

Poor as God's favorites: This view draws on the prophetic literature and the Exodus account. The poor are the ones who are blessed, for theirs will be the kingdom. They are poor because they are oppressed by social systems that keep them poor for the benefit of the non-poor. The poor need justice and help in finding their voice and place in the economic and political system.

Poor as lost souls: This is a category that I am taking the liberty of adding to Mouw's typology. This view draws selectively on the gospels and reflects the dichotomy between the spiritual and the physical of the modern world. The poor are lost. The kingdom is coming when Jesus comes, and that will be soon. The poor need to be saved.

Seen in this light, the conclusions are obvious. First, Christians sometimes are selective in their use of Scripture and thereby support a view of the poor they already hold or that they received from somewhere else. Second, it would seem more fruitful to develop an understanding of the poor that includes all and excludes none of these images. The poor are made in the image of God. They are fallen. Christ did use the poor as a metaphor for himself and our need to serve the less fortunate. There is a bias toward the poor and against the non-poor (see the end of the theology chapter), and the poor are often lost souls.

WHO ARE THE POOR?

This section attempts to integrate a family of definitions drawn from several sources. As we do this, we must keep in mind my opening admonition: any such definition is necessarily flawed because it describes real people using ideas and concepts. The following observations must be held lightly in the palm of our open hand. We must be ready to let the idea go, when our experience with poor people says otherwise.

The poor are people, and we must begin there. Our theological reflections of the last chapter tell us that the poor are whole, living people, inseparably body, soul, mind, and heart. Further, they are persons embedded in families, communities, and the corresponding social systems. Like ourselves, the poor are encumbered selves. Finally, the biblical narrative tells us that the poor are made in the image of God and thus have gifts, skills, and the potential to become kingdom-like, just as we do.

Households

The poor live in households, and some development thinkers believe that we need to view the household as the economic and social unit of importance. Each member helps and contributes, disrupts and consumes, yet they all understand themselves as part of this social unit rather than thinking of themselves so much as individuals. Chambers's definition of the poverty trap, which I will introduce later, assumes the household as the basic economic unit (Chambers 1983, 108). Maldonado reports on the power of Christian conversion for social transformation acting through and changing the culture of the household unit in Latin America (1993, 196). Friedman sees the household as a living social unit with people in dynamic relationship located in a real place (1992, 46). Households are the building blocks of larger social systems. Friedman's analysis is worth developing in greater detail.

Friedman sees households as made up of three-dimensional moral human beings living in dynamic interaction with others. People have obligations to one another as well as needs and wants. Human needs, according to Friedman, include the psychological needs for "affection, self-expression and esteem that are not available as commodities but arise directly from human encounter" (1992, 32). Each household forms a political structure and economy in miniature, the self-same image of the larger social structure of which it is a part. Households exercise three kinds of power:

- *Social power* dealing with access to information, knowledge and skills, participation in social organizations and access to financial resources.
- *Political power* dealing with access to the process by which decisions affecting their future are made.
- *Psychological power* dealing with a sense of individual potency or self-confident behavior (ibid., 33).

Time is the basic resource of the household, according to Friedman, not money. The household allocates the time of individual members to different tasks, areas of life, and domains of social practice in order to live. "Poor households . . . rely heavily on non-market relations both for securing their livelihood and pursuing their life goals" (Friedman 1992, 45). The poor cannot rely on money to satisfy their needs. This often makes poor households invisible to social research.

Using the household as the lens through which we see the poor also allows us to see the poor both as individuals and as embedded in social systems:

> Households are miniature political economies that have a territorial base (life space) and are engaged in the production of their own life and livelihood. Households are *political* because their members arrive at decisions affecting the household as a whole and themselves individually in ways that involve negotiating relations of power. Households have a *territorial base* because people have to have a place to live even if it is only a cardboard shack. . . . Finally, households are conceived as *producers* and thus as collective actor on behalf of their own (and sometimes others') material interests (Friedman 1992, 47).

Because households normally consist of people related to one another in some way, they manifest reciprocity and mutual obligation. Thus there is a moral economy of mutual exchange that operates by moral rules learned largely within the household (Friedman 1992, 48). This moral economy operates, at least in part, outside the market economy and is an important way the poor maintain life and livelihood. Relationships are often more important to life than money.

The idea of the household as the central social unit also resonates with the biblical narrative. The Bible seems to see people in household units, too. Noah and his extended family were saved (Gn 7:1). God distributed the Promised Land fairly according to clans and household units (Wright 1983, 68). Joshua made commitments in the name of his family (Jos 24:15). Lydia and her household were baptized by Paul, as were the Philippian jailer and his family later in the same story (Acts 16:15, 33). One test of leadership is that a deacon "must manage his children and household well" (1 Ti 3:12).

Finally, understanding poverty in terms of a household sets the stage for thinking about the causes of poverty in terms of the larger social systems. I will develop this more, later in this chapter.

The poor and the non-poor

We cannot talk about who the poor are without pointing out the fact that they are always among others who are not poor. Too often we oversimplify and use mental models that assume the poor live in poor communities and that the non-poor live elsewhere—a nearby community, in the city, in the North. This is not true. Even in the poorest communities, there is a small group who are less poor and who occupy positions of relative power and privilege. In any area there is always a small group of communities that are not poor in relation to the other communities in the area. Even in the household unit this is true; there is usually a dominant man who is not poor in comparison to the rest of the household (Anderson 1996c, 8). Therefore, poverty and the poor can only be understood by keeping the relationships between the poor and the non-poor clearly in mind.

Who the poor are not

We must stop for a moment and deal with two things people sometimes say about the poor that are not always true. Some say the poor are lazy, fatalistic, and will not save for the future. Others say the poor are ignorant. Chambers debunks these claims and calls us to be more humble in our judgments. The poor may not save, but this may be for the very good reason that their survival today will not permit it. The poor may appear lazy, but what we may be seeing is their way of conserving limited physical energy. Fatalism may be an adaptation that is prudent, not a giving up. "The appearance of powerlessness, unawareness and acquiescence may be a condition for survival" (1983, 106).

The assertion that the poor are ignorant and stupid does not survive any informed understanding of real poor people. The depth and breadth of their indigenous knowledge frequently astounds us (Chambers 1983, 106; Muchena 1996, 178-79). Their knowledge of local ecology, traditional medicine, and survival skills is considerable. The poor can survive in conditions that would daunt the non-poor. Furthermore, Chambers reminds us that "apparent ignorance and stupidity are part of the strategy of lying low, a stance necessitated in the face of officials who demand obsequious behavior" (1983, 107).

The poor are no more lazy, fatalistic, improvident, stupid, or arrogant than anyone else. All people suffer from these problems, poor and non-poor alike. But only the non-poor can afford to indulge in these behaviors. "People so close to the edge cannot afford laziness or stupidity. They have to work and work hard, whenever and however they can. Many of the lazy and stupid poor are dead" (Chambers 1983, 107).

Which poor?

The poor are not a homogeneous category, and poverty is different for different groups. Poverty means different things to children and youth, to women, to the mentally and physically challenged, and to the old. To think and do well, we need to understand these differences and plan accordingly without increasing the poverty of the community through social fragmentation. Mary Anderson's book *Development and Social Diversity* helps open up this world of differences, while affirming that solidarity among these groups is equally important to effective development.

Children and youth are often an underutilized development resource. Too often they are viewed as helpless, vulnerable, and in need of care. In a sense, we have a mental model that says that the poverty of children is complete; they are simply poor and have nothing to contribute. This makes them all the poorer. We are always tempted to "do for" children, not recognizing the potential for transformation that children represent. I will come back to the potential transformational role of children in the chapter on the tools we use for development.

The poor are often women, and the poverty of women is both a special concern and a special opportunity. These UN statistics are now widely known: women perform two-thirds of the world's work, earn one-tenth of the world's income, are two-thirds of the world's illiterate and own less than one-hundredth of the world's property (Williams and Mwau 1994, 100). There is a great deal of documentation that shows that women and young girls get less schooling, have poorer nutrition, and receive less health care. The poverty of women is physical, spiritual, and social. This must be an area of special concern for those working for human transformation. At the same time, there is another body of research that shows that female literacy is a positive predictor of many good things—lower fertility, lower child mortality, and successful micro-enterprise development. Thus, women offer a special opportunity if we simply keep them in sight and involved as part of the development process. Transformational development that does not include gender analysis and seek the empowerment of women will fail.

WHAT IS POVERTY?

Poverty has been described in various ways and with increasing sophistication. It is important to articulate our view of poverty because our view of poverty strongly influences what we think transformational development is and how we should go about doing it.

Poverty as deficit

In the early days of development thinking, people defined poverty as a deficit, a lack. Poor people do not have enough to eat, a place to sleep, or clean water. Their land is poor, there is no water for irrigation, roads are inadequate, and there are no schools for their children. This view of poverty encourages plans to provide the missing things: food, low-cost housing, wells. The unspoken assumption is that when the missing things are provided, the poor will no longer be poor.

Another kind of deficit has to do with things people do not know or skills they do not have. Poor people may not understand nutrition, the need to

[Handwritten margin note top: UNDERSTAND THE IMPORTANCE OF SAVING, WHY ARE]

[Handwritten margin note right: WE THE WORST. DAMN IT]

[Handwritten margin note left: IF THE POOR CAN'T READ AND DON'T]

boil water, the importance of child spacing, how to read the instructions on a packet of improved seeds. They don't know about sustainable agriculture, running small businesses, the importance of saving money. This view of poverty invites programming that features education and nonformal learning. It assumes that if the poor simply learn enough, they will no longer be poor.

Christians tend to add another dimension to poverty as deficit: the non-Christian poor lack knowledge about God and the good news of Jesus Christ. To make their understanding of poverty holistic, Christians add knowledge of the gospel to the list of other things the poor do not have. Thus proclamation of the gospel is added to the development program.

These views of poverty are true, and, as far as they go, they are correct. People *do* need things—skills, knowledge, and a chance to hear the gospel. However, limiting one's understanding of poverty to this framework also creates some serious problems.

If poverty is the absence of things, then the solution is to provide them. This often leads to the outsider becoming the development "Santa Claus," bringing all good things: food, well drilling, education, and proclamation. The poor are seen as passive recipients, incomplete human beings we make complete and whole through our largess. This unwitting attitude has two very negative consequences. First, this attitude demeans and devalues the poor. Our view of them, which quickly becomes their view of themselves, is that they are defective and inadequate. We do not treat them as human beings made in the image of God. We act as if God's gifts were given to us and none to the poor. This attitude increases their poverty and tempts us to play god in the lives of the poor.

Second, our attitude about ourselves can become messianic. We are tempted to believe that we are the delivers of the poor, that we make their lives complete. We can inadvertently harbor a belief that we are the ones who save. Such an attitude is not good for our souls. *[Handwritten note: we do not save the poor]*

Poverty as entanglement—Robert Chambers

Robert Chambers is a respected development professional working at the Institute of Development Studies at the University of Sussex in England, and is a champion of the Participatory Rural Appraisal (now called Participatory Learning and Action, see pages 173ff.). Using the household as his point of departure, Chambers describes the poor as living in a "cluster of disadvantage." The household is poor, physically weak, isolated, vulnerable, and powerless. Chambers describes these dimensions of poverty as an interactive system that he calls the "poverty trap" (1983, 103-39). Chambers's systems view of poverty has considerable explanatory power and aligns well with experience. Let's examine the respective parts.

1. *Material poverty:* The household has few assets. Its housing and sanitation is inadequate. It has little or no land, livestock, or wealth.
2. *Physical weakness:* The household members are weak. They lack strength because of poor health and inadequate nutrition. Many in the household are women, the very young, and the very old.
3. *Isolation:* The household lacks access to services and information. It is often remote—far from main roads, water lines, and even electricity. It lacks access to markets, capital, credit, and information.
4. *Vulnerability:* The household has few buffers against emergencies or disaster. Its members lack choices and options. They cannot save, and they are vulnerable to cultural demands, such as dowry and feast days, that soak up savings.
5. *Powerlessness:* The household lacks the ability and the knowledge to influence the life around it and the social systems in which it lives.
6. *Spiritual poverty:* With apologies to Chambers, I add this category in the interest of being holistic. The household suffers from broken and dysfunctional relationships with God, each other, the community, and creation. Its members may suffer from spiritual oppression—fear of spirits, demons, and ancestors. They may lack hope and be unable to believe that change is possible. They may never have heard the gospel or have only responded to a truncated version of the gospel that lacks transforming power.

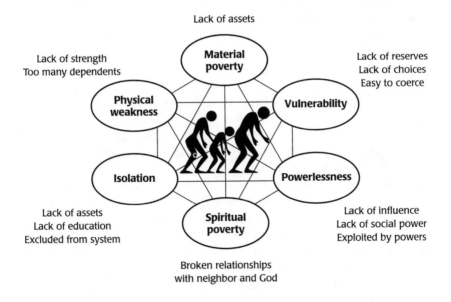

Figure 3-2 : The poverty system of the household.
(Adapted from Chambers 1983, 110)

Chambers's systems approach to poverty is a powerful tool. The interconnection among the six elements of his poverty trap is an important feature. Each is linked to and reinforces the others. A problem in one area means problems in another, and it is easy to see how the result can be greater and greater poverty.

Two of Chambers's system elements need further development: vulnerability and powerlessness. Chambers identifies four elements that contribute to vulnerability of poor households (1983, 114-30). First, they are subject to *social conventions* such as dowry, bride price, feast days, weddings, and funerals. These social requirements create a permanent demand for moneylenders, whose usurious rates ensure permanent poverty. We must note that religious systems often collude at this point by making such conventions part of religious life. Second, natural or manmade *disasters* expose vulnerability. The poor have no reserves, and disasters push them to do things they might not wish to do, such as sell land and livestock. Third, *physical incapacity*—sickness, childbearing, and accidents—reveals vulnerability. These increase physical weakness and result in the sale of assets the people can ill afford to lose. Fourth, there are *unproductive expenditures* for things like drink, drugs, unproductive assets (like radios, shoes, or clothes), and poor business investments. Finally, there is the *exploitation* that takes advantage of vulnerability. Exorbitant interest rates, trickery, coercion, intimidation, and blackmail are used by the powerful (often the non-poor in poor communities) to take what little a poor household has—its assets and even its labor.

Chambers's examination of powerlessness (1983, 131-35) is particularly interesting in that it prepares us for the poverty interpretations of Friedman and Christian that will follow shortly. Chambers points out that powerlessness is often overlooked because it is discomforting to the powerful, even to development practitioners. Powerlessness is an invitation to exploitation by the powerful. Chambers alerts us to three clusters of exploitation. First, the local non-poor often stand as *nets* between the poorer people and the outside world by trapping resources and benefits that were intended for the poor. "It is a notorious commonplace how, almost everywhere in the third world, credit and marketing cooperatives have been dominated by the larger farmers who have used them for their own benefit, at the cost of smaller producers" (1983, 131). Second, *robbery*. The local non-poor—police, politicians, and landowners—use deception, blackmail, and violence to rob the poor who, in turn, lack recourse to justice, "since they do not know the law, cannot afford legal help and fear to offend the patrons on whom they depend" (1983, 133). Finally, there is *bargaining and its absence*. The assets of the poor are bought at far below market value because of distress sales. The poor borrow at exorbitant rates, even when less costly options are available, because they fear that alienating the local moneylender may lead to a lack of credit in the future. The poor are particularly vulnerable to bargaining when it comes to being paid for their labor. The power to withhold work without reason is a powerful bargaining tool.

One important feature is missing from Chambers's analysis of poverty: the impact of spiritual poverty. Each of the elements of his poverty trap has a spiritual side. Powerlessness is not just a problem the poor have with the material world and the non-poor who live in it. The poor often live in fear of the unseen spiritual world of curses, gods, demons, and ancestors. Physical weakness is often associated with spiritual causes. Isolation from God and the Bible is as significant as not having access to government services, markets, and capital. The need to find money to lift curses and ensure the blessing of the spirits contributes to vulnerability in the same way that disasters and social convention do.

There is another, more fundamental level at which we can see the lack of the spiritual. There is a spiritual reality that underlies the entire poverty entrapment system and its six interacting elements. This foundational spiritual reality provides the explanation for (1) the deceptive and dominating activity of the non-poor, (2) the contribution the poor make to their own poverty by destructive behavior within the household, and (3) the poverty of being (we are of no value and are unworthy) and meaning (there are no answers for important questions), especially among the poor. No systems account of poverty is complete without a holistic view of the spiritual and material at the level of people and the social systems within which they live.

Poverty as lack of access to social power—John Friedman

John Friedman, professor of urban planning at the University of California at Los Angeles (UCLA) and a promoter of what he calls "alternative development," describes poverty by focusing on powerlessness as lack of access to social power. Poor households are excluded and need to be empowered. Like Chambers, he begins with the household as the social unit of the poor and sees it embedded within four overlapping domains of social practice: state, political community, civil society, and corporate economy (Friedman 1992, 26-31). Each domain has a distinctive type of power: state power, political power, social power, and economic power.

Each domain also has its own set of institutions. The core of the state consists of the formal executive and judicial elements of government. The core of the political community consists of independent political organizations. In the overlap between the state and the political community domains, Friedman places the legislative and regulatory bodies. The core of civil society is the household. Where the domains of civil society and the state overlap, we find churches and voluntary organizations. The central institution of the corporate economy is the corporation. This domain is also open to and profoundly interconnected with the global economy and transnational corporations. Where the corporate economy overlaps with the political community, we find political parties, protest movements, and environmental groups. Where the corporate economy overlaps with civil society, we find the non-formal economic sector and popular economic groups. These interacting domains are the system within which the poor household struggles to find space, location, and influence.

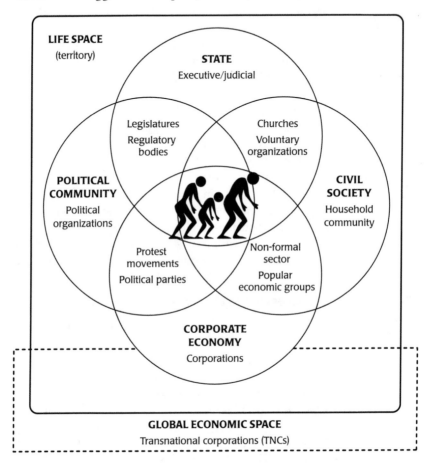

Figure 3-3: Life space for the household and the four arenas
of social practice.
(Friedman 1992, 27)

Friedman then describes eight bases of social power that are available to the poor as avenues for creating social space and influence: social networks, information for self-development, surplus time, instruments of work and livelihood, social organization, knowledge and skill, defensible life space, and financial resources (1992, 67).

Social networks are a big part of poverty

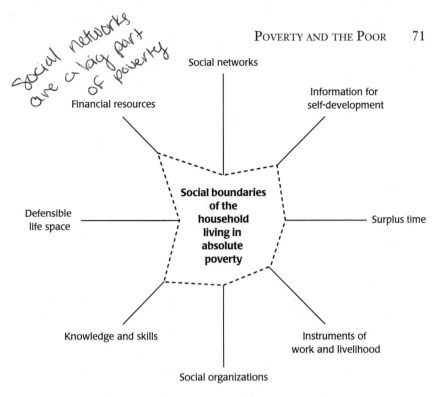

Figure 3-4: Eight bases of social power and the poor household.
(Adapted from Friedman 1992, 67)

Absolute poverty for Friedman is when the values for these eight dimensions are too low for a household to be able to move out of poverty on its own. Friedman's explanation of poverty is a lack of social organization and lack of access to the political process (1992, 66).

> The (dis)empowerment model of poverty is a political variant of the basic needs approach. It is centered on politics rather than planning. . . . The starting point of the model is the assumption that poor households lack the social power to improve the condition of their members' lives.

Friedman's understanding of poverty brings a more sophisticated understanding of how poverty is related to lack of access to social power, in contrast to simply a lack of things or lack of knowledge. It also inserts poor households into a social system that goes beyond the local setting. The role of government, the political system, civil society, and the economy, integrated into the global economy, is now part of the field of play. Poverty is understood as a state of disempowerment. In addition, Friedman has introduced a psychological dimension to poverty and power. These are helpful developments.

Friedman's understanding of poverty alludes to, but does not develop the spiritual dimension of life. There is no explanation for why social systems exclude the poor and become self-serving. A spiritual dimension is needed to account for the fact that social institutions frequently frustrate even the best and most noble intentions of the people who inhabit and manage them. Without a doctrine of principalities and powers, it is unclear why good people cannot make social institutions do what they were set up to do. Furthermore, there is no means to account for the destructive behaviors and poor choices of both the poor and the non-poor, nor for the fact that the poor often exploit each other.

Poverty as disempowerment—Jayakumar Christian

Jayakumar Christian, a long-time Indian practitioner and World Vision colleague, codified his development experience in the form of his Ph.D. thesis (1994). Christian builds on Chambers and Friedman and adds the spiritual side of understanding poverty. Like Chambers and Friedman, Christian sees the poor household embedded in a complex framework of interacting systems. For Christian, these systems include a personal system, which includes psychology; a social system similar to Friedman's; a spiritual/religious system, which is both personal and social; and a cultural system that includes worldview (1994, 334). The poor find themselves trapped inside a system of disempowerment made up of these interacting systems. Each part of the system creates its own particular contribution to disempowerment of the poor, including what Christian terms captivity to

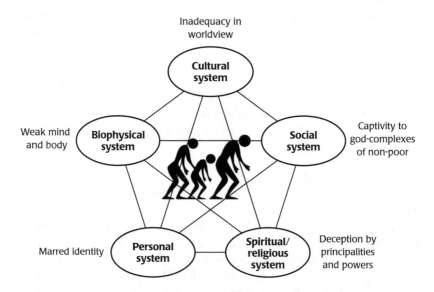

Figure 3-5: Poverty as disempowering systems.
(Adapted from Christian 1994)[1]

god-complexes of the non-poor, deception by the principalities and powers, inadequacies in worldview, and suffering from a marred identity.

Captivity to god-complexes of the non-poor— the socio-economic-political system

Similar to Friedman, Christian argues that the social system reinforces the powerlessness of the poor by exclusion and exploitation, but Christian seeks deeper roots for this (1994, 178). The non-poor understand themselves as superior, necessary, and anointed to rule. They succumb to the temptation to play god in the lives of the poor, using religious systems, mass media, the law, government policies, and people occupying positions of power. These people create the narratives, structures, and systems that justify and rationalize their privileged position. The result is that the poor become captive to the god-complexes of the non-poor.

According to Christian, the non-poor express their god-complexes by:

- Seeking to absolutize themselves in the lives of the poor.
- Citing the "eternal yesterday"[2] as the justification for influencing the "eternal tomorrow" of the poor. "It has always been this way."
- Influencing areas of life that are beyond their scope of influence (e.g., the landlord choosing the names of the children or deciding who will marry whom).
- Claiming immutability for their power over the poor. There will never be power sharing.
- Interacting with other non-poor, safeguarding and enhancing each other's power (1998a, 1-2).

This captivity finds its concrete expression in the interactive working of the social, political, economic, religious, and cultural systems, resulting in a web of lies and deceit (more on this shortly) that mediates power, often with no need of force. Furthermore, this systemic captivity has many levels. The local police, landowners, and religious leaders form the micro-expression or the lowest level of this disempowering system. They, in turn, are linked to and usually subservient to business, political, and judicial leaders at the regional and national levels. This is the macro-level of the god-complexes. These are embedded in global systems represented by transnational corporations, international financial institutions (the World Bank, IMF, etc.), the UN system, and the like, who also play god in the lives of the poor, albeit from a far distance. Finally, Christian follows Wink in reminding us that all these levels exist within a cosmic system in which the principalities and powers work out their rebellion against God and God's intentions for human life in creation.

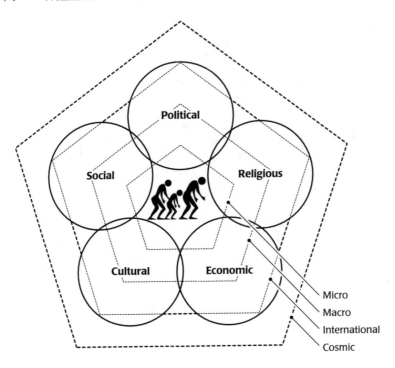

Figure 3-6: Systems framework for the god-complexes
that disempower the poor.
(Adapted from Christian 1994)

Building on Walter Wink, Christian goes on to point out that these god-complexes, especially at the level of systems and structures, have an ideological center, "an inner reality that governs and holds together the structures, systems and people who inhabit them. This inner reality provides the inner logic . . . and interpretations for ultimate values of life and events" (1998, 3). Transformational development that does not assert God's truth over these self-justifying narratives leaves the structural side of poverty and its causes untouched.

This captivity to the god-complexes of the non-poor becomes internalized as the poor acquiesce to what appears to be the normalcy and immutability of their captivity. Salvian, in the fifth century, wrote: "They [the poor] give themselves to the upper classes in return for care and protection. They make themselves captives of the rich, as it were, passing over into their jurisdiction and dependence" (quoted in Oden 1986, 151). I've already mentioned that it took forty years to get the experience of Egyptian slavery out of the collective mind of Israel before nation building could begin. This is an expression of what Christian calls the marred identity of the poor (more on this shortly).

Deception by principalities and powers—the spiritual system

While acknowledging the impact of the fall and sin on individual human beings, Christian also identifies an additional impact of the fall in what he calls deception by the principalities and powers (1994, 252), drawing on and extending Walter Wink. The powerlessness of the poor is reinforced by fear and deceit created by the "god of this age that has blinded the minds of unbelievers" (2 Cor 4:4) and the "trap of the devil who has taken them captive to do his will" (2 Ti 2:26). Both the poor and the non-poor are "in slavery under the basic principles of the world" (Gal 4:3).

The primary expression of this deception is through the ideological center or inner reality of the systems, structures, and legitimating narratives through which the non-poor play god in the lives of the poor. But there is a deeper truth as well.

Christian is also affirming that it is not simply human beings, and the systems within which they live, that create and sustain poverty. There is a cosmic adversary who is working against life. This adversary is "a liar and the father of lies" (Jn 8:44). Any account of poverty that ignores the reality of an Evil One lacks the full explanatory power that the Bible offers.

Inadequacies in worldview—the cultural system

For Christian, powerlessness is reinforced by what he calls inadequacies in worldview (1994, 199, 262). Writing from within a Hindu context, Christian points to the disempowering idea of *karma*, which teaches the poor that their current state is a just response to their former life and something that must be accepted if they hope for a better life the next time around. When the poor are invited to try to change their present condition, their worldview tells them they are being invited to sin.

In another example of a worldview supporting oppressive social relationships, the Brahmin are taught by their Hindu tradition that they were made from the head of God and so are supposed to rule. The haridjan are taught that they were made from the lower parts of god and thus are inferior by nature. Every culture has beliefs that disempower people, discourage change, and label oppressive relationships as sacrosanct and ordained.

Weakness in mind, body, and spirit—the biophysical system

This expression of poverty corresponds to Chambers's category of physical weakness. The biophysical system—mind, body and spirit—is diminished by poverty and powerlessness results because of hunger, illness, and lack of education (1994, 200). Undernourished, sick, and weak bodies and minds are easy homes for captivity to god-complexes, deception, and inadequate worldviews.

The marred identity of the poor—the personal system

Christian concludes his explanation of poverty by pointing out that captivity to god-complexes, deception by principalities and powers, and inadequacies in worldview result in a tragic marring of the identity of the poor. The identity of the poor is marred in two important ways.

First, the poor are systematically excluded as actors. Too often the voice of the poor is regarded as "damaged goods." The powerful do not expect the poor to have anything to offer, since they have been labeled (usually by the non-poor) as lazy, ignorant, or unworthy. Sadly, sometimes the development agency and its practitioners are so full of their own expertise that they treat the poor in a similar way.

Second, a lifetime of suffering, deception, and exclusion is internalized by the poor in a way that results in the poor no longer knowing who they truly are or why they were created. This is the deepest and most profound expression of poverty. The poor come to believe that they are and were always meant to be without value and without gifts. They believe they are truly god-forsaken. "Poor people feel nonexistent, valueless, humiliated" (Wink 1992, 101). Internalization of poverty and the messages of non-value from the non-poor and social systems result in what Augustine Musopole calls a poverty of being: "This is where the African feels his poverty most: A poverty of being, in which poor Africans have come to believe they are no good and cannot get things right" (Musopole 1997).

So deeply embedded is this kind of poverty that the good news is no longer believable. Sitting at a campfire in the Kalahari Desert, I heard a San woman say, in response to hearing the news that the Son of God had died for her sins, that she could believe that God would let his Son die for a white man, and that maybe she could believe that God might let his Son die for a black man, but she could never accept the idea that God would let his Son die for a San woman. This is spiritual and psychological poverty of the deepest kind, the root of fatalism.

When the poor accept their marred identity and their distorted sense of vocation as normative and immutable, their poverty is complete. It is also permanent unless this issue is addressed and they are helped to recover their identity as children of God, made in God's image, and their true vocation as productive stewards in the world God made for them.

I would like to take this idea of marred identity a little farther. Who we are is a question of both being and doing. Christian eloquently calls our attention to the being part of the marred identity of the poor, but does not speak to the issue of doing. I believe that poverty mars both parts of the identity of the poor. The result of poverty is that people who are poor no longer know who they are (being) nor do they believe that they have a vocation of any value (doing).

The web of lies

For Christian, the identity of the poor is distorted, and is kept distorted, by a "web of lies" that entraps the poor in ways far stronger and insidious than physical bonds or material limitations (1994, 264). These lies are a result of god-complexes, inadequacies in worldview, and deception by principalities and powers.

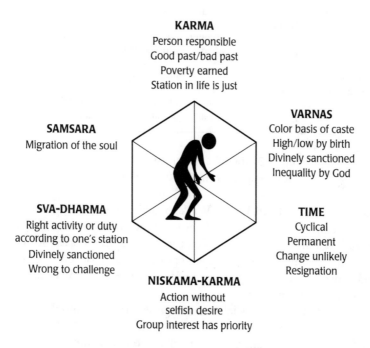

KARMA
Person responsible
Good past/bad past
Poverty earned
Station in life is just

SAMSARA
Migration of the soul

VARNAS
Color basis of caste
High/low by birth
Divinely sanctioned
Inequality by God

SVA-DHARMA
Right activity or duty
according to one's station
Divinely sanctioned
Wrong to challenge

TIME
Cyclical
Permanent
Change unlikely
Resignation

NISKAMA-KARMA
Action without
selfish desire
Group interest has priority

Figure 3-7: The disempowering themes
in the Hindu belief system.
(Adapted from Christian 1994, 241)

Christian's idea of a debilitating web of lies can be used to show the impact of each element of Christian's disempowering themes in the way the poor view the social, political, and social systems within which they live.

Theme	Social System	Lie
Captivity to the god-complexes of the non-poor	Social Political Economic Religious	You are outside the social system. Your purpose is to serve us. You have no assets, nor should you. We will speak to God on your behalf.
Marred identity of the poor	Social Political Economic Religious	We are not worthy of inclusion. We are not worthy of participation. We have nothing to contribute. We are not worthy of God's concern.
Inadequacies in worldview	Social Political Economic Religious	Our place in the social order is fixed. They are supposed to rule over us. Our poverty is ordained. We sinned: God gives us what we deserve.
Deception by the principalities and powers	Social Political Economic Religious	Social systems are not for the likes of you. Political systems are not for the likes of you. Economic systems are not for the likes of you. God is not for the likes of you.
Weakness of mind, body, and spirit	Social Political Economic Religious	I'm not smart enough. I'm uneducated. I'm too weak to matter; I have nothing. I can't understand these things anyway.

Figure 3-8: The all-encompassing web of lies.
(Developed from Christian 1994, 264)

Along these same lines, Walter Wink has articulated "delusional assumptions"[3] that are accepted uncritically by poor and non-poor alike (1992, 95). The non-poor are socialized into a culture with mythic stories, structures, and systems that make their position of power make sense, even seem ethically defensible. The deception is complete. A partial list of Wink's delusional assumptions includes:

- The need to prevent social chaos requires that some should dominate others.
- Men are better at being dominant than women; some races are more naturally suited to dominate others.
- A valued end justifies any means.
- Violence is redemptive; it is the only language enemies understand.
- Ruling or managing is the most important social function.
- Rulers and managers are entitled to extra privileges and wealth.
- Those with the greatest military strength, the most advanced technology, the biggest markets, and the most wealth are the ones who will and should survive.

- Production of wealth is more important than production of healthy, normal people and sound human relationships.
- Property is sacred and property ownership is an absolute right.
- Institutions are more important than people.
- God, if there is a God, is the protector and patron of the powerful.

These delusions are widely believed. They are the way of the world, largely taken for granted by poor and non-poor, Christian and non-Christian alike. The poor, Christian tells us, have internalized a web of lies.

I would like to take this further and argue that the non-poor are no better off. The only difference is that they believe a different set of lies. "The rulers of the earth do not know that they too are held in thrall by the Delusional System. They do not know whom they serve" (Wink 1992, 97). Poverty cannot be addressed fully unless these delusions on the part of the poor and the non-poor are exposed and their respective webs of lies confronted by God's truth. "The church has no more important task than to expose these delusional assumptions as the Dragon's game" (Wink 1992, 96, referring to the Dragon of Revelation 13).

Christian's understanding of poverty adds an additional dimension to the work of Chambers and Friedman. He uncovers the internal nature of poverty, created and sustained by the social systems to which Chambers and Friedman are so sensitive. This inner set of limitations, all lies, drives poverty deep inside, making it very hard to confront and change. "Poverty is the world telling the poor that they are god-forsaken."[4]

One final note. Christian's framework also provides a way of understanding what John Dilulio of Princeton University calls "moral poverty"; he describes "the super-predators," the incredibly violent youth of American inner cities, teenagers who will kill without thought or remorse because they are inconvenienced. Dilulio says that moral poverty is what you get when people grow up

> without loving, capable, responsible parents who teach you right from wrong . . . who habituate you to feel joy at other's joy, pain at other's pain, happiness when you do right, remorse when you do wrong. . . . Poverty is growing up surrounded by deviant, delinquent and criminal adults (1995, 25).

This suggests that in addition to internalizing negative, debilitating lies learned from the social system, poverty can also occur as a result of the chronic absence of experience with love, responsibility and righteousness. Apparently we also need to believe in a web of truth. This is not a problem limited to the inner city of America. Young people in too many parts of the world are being denied this kind of poverty prevention when they are used in the sex trade, abused as child laborers or sent to war as teenagers. We do not know what kind of adults we will encounter in ten years time in places

like Thailand, India, Rwanda, Liberia and Sierra Leone—or in the inner
cities of America.

Poverty as a lack of freedom to grow—Ravi Jayakaran

Ravi Jayakaran, an Indian expert in the use of the Participatory Learning
and Action (PLA) methodology and a colleague of Robert Chambers, describes poverty as a lack of the freedom to grow (1996, 14). Echoing Luke
2:52, Jayakaran pictures the poor wrapped in a series of restrictions and
limitations[5] in four areas of life: physical, mental, social, and spiritual.

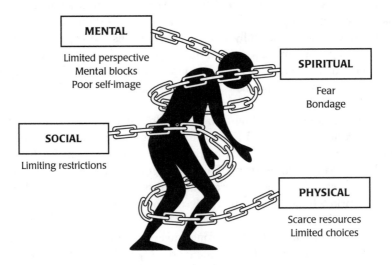

Figure 3-9: Poverty as a lack of freedom to grow.
(Jayakaran 1996, 14)

Jayakaran goes on to point out that behind each of these "bundles of
limitations" lies powerful stakeholders, people whose interests are served
by the limitations and who have a stake in sustaining the illusion that such
limitations can never be changed. We discover these limitations when we
ask the critical diagnostic question: Who is doing what to whom? The micro-expression of these stakeholders is usually local and obvious: moneylenders, local traders and business people, police, government officials, and
priests or shamans. The macro-expressions are often harder to name because they are located elsewhere, usually close to where decisions affecting
the poor are made. In addition to being harder to find and identify, the
higher-level stakeholders usually control the micro-level ones.

Jayakaran adds to our understanding of poverty in two important ways.
First, he locates the causes of poverty in people, not in concepts or abstractions. This is important and is frequently forgotten. It is easy to blame greed,
systems, the market, corruption, and culture, but these are abstractions and

cannot be directly changed. People—the poor and the non-poor—have to change. Second, Jayakaran alerts us to the fact that these stakeholders, the sources of oppression, are often themselves operating within "bundles of limitations" kept in place by still-more-powerful stakeholders. The local non-poor are also the poor held in bondage by another group of non-poor who are operating at a higher level in the system. This staircase of oppression goes all the way from the village to the area, to the nation, and to the global level. Linthicum calls this "systems above systems" (Linthicum 1991, 19). This is the nature of poverty and oppression. Everyone is sinner and sinned against.

Summary

We've looked at poverty as deficit, as entanglement, as lack of access to social power, as powerlessness, and as lack of freedom to grow. All have added important elements to our picture. We can conclude that poverty is a complicated social issue involving all areas of life—physical, personal, social, cultural, and spiritual. At some level, however, we must also conclude that poverty is in the eye of the beholder. We see what our worldview, education, and training allow us to see. We need to be aware of this and work hard at seeing *all* there is to see.

Having said this, I add a word of caution. I doubt there is or ever will be a unified theory of poverty. There is always more to see and more to learn. The corrective is to keep using a family of views to see all the things we need to see. We must work hard to be as holistic as we can be for the sake of the poor.

THE CAUSES OF POVERTY

Having explored the nature of poverty, we can now turn to the causes of poverty. Articulating our understanding of the causes of poverty is important for the simple reason that this is what determines how we respond. Our understanding of why people are poor shapes our understanding of transformational development, the better human future it seeks, and the methods we must apply to get there. This simple chart illustrates the point:

View of cause	Proposed response
The poor are sinners.	Evangelism and uplift
The poor are sinned against.	Social action; working for justice
The poor lack knowledge.	Education
The poor lack things	Relief/social welfare
The culture of the poor is flawed.	Become like us; ours is better
The social system makes them poor.	Change the system

Figure 3-10: How cause shapes response.

Like our understanding of the nature of poverty, our understanding of the causes of poverty tends to be in the eye of the beholder. If care is not taken to understand our unwitting biases, our understanding of the causes of poverty tends to be an outworking of our place in the social system, our education, our culture, and our personality. Our understanding of the causes of poverty also depends on where we start looking at poverty, and more important, where we stop looking.

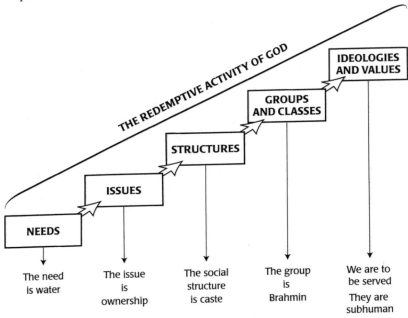

Figure 3-11: From needs to causes.

For example, if we are only concerned with needs, we will only see lack of water. Without further thought, lack of water is the cause of poverty and providing water is the answer. However, behind needs are issues, such as ownership of the water. If this is the cause of the lack of water, then the response is to work on ownership or access. Yet behind issues there are structures, such as caste, that influence who gets access to water, and which often create insurmountable barriers to access. Behind structures are groups who inhabit and enforce the structures by insisting that "it is our water and our right to control its use." Behind these groups are the ideologies and values that inform the group and shape the social structure, the unspoken assumptions that "we are to be served and they are subhuman and aren't supposed to drink where we drink." This is worldview.

This kind of social analysis deepens our understanding of what causes poverty. It allows us to discover much of what Chambers, Friedman, Christian, and Jayakaran say we must see. We raise our view from physical need and the individual person to the social and cultural systems within which the poor live. We begin to understand that ideas, values, and worldviews also need to change. This is good.

There is a downside, however, against which we must guard. Sometimes this kind of analysis results in the development practitioner ignoring the immediate need and instead going single-mindedly after the underlying causes. While ideas and values must be addressed, leaving the poor without water or with even angrier custodians of water is questionable good news. There can also be a tendency to be caught up in the world of ideas: Change the ideas or the worldview and you change the world. This can lead to depersonalization, forgetting that the web of lies and the value systems that created it are believed by human beings; they do not live in abstractions like "systems" or "ideologies" or "worldviews." At the end of the day, people are the cause of poverty, and it is people who must change for things to change.

Physical causes of poverty

There are physical causes to poverty. This is obvious. Chambers's categories of material poverty and physical weakness speak to this. People need food, shelter, water, and clean air. They need an environment that supports life. Money, land, and livestock are helpful assets to have. If these things are wholly or largely absent, poverty is the result.

There has been a recent addition to the physical causes of poverty offered by Jared Diamond, a physiologist with a background in linguistics, archeology, and ecology (Diamond 1997). Diamond looks not at the biology of humans, but at the biology that surrounds humans. He is looking for an alternative to the kind of social Darwinism that explains the world map of development by implying that some races are better than others. Diamond claims to show that *geography*, the quality of land, climate, and native plant species; *guns and capital*, which allow exploration and domination; and *germs*, carried by the urbanized and now immune explorers, hold more explanatory power for economic, political, and cultural progress, than the claim of superior racial characteristics.

Social causes of poverty

The physical causes of poverty intensify and are intensified by the social causes of poverty. "There are large-scale social practices and a whole system of social roles, often firmly approved by the members of society generally, that cause or perpetuate injustice and misery" (Wolterstorff 1983, 24). This is developed by Chambers and then more fully by Friedman. Christian's framework points to these systems as the tools and legitimating narratives of those who play god in the lives of the poor by creating the web of lies. Jayakaran identifies the social causes of poverty by pointing us to the stakeholders that stand behind each limitation to growth.

a lot of the poor don't have friendships. I wouldn't be able to function w/out friends

In a discussion of the social causes of poverty, we must also note the work of Emmanuel Todd, the French demographer. Todd has established a statistical (thus not necessarily causal) relationship between family structure and the status of women within family structure in relationship to cultural development, measured by literacy level (1987, 25). Todd comes to this thesis by seeking an explanation for why the world map of development is the way it is. Why does there seem to be progress in one part of the world and not in others? Why did Europe take off in the nineteenth century and the Asian tigers in the late twentieth century? Todd ends by predicting "high cultural potential" for nations with authoritarian family structures, like Germany and Japan, and "low cultural potential" where family structures are weak or patrilineal, like the Arab world and North India (Todd 1987, 180). Although cultural determinism is unattractive and inadequate as a full explanation, Todd's work may reflect to some degree Christian's idea that inadequate worldviews contribute to poverty.

Mental causes of poverty

Some of the causes of poverty have to do with the mental condition of the poor. At the simplest level, it is obvious that poverty is caused in part by lack of knowledge and technical information. The existence of debilitated mental states due to poor nutrition, illness, alcohol, or drugs also creates and sustains poverty. But we need to go deeper. We are all familiar with the feeling of hopelessness that is so often deeply embedded in the minds of the poor. Where does this debilitating attitude come from? There are two responses.

First, we need to remind ourselves that poverty can exist within the mind and spirit in the form of a poverty of being. Christian is right to call our attention to the reality of the web of lies that the poor believe and, by believing, disempower themselves. Maggay provides a highly literary description of this kind of poverty:

> [It is] the spirit that always denies, the annoying yet darkly seductive doubt that constantly questions the best we believe. The result for some is a creeping disillusionment, an intemperate realism, that in the end takes away the spring and lightness in our step, stoops our shoulders and makes us bitterly huddle in corners (Maggay 1994, 97).

The identity of the poor is marred on the inside. This is the deeper, more insidious, cause of poverty.

Research done in World Vision development programs in Tanzania illustrates the dilemma created by these internalized deceptions (Johnson 1998, 154-55). Examining the causes of poverty in an area development program, the view of the community differed considerably from the view of World Vision staff.

Cause	Community view	WV Staff view
Ignorance	Agree	Disagree
Laziness	Agree	Disagree
Lack of entrepreneurial spirit	Agree	Disagree
Lack of community spirit	Agree	Dasagree
Injustice	Disagree	Agree

Figure 3-12: Community *vs.* staff views.

In every case the community blamed itself for its poverty, having internalized the very descriptors of the poor that Chambers warns development workers to avoid (Chambers 1983, 107).

We need to be careful, however, lest we imply the poor make themselves mentally poor. This is not the case. Wink reminds us that "powerlessness is not simply a problem of attitude. . . . There are structures—economic, political, religious, and only *then* psychological—that oppress people and resist all attempts to end their oppression" (1992, 102).

Second, Christian suggests that this hopelessness has its roots in the distorted history of the poor and in the actions of the non-poor in making and writing history (1998a, 15). What has happened or not happened has the power to shape what we think can happen in the future. The way the poor remember their history shapes the day-to-day life of the poor today. In this way, the past can become a limitation on the future. This is exacerbated by the fact that history is usually written or told by the non-poor, and they do it in a way that legitimizes their role while often writing the poor out of the story. Being dismissed to the sidelines of their own history increases the poverty of the poor. Those who "do not make history . . . tend to become the utensils of the history makers as well as mere objects of history" (Mills 1993, 162).

Poorly thought through development interventions can exacerbate this distorted view the poor have of their own history. Friere has exposed the negative contribution that educational systems can have if they teach the poor to read their world and their past through the lenses that the powerful, the history makers and writers, lend to them in the form of the educational system. Friere's *conscientizacao* strategy for literacy and education was designed to allow "each man to win back his right to say his own word, to name the world" (1990, 13). History making and history telling are tools for making the poor captive to the god-complexes of the non-poor.

Spiritual causes of poverty

The spiritual causes of poverty are often overlooked or undeclared by development academics. I have already pointed out how Chambers and Friedman ignore the power of the spirit world, shamans, and witchcraft and their very significant contribution to making and keeping people poor. Money is spent on charms for protection and time is lost to feast days, all in an attempt to manage these power relationships. Technical improvements are refused for fear of the reaction of ancestors or the spirit world. Furthermore, while there are lots of references to oppression, deceit, malfeasance, corruption, violence, fatalism, alcohol, and broken and unjust relationships in the development literature, the spiritual dimension seldom surfaces in the explanatory schemes. As we have noted, Christian adds the principalities and powers and their active deception to his variation of Friedman's framework for powerlessness as the cause of poverty. Maggay supports this view:

> Social action is a confrontation with the powers that be. We are, ultimately, not battling against flesh and blood, nor merely dismantling unjust social systems; we are confronting the powers in their cosmic and social dimensions (Maggay 1994, 82).

Jayakaran actually names the spiritual as a cause of poverty. This is the reason I have adopted his framework for this section on the causes of poverty.

So what can we say about poverty and its causes at the end of this review of four major contributors to the conversation? First, poverty is a complex, multifaceted phenomenon. There are unlikely to be any simple answers. Second, understanding poverty requires that we be multidisciplinary; we need the tools of anthropology, sociology, social psychology, spiritual discernment, and theology, all nicely integrated. Third, the works of Chambers, Friedman, Christian, and Jayakaran need to be seen as complementary views, each adding something to the other.

A HOLISTIC UNDERSTANDING OF POVERTY

I would now like to pull together material from the chapter on the biblical story and the material on poverty and its causes. We need to look for an integrating frame that is both biblical and inclusive of the work of Chambers, Friedman, Christian, and Jayakaran.

The nature of poverty is fundamentally relational

This is the point of departure: Poverty is a result of relationships that do not work, that are not just, that are not for life, that are not harmonious or enjoyable. Poverty is the absence of shalom in all its meanings.[6] All four poverty frameworks provide explanations that rest on the idea of relationships that are fragmented, dysfunctional, or oppressive. Chambers's poverty trap,

Friedman's access to social power, Christian's framework for disempowerment, and Jayakaran's lack of opportunities to grow, all have at their foundation relationships that lack shalom, that work against well-being, against life and life abundant.

There is an interesting confirmation of this in an account by Desmond D'Abreo, a leader of Development Education Services (DEEDS) in India. He led a series of exercises in exploring the root causes of what he calls underdevelopment by asking communities in rural India to develop a web diagram reflecting their understanding of the origins of some of the problems they had identified in an earlier exercise. In explaining the causes of both drunkenness and illiteracy, the underlying causes came out the same: selfishness and systemic injustice, both relational categories (1989, 107-9).

Understanding poverty as relationships that don't work as they should is consistent with the biblical story as well. The scope of sin affects every one of the five relationships in which every human lives: within ourselves, with community, with those we call "other," with our environment, and with God. Each of these broken relationships find expression in the poverty systems we have covered earlier in this chapter. Jayakumar Christian is right when he asserts that, at its core, poverty is relational.

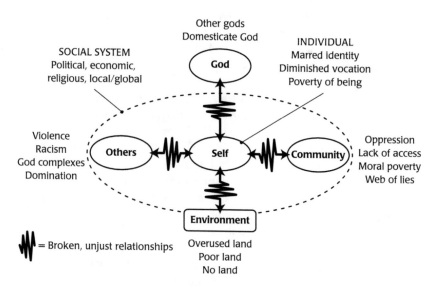

Figure 3-13: A relational understanding of poverty.

At the center of this relational understanding of poverty is the idea of the poor not knowing who they are or the reason for which they were created. When people believe they are less than human, without the brains, strength, and personhood to contribute to their own well-being or that of others, their understanding of who they are is marred. Similarly, when the poor do not believe that they have anything to contribute, or that they cannot be productive, their understanding of their vocation is distorted as well. With marred identities and distorted vocations, the poor cannot play their proper relational role in the world, either within themselves or with those around them.

The cause of poverty is fundamentally spiritual

What causes this distortion and injustice in our relationships? What stands between us and God? What divides us inside ourselves into competing, conflicting voices? What separates us within our community, with some doing well and others suffering? What causes us to exclude and sometimes demonize the "other"? Why do we abuse the earth? What is it that works against life, against shalom? The answers to these questions provide us with an explanation of the causes of poverty. Any theory of poverty must have answers.

For the Christian, the biblical story provides an unambiguous answer. Sin is what distorts these relationships. Sin is the root cause of deception, distortion, and domination. When God is on the sidelines or written out of our story, we do not treat each other well.

Why does the poverty trap work as it does? Why are the poor denied access to social power? What is at the root of the web of lies and the disempowerment that results? Why are there constraints to growth, with a group of people standing behind each limitation and restriction? Because of deceptive and dominating relationships, because we are unable to love God and neighbor, because of sin. We work for what we think life is for. We try to provide our own abundant life. Without a strong theology of sin, comprehensive explanations for poverty are hard to come by.

One other point, a hard thing to say. If it is true that sin is the fundamental cause of our lack of shalom, of our world of dominating relationships, then there is good news and bad news. The good news is that through Jesus Christ there is a way out of sin toward transformation. The bad news is that if this news is not accepted, there is a sense in which those who refuse sit wrapped in chains of self-imposed limitations.

For the Christian development worker, there is an obvious implication. There can be no practice of transformational development that is Christian unless somewhere, in some form, people are hearing the good news of the gospel and being given a chance to respond. How one does this in a sensitive, appropriate, and non-coercive way is also very important and will be explored in the chapter on Christian witness.

POVERTY OF THE NON-POOR

A chapter on poverty is not complete unless we make some comments on the poverty of the non-poor. They have their own set of problems, not the least of which is that God hates idolatry, injustice, and the fact that some people attempt to play God's rightful role in the lives of others.

We need to begin with the observation that the non-poor have a great deal in common with the poor from the biblical perspective. The non-poor are also made in the image of God, are also fallen, and are also being offered redemption. Sadly, it is harder for them to hear this good news than it is for the poor. This is true partly because they enjoy, knowingly or not, playing god in the lives of the poor.

But there is a much deep irony here. The non-poor suffer from the same kind of poverty as the poor, only this poverty is expressed in the opposite way. The identity of the non-poor is also marred, but with a marring of a different kind. When the non-poor play god in the lives of other people, they have stopped being who they truly are and are assuming the role of God. Losing sight of their true identity leads to the non-poor misreading their true vocation as well. Instead of understanding themselves as productive stewards working for the well-being of their community, they act as if their gifts and position are somehow rightfully theirs, or earned by merit, and hence are solely for themselves and for their well-being.

The non-poor are poor in another way that is also a mirror image of the poverty of the poor. It seems as if having too much is as bad for us as having too little. Too little food makes us weak and susceptible to disease; too much food makes us overweight and susceptible to heart disease and cancer. The water in the Third World is dirty and bad for our health; the water in the West is bad for our health because it is increasingly polluted with chemicals. The poor have inadequate housing; the non-poor are often slaves to their houses. Octavio Paz has observed that the rich have too few fiestas and are poor, while the poor have too many fiestas and are also poor (Parker 1996, 107). Koyama puts this "too much is poverty" idea nicely:

> Man cannot live without bread. But, man must not live by this essential bread alone. Bread-alone, shelter-alone, clothing-alone, income-alone, all these *alones* damage man's quality of life. Strangely, these good values contain danger elements too. Man is supposed to eat bread. But what if bread eats man? People are dying from over-eating today in affluent countries. Man is supposed to live in the house. But what if the house begins to live in man? . . . Man needs bread plus the word of God (1979, 4-5).

The idea of too much or too little being two sides of the same problem reminds us of Proverbs 30:8-9:

> Give me neither poverty nor riches, but give me only my
>   daily bread.
> Otherwise, I may have too much and disown you and
>   say, "Who is the LORD?" Or I may become poor
>   and steal, and so dishonor the name of my God.

The activity of the non-poor in safeguarding their privilege and power also creates a poverty unique to the non-poor. When we misuse a social system for our benefit, it is hard to believe that our friends are not doing the same. When domination is the goal, we have to keep winning in order not to lose.

> The more a rich man possesses, the more worry he has. . . . He fears the failure of his revenues. . . . He fears the violence of the mighty, doubts the honesty of his household, and lives in perpetual fear of the deceptions of strangers (Hugh of St. Victor, quoted in Oden 1986, 155).

When we get so far out of touch with what is real and true, when we believe in the delusional assumptions of Wink and think that the web of lies is a web of truth, we are becoming crazy, we don't know what is real anymore. We are losing our soul.

At the end of the day, the poverty of the non-poor is the same kind of poverty as the poor, only differently expressed. The poverty of the non-poor is fundamentally relational and caused by sin. The result is a life full of things and short on meaning. The non-poor simply believe in a different set of lies. The only difference is that the poverty of the non-poor is harder to change. "A bank account and abundant diet somehow (I cannot explain it quite satisfactorily) insulate man from coming to feel the primary truth of history" (Koyama 1974, 23). This is what Jesus was trying to say when he compared a rich man getting into the kingdom as a camel trying to go through the eye of a needle.

4

Perspectives on Development

To this point, we have described the biblical narrative as the normative story that frames our individual stories and the stories of the communities in which we live and work. We have also explored several different ways of understanding the nature of poverty and its causes. Our next step will be to review how development is understood by some important Christian and non-Christian contributors to development thinking. As before, we will discover that there is much to learn from those who study development professionally as well as from Christian practitioners.

WHO WILL SAVE US?

This is another way of asking which story will inform our understanding of transformational development. It is important that the development practitioner and the community answer this question and not simply assume that everyone shares the same answer. After all, there are a number of competing stories claiming to provide the answer; some of them are quite subtle and seductive.

For most of the last two centuries modernity has put forth the claim that human progress is the inevitable outcome of applying human reason and modern science, the means by which "the fissures of the world could be repaired and the world can be healed" (Volf 1996, 25). What the myth of human progress ignores is that evil lies at the bottom of these fissures, and evil bends human reason to other ends. The modern story of the West has no antidote for evil. Modernity sets its hopes "in the twin strategies of social control and rational thought" (ibid., 26), neither of which has power over evil.

The three remaining horseman of modernity at the end of the twentieth century—capitalism, science, and technology—still offer to save the poor. The claim is made that things are getting better, at least a little. In its summer 1997 advertising campaign on CNN, CARE associated itself with the good news that the number of people living in absolute poverty has decreased from 60 percent in 1960 to less than 30 percent today. The 1995 United Nations Development Report claims that in the last thirty years the developing world has improved as much as the industrial world did during the whole of the nineteenth century (1995, 15). Yet improving conditions are not enough to support the claim that modernity will save the poor.

Cristian Parker, a sociologist of religion in Chile, reflecting on the poverty of Latin America and the impact of modernity and unbridled capitalism from the North, argues that capitalism "carries within itself the limits of its own horizon, since it has no possible escape from its own golden calves and shatters on the ultimate unsatisfaction [sic] of vital human needs, including the deepest longings of the human being today" (1996, 256).

Parker goes on to note the continuing energy and staying power of popular religion in Latin America and wonders why this should be so.[1] He suggests that popular religion is answering questions and meeting needs that economic growth alone cannot. Parker argues that the worship of pragmatism, assessing everything only in terms of what works, and the ethic of freedom, understood as the right to be indifferent to others in your community, are reflections of a "crisis of civilization" (1996, 258). He goes on to say:

It is a crisis because of the manner in which the dominant modern mentality unfolds in its relationship with nature—in the relation to human beings with one another, with things and with the transcendent. It is the crisis of instrumental rationality carried to its ultimate expression. . . . It is a sacrilegious, perverse conception . . . in view of the fact that it sets up reason as god of the intellect in order to legitimate actions oriented toward ends without any consideration of the value of the means, ultimately leading to the unscrupulous self-destruction of persons and their cultural and natural surroundings. It is modern human beings who are in crisis, since their relation with themselves and the ecosystem is in crisis. Human beings are splitting, have sundered, their original harmony (1996, 259).

The development practitioner must understand that the fundamental claim of capitalism, science, and technology is a lie: they cannot save. Saving is not within their power. Economic growth, modern medicine, agriculture, water development, and the technologies that support them are tools, provisions of a good God. We must use them sensitively and appropriately. They can enhance life and make people more productive. But they cannot save. "The unshakable hope of the 1960s, placed in development and freedom and expressed in the liberation projects of the 1970s has evaporated. . . . Latin America and the world . . . need to rethink . . . to reinvent hope on a different foundation" (Parker 1996, 248).

The wisdom of the cross offers a different basis for hope. The cross teaches that salvation does not come from right thinking or the right technique, but by divine action making right what we cannot make right ourselves. We are told that "the foolishness of God is wiser than man's wisdom and the weakness of God is stronger than man's strength" (1 Cor 1:25). The foolishness and weakness being referred to is the message of the cross, "the power of God" (1 Cor 1:18). The development worker must never forget this basic truth about who can save. The claims of modernity are seductive, and we encounter them every day in the things we read, listen to, and study. Our professional training as development specialists is predicated on the idea that the stories of the market, science, and technology can save others. This is not true, and we must guard against this deception. These things are tools and they can help, but they cannot save.

There is one other possible source of salvation that needs to be debunked, lest we do harm unwittingly. It is understandable that the poor may believe that the development worker or the development agency will be the one who saves. After all, we come in power with money, technology, and technical knowledge. We seem to understand why things are as they are and how to change them. Helping the poor set aside this perception is a significant methodological challenge for the development worker. I will come back to this important issue in the chapter on development practice.

SHAPING OUR VIEW OF TRANSFORMATION

Just as we saw with the causes of poverty, our point of view tends to determine how we think about human transformation. We need to make explicit our point of view and then see if we can enlarge it. There are several ways in which this takes place.

Transformation from what and to what?

One way to make explicit our assumptions is to take note of what we believe people are being transformed *from* and transformed *to*.

From what?	To what?	Which relationship?
Lost soul	Saved soul	With God
Dying body	Nourished body	With self
Sick body	Healed body	With self
Broken mind	Restored mind	With self
Unjust social system	Just social relationships	With community and others
Violence	Reconciled relationships	With community and others
Decaying creation	Sustaining world	With environment

Figure 4-1: Transformation from? To?

If we see people as lost souls, then transformation is about saving souls. If we see people as dying from hunger, then transformation is about feeding. If the problem is unjust systems, then the tools of transformation are community organizing or political activism. And so it goes, a series of views of poverty and differing approaches to transformation to restore what is missing. Note that each has to do with a relationship that is not what it should be.

Each of these views is true, but each is also incomplete. If we can accept that biblical transformation addresses all these dimensions of human life, we can take another step toward a more comprehensive, holistic view of transformation. If we do not, we reduce transformation to evangelism to save the soul; to social work, medicine, or psychology to save the person; to political activism or peacemaking to restore the social system; and to environmentalism to save nature.

Levels of the problem

In the chapter on poverty and the poor, we discovered that our understanding of poverty depends on the level at which we examine any given situation. As we dig deeper, our understanding of its causes change. The way we understand the causes of poverty also tends to determine our response to poverty. If we see poverty as hungry children, the response is social welfare; we need to feed them. If we see poverty as lack of knowledge of nutrition and low agricultural production, the response is community development that teaches new skills and provides new seeds. If we go a level deeper and see poverty as an issue of land tenure and local marketing systems that favor cash crops over food, then the response is to work for policy change, government intervention, and community organizing. Once again, we need to resist the temptation to choose one view over the others. All call for a response. Transformational development takes each seriously.

WHAT IS DEVELOPMENT?

As with the section on understanding poverty, it is helpful to review several different perspectives on what development is and what's involved in causing it to happen. Each view has something to teach us and hence is important to our attempt to create a Christian framework for transformational development. The key will be to identify the transformational frontiers in each view. Transformational frontiers are those areas at which a transformational strategy might be focused to bring about sustainable change in the direction of the kingdom of God.

Development as transformation—Wayne Bragg

In the evolution of development thinking of evangelicals, the Wheaton '83 consultation entitled "A Christian Response to Human Need" was noteworthy. Wayne Bragg, former director of the Hunger Center at Wheaton College, wrote a seminal paper in which he argued that transformation was the biblical term that best fit a Christian view of development (1983, 37-95). While not a development theory per se, Bragg called for an understanding of development that went beyond social welfare by including justice concerns, something controversial for evangelicals at that time. Bragg listed what he called the characteristics of transformation, each a transformational frontier:

- *Life sustenance*, or the meeting of human basic needs.
- *Equity*, meaning equitable distribution of material goods and opportunities.
- *Justice* within all social relationships, including democratic participation.
- *Dignity and self-worth* in the sense of feeling fully human and knowing we are made in the image of God.
- *Freedom* from external control or oppression; a sense of being liberated in Christ.
- *Participation* in a meaningful way in our own transformation.
- *Reciprocity* between the poor and the non-poor; each have something to learn from the other.
- *Cultural fit* that respects the best in local cultures and that treats them as creative.
- *Ecological soundness.*

Bragg added some important new ideas to the evangelical conversation about development. Just social systems and opportunities for all had not been squarely on the evangelical development agenda. At the time they were deemed "too political," and most evangelicals had not yet formed a theology of political activism.[2] The inclusion of freedom and participation were just gaining an understanding. Learning from the poor and seeing all cultures as made by God and being creative sources of transformation were also important. Ecology was a new issue for evangelical development thinking at that time.

Bragg's views have some weaknesses as well. There is a strong redistributionist tone that is no longer viewed as positively as it once was. Bragg, like many evangelicals working in development at the time (including the author), also underestimated the importance of wealth creation. Finally, Bragg's view of the poor tended to be somewhat romantic. There was no space for the contribution the poor make to their own poverty; all sin, including the temptation to oppress others, seemed to belong only to the non-poor.

People-centered development—David Korten

David Korten is director of the People-Centered Development Forum and the author of *Getting to the 21ˢᵗ Century*, an important book on development in the early 1990s. Korten contrasts what he calls people-centered development with the economic growth-centered development promoted by many Western governments.

Growth-centered development	People-centered development
Material consumption	Human well-being
Wants of the non-poor	Needs of the poor
Corporation or business	Household
Competition	Community
Export markets	Local markets
Absentee ownership	Local ownership
Borrowing and debt	Conserving and sharing
Specialization	Diversification
Interdependence	Self-reliance
Environmental costs externalized	Environmental costs internalized
Free flow of capital and services	Free flow of information

Figure 4-2: Two visions of development.
(Adapted from Korten 1991)

Korten believes the world at the end of the twentieth century is suffering from a threefold crisis: poverty, environmental destruction, and social disintegration (1990, 114). He defines development as "a process by which the members of a society increase their personal and institutional capacities to mobilize and manage resources to produce sustainable and justly distributed improvements in their quality of life consistent with their own aspirations" (1990, 67).

Korten's key phrases are "process," "capacities," "sustainable and just," and "consistent with their own aspirations." Development is not something arrived at, an end point; it is a continuing process. This process, according to Korten, should be driven by three principles: sustainability, justice, and inclusiveness, each a transformational frontier.

By "sustainable," Korten means that any good development must sustain and nurture the environment. By "justice and inclusiveness," Korten addresses the problem of the social disintegration and disenfranchisement that accompanies (and causes) poverty and the fact that governments and social systems are biased in favor of the powerful, who are also the major consumers.

Finally, for Korten, "consistent with their own aspirations" means that the people should themselves decide what the improvements are and how they are to be created. The development program must not come from the outside.

One of Korten's other major contributions is calling attention to the fact that a development agency must have some kind of philosophy of development and that this philosophy is a response to the agency's understanding of the causes of poverty. His call to make these assumptions explicit and to review them critically in light of the agency's experience is very important.[3]

> In the absence of a theory, the aspiring development agency almost inevitably becomes an assistance agency engaged in relieving the more visible symptoms of underdevelopment through relief and welfare measures. The assistance agency that acts without a theory also runs considerable risk of inadvertently strengthening the very forces responsible for the conditions of suffering and injustice that it seeks to alleviate through its aid (1990, 113).

Korten then creates a typology of development responses, each reflecting how the problem of poverty is understood.

Korten moves problem definition from shortage of things to shortage of skills and local inertia, to failure of social and cultural systems, and finally to an inadequate mobilizing vision. The development response changes accordingly from feeding people to empowering communities, to developing sustainable social systems,[4] and finally to mobilizing people's movements. Korten describes these responses as four generations of development strategy that move from responding to symptoms (relief) to addressing underlying causes.

Most development agencies began at Korten's first level and have moved to the second level: community development. A few have begun to work at the third level: working for sustainable systems. Korten's prophetic call is to move to his fourth level: promoting people's movements. This is his answer to transforming the lives of the poor.

Korten's understanding of development has made some helpful contributions. Development as a process and not an end is an important idea. He also adds critical concerns for just social systems and a sustainable environment. While there are things to argue about in Korten's view of people-centered development, its contrast with growth-centered development is helpful in disclosing the blind spots of this prevailing view.

Korten addresses the spiritual aspect of development in an interesting though limited way. He acknowledges that "questions relating to the uses of power, values, love, brotherhood, peace and the ability of people to live in harmony with one another are fundamental to religion and to the role of church in society" (1990, 168). After Charles Elliot (1987), Korten goes on to say that "the human spirit must be strengthened to the point that greed and egotism play a less dominant role" (1990, 168). Korten is struggling to find a way to help those who accept the growth-centered approach to development to change their view. How will the values of just distribution and

	Relief and Welfare	Small-scale, self-reliant local development	Sustainable systems development	People's movements
Type of problem	Shortage of things	Shortage of skills and local inertia	Failure of social and cultural systems	Inadequate mobilizing vision
Time frame	Immediate	3-5 years	10-20 years	Indefinite
Scope	Individual and family	Neighborhood/village	Region and nation	National and global
Chief actors	Development agency	Development agency and community	All relevant public and private institutions	Networks of people and organizations
Role of agency	Doer	Mobilizer and teacher	Catalyst	Activist and educator
Management style	Logistics management	Community self-help	Strategic management and systems development	Linking and energizing self-managed networks

Figure 4-3: Korten's typology of development responses.
(Adapted from Korten 1990)

sustainability be taught or caught? He concludes by noting that values for-mation, including reordering power relations, "has long been the essence of all great religious teaching" (1990, 168).

Korten seems to understand that value change is hard work and that it is spiritual work. He also affirms that, while religious institutions do not have the best of records living out their own values in these areas, they are none-theless the most likely candidate for help on this transformational frontier. Having bravely acknowledged the possible role of the faith-based organiza-tions in the process, Korten stops short of declaring himself on the issue of evangelism and conversion. One gets the feeling that he would prefer faith-based value formation as long as that did not include asking people to change their religious orientation.

Korten leaves some other questions unanswered as well. He may be overly optimistic in expecting that a quality of life that is quality for all will emerge if its definition is left solely to local aspirations. Local aspirations are shaped by local culture, local worldview, and local social structures. As Christian has reminded us, accepting local worldviews uncritically is sometimes a source of poverty, not an answer to it. Finally, Korten's fourth-generation strategy calls for an adequate mobilizing vision but then is mute on the critical questions: Whose vision? What makes a vision adequate? Where does the vision come from?

Finally, while very helpful, there is also something worrisome about Korten's typology of development responses. He develops his four genera-tions of strategy as a story of evolution, a social learning process whereby agencies learn to move from symptoms to causes. Does he expect develop-ment agencies to cease working at the lower levels (symptoms) and focus solely on causes? Is the ideal development agency a fourth-generation agency? Or, does he expect development agencies to work at all four levels at once? Can any agency be effective working on this many fronts? Or should development agencies partner with relief agencies and advocacy groups, forming consortiums that together can work at social welfare, relief, com-munity development, sustainable systems, and people movements? Finally, the evidence that people movements create sustainable societal change is limited.

Alternative development:
Expanding access to social power—John Friedman

John Friedman's understanding of development follows closely from his definition of the cause of poverty: limited access to social power. Alterna-tive development for Friedman "is a process that seeks the empowerment of the households and their individual members through their involvement in socially and politically relevant actions" (1992, 33). Empowerment in-cludes an emphasis on local decision making, local self-reliance, participatory democracy, and social learning. It pursues the "transcendent goals of inclusive democracy, appropriate economic growth, gender equality and sustainability" (1992, 164). Friedman explains using the schema developed in the poverty chapter.

Recalling the eight bases for enlarging social power (see Figure 3-4), Friedman's view of transformation calls for working with the household so that it is empowered to increase the envelope of its social power—the transformational frontier—outward along the eight lines of social power by building, empowering, and nurturing social networks and social organizations.

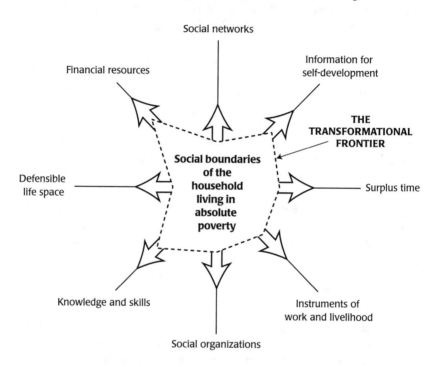

Figure 4-4: Transformation as expanding the frontiers of social power. (Adapted from Friedman 1992, 67)

Social organizations include formal and informal groups to whom the household belongs, "including churches, mother's clubs, sports clubs, neighborhood improvement associations, credit circles, discussion clubs, tenant organizations, syndicates and irrigation associations" (1992, 68). Social networks, for Friedman, "are essential for self-reliant actions based on reciprocity" and include family, friends, and neighbors.

Keeping in mind Friedman's four domains of social practice (see Figure 3-3), Friedman believes that, in the last part of the twentieth century, the domain of the state is shrinking because of the popularity of neo-liberalism, while the domain of the economy is expanding as it is linked and incorporated into the global economy. In Friedman's view, this leaves two major transformational frontiers that are critical to empowering the household: the domain of the civil society and the domain of the political community (see Figure 4-5). Alternative development works to expand these two domains, thus creating more life space for the poor.

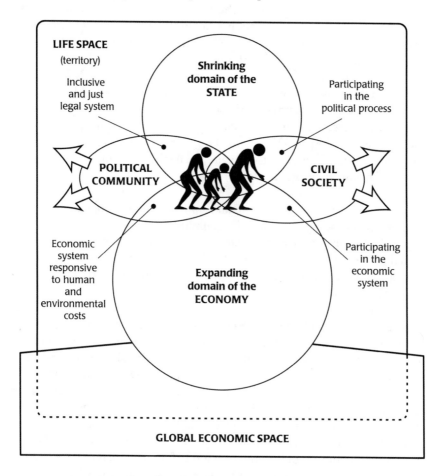

Figure 4-5: Transformation as expanding the social
and political power of households.
(Adapted from Friedman 1992, 27)

Where civil society overlaps the domain of the state, the transformational frontier is expanding household participation in democratic processes. Where civil society intersects with the economy, the frontier is increasing household participation as productive citizens with a stake in society. Where political community overlaps with the state, the transformational frontier is creating a more responsive, inclusive, and just legal system. Where political economy intersects with the corporate economy, the frontier is creating an economic system that is more responsive to human and environmental costs.

Friedman believes in a bottom-up approach to empowerment, in contrast to one mediated by government or even by the development agency. His logic works like this. The poor must take part in meeting their own needs. To do so, they must acquire the means to do this. The means should be the result of "the hurly burly of politics in which the poor continuously press for the support, at the macro level, of their own initiatives" (1992, 66). However, he acknowledges that this is not enough: "Although an alternative development must begin locally, it cannot end there" (1992, 7).

The question is how one gets from a bottom-up, household-centered approach to development to accessing social power, especially political power. Friedman suggests that this can be done by "scaling up" the micro development projects of the past.[5] While small is beautiful, it is also often invisible, Friedman argues. The key is to "expand the territorial scope of alternative projects" by linking projects into

> networks, coalitions, federations and confederations of popular organizations and non-governmental organizations. These ensembles serve as vehicles for information exchange, technical and political support, and political lobbies, establishing the civil society of the disempowered as a significant actor outside the traditional system of party politics (1992, 142).

Friedman's view of alternative development is very helpful by placing social power—both economic and political—in the center of the development agenda. Friedman locates the household in a social systems perspective, making clearly visible the need for households to be able to participate in both the political and economic system if there is to be sustainable change. Like Chambers, Friedman begins with the household and insists that the larger social power agenda not displace real help now: "If social and economic development means anything at all, it must mean a clear improvement in the conditions of life and livelihood of ordinary people" (1992, 9).

Friedman's approach also gives considerable substance to what Korten calls "sustainable systems," while nonetheless accepting the current global economic system of accumulation as a given, rather than hoping it will somehow go away or that local realities can somehow act as if it were not there.

> The objective of an alternative development is to humanize a system that has shut them [the poor] out, and to accomplish this through forms of everyday resistance and political struggle that insist on the rights of the excluded population as human beings, as citizens, and as persons intent on realizing their loving and creative powers within.

Its central objective is their inclusion in a restructured system that does not make them redundant (1992, 13).

This is why Friedman makes a point of linking access to social power to the ability to use real political power. Without serious political power and the knowledge to employ it meaningfully, the open-ended local economy linked increasingly to the global economy becomes the only power that matters.

Friedman's approach has some blind spots. He essentially takes a Western liberal stance that assumes that the good in people will somehow find a way to work in favor of good in social systems. This view does not explain why things are not working more justly and with more access, nor is there a remedy for such poverty-sustaining behavior. That social systems tend to become self-serving and that the non-poor are not troubled enough by the current state of affairs to seek remedies are not addressed. He does not acknowledge the deceit and violence to which the non-poor will resort to keep things as they are. Nor does he mention the effect of worldview in perpetuating poverty and sustaining the privileged status of the non-poor.

The spiritual side of life is largely neglected in Friedman's alternative development. Life is more than having access to social power. While Friedman talks of "improving the conditions of life and livelihood"—and life and livelihood could include spiritual well-being—Friedman's approach to development does not appear to extend this far. Life space must include the spiritual domain in addition to state, civil society, economy, and political community. Access to spiritual power is as important to the poor as social and political power, in fact, more so in many traditional rural communities. While Friedman does include the church in his understanding of civil society, it sounds like the church as a social institution, not as a sign of the kingdom. Perhaps Friedman would include the spiritual in the category of household power he calls "psychological," but he does not say so, nor would this be fully adequate. In spite of this lacuna, Friedman's contributions should not be down-played. In fact, his proposal should provoke us in a constructive way.

Friedman poses a challenge to Christians, particularly evangelicals, who are for the most part nervous about political engagement. This needs to be overcome. If Christians cannot develop a truly Christian theology of political engagement on the part of the excluded, then they will have nothing to offer the poor in this critical area of life. This challenge is not so much a biblical issue as it is one of cultural captivity.

The Old Testament is full of political stories, including God's proposal for the political and social life of pre-monarchy Israel.[6] These accounts create no division between religious and political life. The challenge is to overcome the twentieth-century captivity to modernity on the part of the church (and its theology) and to rediscover a biblical approach to life in the public square. The Western church tends to sees the church as doing spiritual work, while political work is done in the material world (see Figure 1-1). The consequence of this view of the world is twofold. Some believe that the work of the church is solely spiritual, and hence politics in the material world is of the devil and should be spurned. Others, believing in God's rule in the material world, nevertheless accept the dichotomy and express their Christian faith on Sunday morning and treat Monday through Friday political life as if their faith and the Bible had nothing to say. Either way, there is no biblically seamless spiritual/physical view of political engagement.

Development as responsible well-being—Robert Chambers

Fourteen years after Chambers published his poverty trap to help us understand how poverty entraps the poor, he published *Whose Reality Counts? Putting the First Last*, in which he presents his framework for the outcome of successful development. Taking note of the fact that development thinking has undergone a significant shift "from things and infrastructure to people and capacities" (1997, 9), Chambers presents five words that he believes describe the current development consensus: well-being, livelihood, capability, equity, and sustainability.[7] He links these transformational frontiers into an interactive system reminiscent of his poverty trap.

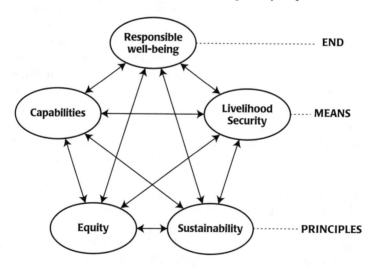

Figure 4-6: Transformation as responsible well-being.
(Chambers 1997, 10)

For Chambers, the objective of development is *responsible well-being* for all. He describes well-being as quality of life; its opposite is ill-being. This moves him beyond the limiting categories of wealth and poverty. "Well being is open to the whole range of human experience, social, mental and spiritual as well as material.[8] It has many elements. Each person can define it for herself or himself" (1997, 10). Chambers also makes the significant observation that while poverty and ill-being may be associated closely, wealth and well-being are not: "Amassing wealth does not assure well being" (1997, 10).

There are two things that Chambers claims are basic to responsible well-being: *livelihood security* and the *capabilities* by which livelihood security and responsible well-being are achieved. Chambers defines livelihood security as:

adequate stocks and flows of food and cash to meet basic needs and to support well being. Security refers to secure rights and reliable access to resources, food and income and basic services. It includes tangible and intangible assets to offset risk, ease shocks and meet contingencies (1997, 10).[9]

Chambers's capabilities category is broad and rich. He includes what people are capable of being as well as what they are capable of doing, and thus values formation becomes part of the conversation. People's capabilities are enlarged "through learning, practice, training and education," with the outcome being "better living and well being" (1997, 11).

The two final categories of Chambers's interactive systems approach to well-being are the principles *equity* and *sustainability*, both of which are to guide the process of increasing capabilities and livelihood security. Equity, for Chambers, means that the poor, weak, vulnerable, and exploited come first. Equity includes "human rights, intergenerational and gender equity and the reversals of putting the last first and the first last" (1997, 11). Sustainability is important as well: "To be good, conditions and change must be sustainable—economically, socially, institutionally and environmentally" (1997, 11).

All of this works within an interactive framework. Well-being cannot be achieved at the expense of some in the community because this violates the principle of equity. Well-being that is not sustainable is not well-being. Increasing capabilities must include the valuing of equity and sustainability as well as helping people define what well-being is for them. Overcoming the various elements of the poverty trap is the road to well-being and the guarantee of sustainability.

Chambers then explores the issue of the power and the will to make the changes necessary to move toward well-being for all. He notes that there is considerable reason for cynicism, but also points to some evidence for hope. The world is changing rapidly at the end of the twentieth century, modernity is waning, and some are making choices that are helpful. At the end of the day, Chambers rests his framework for change on personal choice.

The actions of TNCs (transnational corporations), of currency specu-
lators, of UN agencies, of governments, of NGOs are all mediated by
individual decisions and action. The point is so obvious and so universal that it pains to have to make it. . . . People can choose how to
behave and what to do. The assumption of pervasive selfishness and
greed in neoliberal and male-dominated thought, policy and action
supports a simplistic view of human nature. This overlooks or under-
estimates selflessness, generosity and commitment to others, and the
fulfillment that these qualities bring (1997, 13).

Chambers's well-being framework for development is helpful. It insists
on basic needs being met and speaks to transformational training and the
importance of sustainability. He also makes space for both spiritual well-
being and value change. His concept of equity is supported by the concept
of the upside-down nature of the kingdom of God (Kraybill 1978).
Chambers's focus on the importance of individual choice and holding people
in positions of power accountable, rather than blaming unjust behavior on
abstractions and systems, is also an important correction. There is much
here that is fully consistent with the biblical narrative.

There are some transformational frontiers that are hard to find.
Chambers's framework does not address the fear of spirits, oppressive land-
lords, shamans, and the like, yet these suppress the will to change. The
contribution of worldview to ill-being is not mentioned. There is no comment on how one deals with those who already believe they have well-being
and do not wish to examine the truth of their claim or concern themselves
with those who are not as well off as they are. The spiritual dimensions of
powerlessness are also not addressed in any obvious way. Finally, like Friedman, the underlying worldview is that of Western liberalism and its belief
that there is enough good in people so that human political processes can
correct themselves if we work at it long enough.

Development as a kingdom response to powerlessness—
Jayakumar Christian

I will now turn to the proposal of Jayakumar Christian. As we would
expect, it reflects Christian's systems view of powerlessness (see Figure 3-
5). Christian sees each area of his "web of lies" as a transformational frontier. The response to each is to declare truth and righteousness while doing
good works.

Christian's proposal rests on the assumption that the powerlessness of
the poor is the "result of systematic socio-economic, political, bureaucratic
and religious processes (systems) that disempower the poor" (1994, 335).
The proper transformational development response must reverse the pro-

cess of disempowerment with a kingdom of God response that includes three commitments:

1. Dealing with the relational dimensions of poverty "by building covenant quality communities that are inclusive . . . challenging the dividing lines . . . popular community organizing efforts that exploit issues and numbers . . . pointing toward the coming of the kingdom" (1994, 336).
2. Dealing with forces that create or sustain powerlessness at the micro-, macro-, global, and cosmic levels.
3. Challenging the time element in the process of disempowerment by rereading the history of the poor from God's perspective, providing "a prophetic alternative to the distortions that the winners perpetuate . . . challenging the captivity of the poor to the belief that they cannot change their present reality" (1994, 336).

For each of the elements of the web of lies that entraps the poor, Christian outlines a kingdom response. For the *captivity of the poor to the web of lies*, Christian calls for development processes that allow the poor to discover the lies and find the truth. This is not easy work.

This web has several spiders. It includes the non-poor and the poor, the world views of persons in poverty relationships, the principalities and powers and the spiritual interiorities within structures and systems (1994, 342).

Truth and righteousness must be established and the source of this truth is the "continuous study of the Word of God" (1994, 343). Development workers need to live lives that are consistent with that truth and that unmask the lies. The truth of the kingdom of God

is the only thing that will reorder the relationship between truth and power. It will seek to establish truth with a capital "T", truth about self, truth in public and private life and truth about power (1994, 343).

Responding to the *captivity to the god complexes of the non-poor*, the truth is declared that the kingdom of God is the only alternative that promises liberation. Wink would also add exposing the idolatry of the non-poor and unmasking the powerlessness of their idols to provide well-being. As Koyama reminded us, the idols of the non-poor can only save themselves, they cannot save us.

For the low self-confidence resulting from the *marred identity* of the poor, the kingdom response "clarifies and heals the marred identity of the poor. It goes beyond issues of justice and dignity to deal with the underlying marring of identity of the poor" (1994, 339). Christian proposes that we do our development work in a way that shows the poor that we value them. We need to work as barefoot counselors, listening, talking, and loving. Their history of exclusion and disrespect needs healing. We need to proclaim the good news that the poor are made in the image of God, that God calls them his children, and that God values them as much as God values the non-poor.

For *inadequacies in worldview*, Christian insists that we must go beyond concerns for cultural sensitivity. There are elements in every worldview that are not for life or for the poor. Christian, as an Indian, is especially concerned for issues of religious sanctions for oppressive relationships and the idea that the poor should not desire change. Caste and karma are heavily biased against the well-being of the poor. The kingdom response is an "encounter of world view and religion, with the Bible as the basic frame of reference" (1994, 340).

For *deception by principalities and powers*, Christian calls for the practices of prayer and fasting as important tools for social action. "There is a need to rediscover the potential of prayer and fasting to move mountains and cause the devil and his forces to fall from heavenly places (Lk 10:18)" (1994, 341). Grassroots development workers must have the spiritual disciplines necessary to equip them with the "whole armor of God" (Eph 6:10-12).

How does one establish truth and righteousness? Christian suggests the following (1994, 342-43). First, the tools of social analysis help by establishing who is doing what to whom. The poor, then, need a chance to discover who they truly are by reflecting on the word of God and by being treated as valuable human beings with something to contribute. The truth of the kingdom also needs to be declared in public by the church, the community that is supposed to be the sign of the kingdom. The truth also needs to be told about power: power belongs to God and to God alone. This takes us beyond the idea of "power to the people." Finally, worldview needs to be examined against the whole of the biblical narrative to see where it reinforces powerlessness and works against life and well-being.

How does all this relate to the models of development proposed by Korten, Friedman, and Chambers? Has Christian spiritualized the whole exercise? No. This would be a profound misunderstanding of Christian's proposal. Christian is standing on the shoulders of Chambers and of Friedman, in particular. Their frameworks are carefully covered in his thesis, and both address the issue of powerlessness. Powerlessness was one of the five interacting elements in Chambers's poverty trap and Friedman uses powerlessness (in terms of social power) as the central frame for his understanding of poverty and his response. Christian takes both views seriously and even extends them.

> As a people concept, powerlessness describes the experience of persons in households and communities. As a people concept, powerlessness is about real people living in real living space with micro, macro,

global and cosmic dimensions. As a time related concept, it encompasses the forces in history, present realities and perceptions about the future.[10] As a spatial concept, it includes geographical location, nature and environmental dimensions (1994, 332).

Christian calls for a thorough mapping of the expressions of powerlessness, including those of Friedman, and then goes beyond into areas Friedman does not consider. Christian's mapping exercise, done by the poor themselves, is part of the process of unmasking the lies to which the poor are captive.

What Christian intends is to add to the others and especially to Friedman. He does not take issue with them at any point other than to show that their analysis and proposals do not go far enough. Christian is attempting to fill in the spiritual blind spot in a broad and holistic way, and by so doing make their proposals (Friedman's, in particular) stronger and more complete. Without addressing the web of lies, it is hard to see how any development process can be sustained.

What about Korten's development strategies? Or Friedman's concern that development must lead to "clear improvement in the conditions of life and livelihood of ordinary people," and belief that the poor need greater access to social power? What about Chambers's sustainable livelihood and capacity building as the means of achieving well-being? Christian accepts these contributions, and his work in development programs in India reflects this. If asked why he did not speak specifically to such things, he would argue that, as important as they are, they are means, not ends.

The end of development for Christian is true identity, the restored identity of the poor as "children of God with a gift to share" (Sugden 1997, 187). We are to be citizens of the kingdom, people living in just and harmonious relationships with God, self, each other, and the created order. Of Jayakaran's four dimensions of poverty, the spiritual and mental dimensions are the keys for Christian. In addition to the transformational frontiers of Chambers and Friedman in the material order and the domains of social power, the transformational frontiers for Christian are inside the mind of the poor, with the disempowering deceptions that have spiritual roots.

There has been a great deal written in the last fifty years about eradicating poverty, mostly dealing with its physical and social dimensions. Korten, Chambers, and Friedman are among the more recent. This is well and good. Christian development workers should and must take these lessons seriously and apply them to the physical and social dimensions of development. The poor are entitled to the benefits of this thinking. Christian would agree. He would go on to ask, however, what it is that believers in Christ bring to the conversation because they are Christian. His answer is the kingdom of God as the location of everyone's true identity: no more lies, a restored image, a transformed worldview, truth and righteousness established. In the next chapter I will come back to this question of recovering identity as one of the goals of human transformation.[11]

There are two ways in which Christian's proposal could be extended. The first has to do with the vocation of the poor. In Chapter 2 we noted the importance of framing identity in terms of both being (who we are) and doing (what we do). Christian has correctly identified the marring of the identity of the poor, which has to do with being. To this I would add that the identity of the poor has also been marred with respect to their doing or their vocation. The poor have been taught to believe that they are supposed to be slaves or that it is part of the scheme of things that they should do the work of untouchables or bonded laborers. They do not believe they are intended to be creative and productive stewards. To poverty of being we must add poverty of purpose.

Second, Christian expresses little sympathy for the non-poor because of the way they participate in the disempowering systems that create and sustain poverty when they play god in the lives of the poor. While this is appropriate and correct, it fails to take note of the fact that the non-poor also live in a web of lies, ones that support their sense of privilege.[12] In this sense, the non-poor also suffer from a marred identity and sense of vocation, only not in the diminished way experienced by the poor. The non-poor suffer from an overinflated view of who they are when they play god in the lives of the poor. They also have forgotten their true vocation when they use their gifts not to serve but to control and oppress.

Christian's approach is also ambitious. What is being proposed cannot be accomplished this side of the second coming of Christ. We can respond to this in two ways. There is the danger of establishing expectations that permanently disappoint the poor and that become an intolerable burden for the development practitioner. On the other hand, committing oneself to an unattainable ideal, the kingdom of God, also creates an absolute demand for faith, since "faith is being sure of what we hope for and certain of what we do not see" (Heb 11:1). We know we cannot bring the kingdom, and yet we are committed to work for its coming. Living and working in the sinful here and now, while believing in the coming of the sinless kingdom, is a uniquely Christian stance. Care needs to be taken that we understand that we are being asked by God to be obedient, not successful.

5

Toward a Christian Understanding of Transformational Development

It is time to try to pull the material in the preceding chapters together and create a framework for transformational development done by Christians. To do this we need to recognize who owns the development task and place this task within the biblical narrative. I will then pose answers to these questions: What better future? What are the goals of transformation? What process of change? What is sustainability? In what ways do we need to think holistically? All of this will then be placed into a framework for thinking about and planning transformational development.

WHOSE STORY IS IT?

There is a sense in which every development program is a convergence of stories. We bring our story and join the story that is already there, the community's story. As Christians we bring more than one story. We bring our personal story and the story of the culture from which we come (which includes the story of our development institution) along with our understanding of the biblical story, the story of God at work in history. Within the community there are also two stories, the history of the community and the story of God at work in the community. If there are Christians there, the church or churches are the primary bearers of this story. If there are no churches, God has nonetheless been working in the community since the beginning of time, with God's story being hidden or only partly known or recognized.

This convergence of stories raises two very important questions: First, when we speak of transformational development, we must be clear as to whose story it is. Second, we must also affirm which story is normative to all the stories that are converging in a particular time and place.

111

Whose story it is is simply answered but often hard to live out. The transformational development story belongs to the community. It was the community's story before we came and it will be the community's story long after we leave. While our story has something to offer to the community's story, we must never forget that, at the end of the day, this is not *our* story. We all know this, and development literature affirms this consistently. It is in the day-to-day work of development that we are tempted to forget and compromise, all in the name of being helpful or efficient. Forgetting whose story it is means that we further mar the image of God in the poor. When we usurp their story, we add to their poverty.

To frame the stories that are converging in a particular time and place, we must remind ourselves of the larger, foundational story of which all of these converging stories are a part. Transformational development takes place within the larger story of creation, fall, redemption, and the second coming of Christ, at which the final judgment will be made. Therefore, the community and everyone in it is facing a choice.

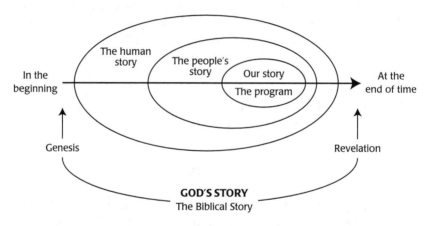

Figure 5-1: Development in the context of the biblical story.

Which trajectory do they wish to choose as the frame for their better future? By declining to choose, a choice is made: the trajectory in biblical terms is toward death, even if things improve a little now. Professional development work can improve material, mental, and social life within the lifetime of the community members without changing the ultimate outcome of the bigger story. Only by accepting God's salvation in Christ can people and the community redirect the trajectory of their story toward the kingdom of God. This is the bottom line of every community's story, poor and non-poor. No Christian development practitioner can ignore this bottom line. This demands that we answer the question, What is the nature of the better future toward which the community and we aspire?

WHAT BETTER FUTURE?

The quest for transformational development, therefore, begins with the need to articulate the better future the community decides it wishes to pursue. Making the better future clear requires a process that allows the community to clarify for itself what really matters and why it matters. What is well-being? What is abundant life? What is the community for? What vision will beckon the community members toward becoming who they truly are? What claims does God make on the community? What claims do the members of the community need to make on each other? For what are human beings responsible? What will create joy at the end of the day? In the section on the biblical narrative, the answer became clear: The unshakable kingdom and the unchanging person are the best better future and the means to get there. This is God's better future toward which everyone is invited to move. The kingdom of God is the future that has already invaded history and that is growing, albeit like leaven, in the present. Like gravity, this emerging kingdom is real; it can be ignored only by accepting significant risk.

What does this mean in concrete terms? As we have developed the idea, the kingdom vision for the better human future is summarized by the idea of shalom: just, peaceful, harmonious, and enjoyable relationships with each other, ourselves, our environment, and God. This kingdom frame is inclusive of the physical, social, mental, and spiritual manifestations of poverty, and so all are legitimate areas of focus for transformational development that is truly Christian. Therefore, immunizing children, improving food security, and providing potable water can be part of a kingdom future if the community says they need to be. Reconciliation, peace-building, and values formation toward the end of including everyone and enabling everyone to make their contribution is potentially part of the emergence of the kingdom in the community. Working to make social systems, and those who manage and shape them, accountable to work for the well-being of all can also be part of moving toward the kingdom. Stress counseling, critical incidence debriefing (see page 166), and simply listening and being with those whose poverty begins in the inner heart or broken spirit is kingdom business too. Whatever heals and restores body, mind, spirit, and community, all can be part of the better future toward which transformational development should point.

Another way of saying this is that any better human future must be about life and life abundant. Ellul has reminded us that "what matters is to live, not to act. . . . In a civilization which has lost the meaning of life, the most useful thing a Christian can do is to live" (1967, 92,94). The Mexican poet and essayist Octavio Paz puts it more sharply: "Progress has peopled history with the marvels and monsters of technology, but has depopulated the life of man. It has given us more things but not more being" (1972, 8). Life abundant is about living, not simply having.

Abundant life means no limits to love, no limits to justice, no limits to peace (Hall 1985, 99). Anything that is for life, that enhances life, or that celebrates life is pointing toward the kingdom. Africans pray for "life as well as the means to make life worth living" (Okorocha 1994, 79). Latin Americans are looking to a revitalized, celebratory view of life in which "space for spiritual quests is opened up" so that common people can find a God

> who walks with the human being in the latter's quest for a sound, gladsome, radiant well being, a well being in the spirit of the carnival—an individual and collective well-fare, from which the category of accumulation and worldly "success" is radically absent (Parker 1996, 262).

The key to moving toward this better future of shalom and abundant life is the discovery that the community's story, and our story, can in fact become part of this larger story, the story of God's redemptive work in the world. Getting to a sustainable better future requires becoming part of the plan God has already declared. With God's help we can recompose our own stories so that we discover our true identity and true vocation, namely, being God's children journeying toward God's kingdom.[1]

Both the poor and the non-poor need to respond to the only vision that promises life in its fullness and relationships that work for justice and peace. This is a vision for transformation that is equally interested in being as well as having. Knowing who we truly are and pursuing our true vocation is the key to more life, not just more things or even more knowledge.

Being clear on God's better future is important to Christian development workers as they help communities develop their view of the better future they wish to seek. Seeing the development story of the community as part of God's larger work in history "offers to all people the possibility of understanding that the meaning and goal of history are not to be found in any projects, programs, ideologies and utopia" (Newbigin 1989, 129). At its best, a ten- to fifteen-year development project will bring limited good, none of which will be sustainable in the long term, unless fundamental choices are made about redirecting the community's story.

Envisioning a better human future is hard work for both the poor and the non-poor. The web of lies believed by the poor has convinced them that there is no better future, at least not in this world. The act of getting the poor to believe in the possibility of a better future is a major transformational frontier, a "prophetic act," in Jayakumar Christian's words. This is also hard work for the non-poor, for they believe they are already on the way to or part of a better future. It is very hard for them to believe that there is anything more. It is even harder to get them to consider change—after all, it is fun playing god in the lives of other people.

There is encouragement here. This vision of the best human future is not modernity's story of inevitable human progress or the mind-dulling, hope-destroying acceptance of the relativistic pluralism of post-modernity. The good news is that we do not have to create our own better future, nor do we have to accept that there is no better future. We do not have to accept a better future in which some have a lot and others are left at the side of the road, as if God only had enough to give gifts to some and not to others.

One final note. Any vision of a better human future that is Christian must include a vibrant, growing, living Christian community that is eagerly and joyfully serving God and the community. It is impossible to imagine a transforming community without a transforming church in its midst. Such a church is in love with God and with all its neighbors, celebrating everything that is for life and being a prophetic voice, telling the truth about everything that is against or that undermines life. More on the church later.

THE GOALS OF TRANSFORMATION

Changed people: Recovering true identity and discovering true vocation

A central tenet in Jayakumar Christian's view of transformation is the recovery of the true identity of the poor. A web of lies results in the poor internalizing a view of themselves as being without value and without a contribution to make, believing they are truly god-forsaken (Sugden 1997, 183-201). No transformation can be sustainable unless this distorted, disempowering sense of identity is replaced by the truth. Healing the marred identity of the poor is the beginning of transformation.

Vinay Samuel takes us another step by pointing us beyond identity (Who am I?) to the importance of dignity (What am I worth?). Samuel's addition of dignity points us toward the idea of vocation in addition to that of identity. Both identity and vocation are critical from a biblical perspective. We must know who we are and the purpose for which we were created. Therefore, restoring identity and recovering vocation must be the focus of a biblical understanding of human transformation. The transforming truth is that the poor and non-poor are made in God's image (identity) and are valuable enough to God to warrant the death of the Son in order to restore that relationship (dignity) and to give gifts that contribute to the well-being of themselves and their community (vocation).[2]

While the agenda for the poor and the non-poor are the same, the issues of each are different. The poor suffer from a marred identity and a degraded vocation. The non-poor, on the other hand, suffer from god-complexes and an inflated vocation. The challenge to the poor is to recover their identity as children of God and to discover their vocation as productive stewards, discovering that they have been given gifts to contribute to social well-being. The challenge for the non-poor, including the development agency,[3] is to relinquish their god-complexes and to employ their gifts for the sake of all human beings rather than using their gifts as a source of power or control.

	Identity	Vocation
Poor	Believing that they are made in the image of God and are God's children.	Believing they have gifts to contribute and that they are called to be productive stewards of creation.
Non-poor	Laying down their god-complexes and believing that they are made in God's image and are not, themselves, gods.	Believing that their gifts are for sharing, not control, and that they are to lead as servants, not masters.

Figure 5-2: Identity and vocation:
The transformational frontiers for the poor and non-poor.

This is an important shift in the focus of transformational development. The point of greatest transformational leverage is changed people. "It is a transformed person who transforms his or her environment" (Musopole 1997, 2). Isaiah quotes God as saying that when the poor hear the good news and receive freedom and release, they become "oaks of righteousness . . . that rebuild the ancient ruins and restore the places long devastated (Is 61:3-4). People, not money or programs, transform their worlds.

The fulcrum for transformational change is no longer transferring resources or building capacity or increasing choices, as important as these things are. But these things count only if they take place in a way that allows the poor to recover their true identity and discover the vocation God intends for them. This is important enough to say negatively to make the point. As good as transferring resources or building capacity or increasing choices can be, the process by which they are achieved can rob them of any goodness. A flawed process can make the poor poorer by further devaluing their view of themselves and what they have.

Transforming people begins with helping people discover that "their human dignity and identity are intrinsically related to God in Christ through his redemptive purpose in salvation history" (Bediako 1996a, 8). The moment people discover who they truly are is the moment in which their story takes on a new trajectory as a new future breaks in that cannot be contained, even by the cleverest of lies. With a recovered identity, the next step is the development of character, instilling and forming values that permit a better vision of the future and that allow the poor to love others as themselves, seeking to be life-enhancing for all. Finally, with a rediscovered identity and a character to match, transformational development works to empower people to live out these values in search of their new vision. This means teaching people to read, to understand and interpret their context, to figure out what and who is contributing to their current situation, and then to decide what they want to do about it.[4] Transformation begins with a changed person. All other transformational frontiers are now more easily breached in a more comprehensive way with a greater hope of being sustainable.[5]

Finding that their story makes most complete sense and finds its best hope for the future in God's larger story opens up and invites a wide range of transformational responses. The web of lies is unmasked for what it is, an enormous deception serving the interests of both the evil one and the non-poor (who choose to ignore their complicity). Bediako speaks of opening "the eyes of people and of societies to see those realities—personal and collective—in beliefs, world views and ethical choices, which continue to resist God" (1996a, 9). If poverty is the world trying to tell the poor they are god-forsaken, then transformation is the declaration that they are made in God's image, that God allowed his Son to die for them, and that God has given gifts to the poor so that they can fulfill God's creation mandate that they too may be fruitful and productive.

Helping people recover their true identity and vocation also requires that they learn to reread their history. God did not come into the life of the community with the arrival of the missionaries and certainly not with the arrival of the development agency. God has been active in the story of the community since the beginning of time. Although God is never without a witness (Rom 1:19), God was not always recognized for who God is or for what God has done. For the community to move into a new future, it must rediscover and recover its past, albeit understanding it in a different way. "The great travail of Christian Africa is over the conversion of the African past. Perhaps no conversion is complete without the conversion of the past" (Walls 1996, 53). This is important because the community needs to make the universal gospel story, the true story of history, its own story as well. "Once this basic, universal relevance of Jesus Christ is granted, it no longer is a question of trying to accommodate the Gospel in our culture; we learn to read and accept the Good News as *our* story. Our Lord has been, from the beginning, the Word of God *for us* as for all people everywhere" (Bediako 1994, 101).

For a Christian understanding of transformational development, restoring identity and vocation is the goal. This is the only path that leads toward life and that holds the promise of shalom. We must work alongside the poor and non-poor alike, helping them and helping ourselves uncover and accept our true identity as children of God. We must both work toward the recovery of our true vocations as productive stewards of God's earth, obedient to the claims and promises of Christ and his kingdom.

Just and peaceful relationships

Our identity and vocation are expressed through our relationships. Thus, recovering identity and discovering vocation require that transformational development focus on restoring relationships. From the chapters on the biblical narrative and the nature of poverty we have identified a relational framework that links everyone to God, to themselves, to their community, to those who are "other," and to the environment. This is an important framework for thinking about transformational frontiers.

The central relationship in need of restoration is one's *relationship with the triune God*, the God of the Bible. The good news is that God desires this restoration and has already taken the steps necessary for this relationship to be restored. There is very little for us to do except say yes to God's invitation to faith in Jesus Christ. I have already implied that restoring relationships with God, accepting God's story as the story in which ours finds a home and makes sense, is the transformational point of maximum leverage for change. If people are seeking God, many other good things will follow and become possible. If they are not, the horizons of change are more limited and difficult.

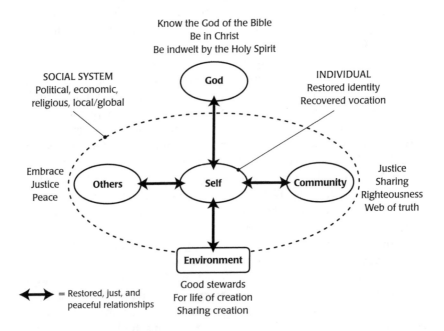

Figure 5-3: Transformed relationships.

Being in a healthy *relationship with oneself* is also an important transformational frontier. Many have suffered from the disempowerment that arises from a web of lies inside the mind, lies about oneself. Some of these lies arose externally and were internalized. Others are lies we told ourselves. These competing and conflicting voices inside ourselves are the root of the mental dimension of poverty. Seeking peace within ourselves requires truth and justice within ourselves as well. This is the task of Christian psychology. Finally, within oneself is the location of character and values formation. "Development has to start with the development of character that is according to the values of the kingdom of God" (Musopole 1997, 3).

The quality of *relationships within one's community* is also important. There are many things that need changing that can only be addressed by the community working together. It is hard if the community is divided or cannot work together. Seldom can single individuals or households sustain change if they are working alone. The primary transformational divide within a community of people who share a common history and culture is between the poor and non-poor. Each is enmeshed in its own web of lies, and the non-poor have a great deal invested in accepting things as they are. In addition, the worldview of a cultural group can legitimate the current conditions of the both poor and non-poor, adding another reinforcement to this separation. For example, in the Hindu context, the oppressive dimension of caste is reinforced by a religious worldview that says that *karma* is the just cause of both the wealth of the oppressor and the suffering of the oppressed (Sugden 1997, 184).

Healing the divide between the poor and non-poor is critical to significant long-term change. This means that the poor need help to recover their true identity and vocation while the non-poor need help to deal with the god-complexes that he or she has accepted to justify their privileged position in relationship to the poor. The divide between the poor and the non-poor is exacerbated by the fact that, even though they share a common language, culture and place, the poor have become "other" to the non-poor and vice versa.

Being at peace with *those who are "other" to us* means adding the ministry of reconciliation to the transformational agenda. Yet reconciliation is often very hard because the most frequent reason for declaring someone "other" is that they have done harm to you and your community. Miraslav Volf has made an important contribution to our understanding of identity, otherness, and reconciliation in *Exclusion and Embrace*. Volf explains that the beginning of reconciliation and hence the path to justice and peace is the embrace of the other, in spite of all that the other has done. "There can be no justice without the will to embrace" (1996, 216). This call transcends the issue of who is right or wrong, who is righteous or unrighteous. We must embrace the other because this is what Christ did and continues to do. Yet,

Volf explains, the embrace is not complete "until the truth is said and justice is done" (1996, 216).

This requires a particular kind of stance toward the other, a way of understanding them. The will to embrace sheds light; its metaphor is the open arms of the father whose son made himself wholly other (Lk 15:11-31). The will to exclude creates blindness. Its metaphor is the clenched fist; there can be no good in the other, only evil. With the will to embrace comes the possibility of seeing that there is some good in the other, bringing hope that this may be a point of convergence, a way of coming together. This insight of Volf's may have particular value when we think about creating a new kind of relationship between the poor and the non-poor.[6]

Finally, the community must be in a *healthy and respectful relationship with the environment* on which it depends for food, water, and air. At the heart of our true vocation is the call to be stewards, caring for the world in which God has placed us so that it is productive and supportive of life. We need to transform our metaphor for our relationship with nature from one of masters of nature to the idea of being stewards of God's creation. Christians knew this once. In the Celtic tradition of the sixth and seventh centuries, "we find a holy intimacy of human, natural and divine. . . . We see everywhere . . . an abandonment to spiritual work and simultaneously a cultivation of the earth" (Bamford and March 1987, 19).

Summarizing, to move toward a better human future we must encourage and develop relationships that work, relationships that are just, peaceful, and harmonious. This is the heart of shalom and the only way leading toward abundant life for all. Thus transformational development that enhances life works to promote relationships that work as well as they can in a world of fallen people. Life and relationships are inseparable. "Development should aim at a blessed life, a life at peace with itself, others, the environment and with God" (Musopole 1997, 3).

WHAT PROCESS OF CHANGE?

Starting with the end in mind is not enough, however. The process by which we get there matters, too. This is because God has imposed some limitations on our choices. Some means are better than others. Some means actually help us live the future before it gets here. Some means have to be given to us, we cannot get them for ourselves. Therefore, we also have to answer the question, To what process of change do we aspire?

There are a variety of choices. Some look to governments as the means of transformation. Some believe that hard work and a free market are the best tools for change. Others believe transformation depends solely in the work of God and the power of the Holy Spirit. Still others look to human reason and technology. Some believe the resources lie within us, while others believe we must get the resources for change by taking them from others, through government taxation or even more direct means.

Affirming the role of God

A Christian process of change must begin with an affirmation that, at the most fundamental level, transformation takes place because God wants it and is enabling it. At the end of the day, any transformation, justice, and peace will be because God made it so. We are not the authors of change, nor the primary actors.

It is the action of God, the triune God—of God the Father who is ceaselessly at work in all creation and in the hearts and minds of all human beings whether they acknowledge him or not, graciously guiding history toward its true end; of God the Son who has become part of this created history in the incarnation; and of God the Holy Spirit who is given as a foretaste of the end to empower and teach the church and to convict the world of sin and righteousness and judgment (Newbigin 1989, 135).

Affirming the role of human beings

Having said this, however, we must also go on to say that change takes place because human beings commit themselves to the process of change and invest whatever gifts and resources they have to the process. God gives us real choices over all elements of our lives. People must make the choice to seek transformation and then invest themselves in making it happen. Thus, a Christian understanding of the process of change centers on the decisions and actions of human beings. This has several implications.

First, the change process belongs to those who are in need of change. If God will not impose change, then neither should we. The beginning of healing the marred image of the poor is to insist that they alone have the right to describe their current reality and to shape the vision of their better future. Second, since not all choices made by people are good ones, and since broken relationships are part of the problem, any Christian process of change must include processes of repentance and forgiveness. Finally, a process dependent on human beings can only go as fast as human beings can go. The pace must be set by the people. Koyama (1979) has spoken eloquently about the "three-mile-an-hour" God, who has graciously adjusted his pace to ours.

Focusing on relationships

This should not be a surprise. Yet sometimes we are unclear as to the importance of beginning at the right place. There is a temptation to begin with the problem or with the research that allows us to understand the problem. Getting on with the work of analysis and planning is tempting to all of us. Yet we must not yield. Paraphrasing Koyama, we can know a poor person, but we cannot know poverty (1974, 129). We must begin with people, not abstractions, data, analysis, or technique. Without transforming relationships there is unlikely to be much transformation.

Keeping the end in mind

When we focus on the process of change, there can be a temptation to value effectiveness over everything else. We need to remember that the goal of human transformation is the discovery of true identity and vocation. Meaning matters more than efficiency. Reflecting on Israel's making of the golden calf because Moses was too long on the mountain, Koyama tells us that Israel's pragmatism, driven by a sense of urgency, resulted in "theological impatience and technological efficiency." The result was "disfigurement of their own history and the loss of their own identity" (Koyama 1985, 139). Valuing efficiency or effectiveness over discovering meaning creates poverty.

Recognizing pervasive evil

With all the talk about God's role and a better human future pointing toward the kingdom of God, there is a danger that we may slip into a romantic optimism about the success of our efforts with the poor. While God will have the final say and the kingdom of God will prove to be the only unshakable kingdom at the end of time, getting there will not be easy. To get to the joy of Easter morning, Christ had to suffer through Good Friday.

The Evil One is in the world working actively against life and shalom. This evil works through the sin in human beings, encouraging bad choices by promoting a web of lies. The Evil One also works a campaign of deception and domination through the political, economic, social, and religious structures of the world by subverting them in the pursuit of their intended missions. No Christian process of change can underestimate this opposition or deny itself the spiritual tools with which to battle against this foe.

In societies in which fear of spirits and the unseen is pervasive, the deception of the Evil One assumes a deeper, more pernicious role. People test the gods and spirits, and those who claim to speak for them. The spirits who respond to sacrifices are moved up the hierarchy of power and receive more sacrifices, money, and attention. Those who prove less reliable or unapproachable move down. This is a framework of lies, a deceptive order that disempowers the poor and enriches and empowers those who claim to be the intermediaries linking this world to the next. Such a deceptive framework undermines human initiative and takes the place of the true God. This is evil at work against life.

Seeking truth, justice, and righteousness

If the most fundamental cause of poverty is the impact of sin, then dealing with sin must be part of the Christian process of change. While we must deal with the individual nature of this sin, we must also address its consequences as expressed in relationships that are based on a web of lies and that promote disempowerment of the poor and domination by the non-poor. This means that a Christian process of change must center on truth-telling[7] and the promotion of justice and righteousness (Christian 1994). The truth must be discovered about the way the poor contribute to their own poverty, and the truth must be discovered about how poverty is created by the god-complexes of the non-poor, inadequacies of worldview, and deception by the principalities and powers. Only in repenting in the face of God's truth can relationships be restored so that life, justice, and peace (shalom) can be restored. Thus, in a Christian process of change, every development action and process must be tested for its contribution to truth and justice.

Addressing causes

No process of human and social transformation can be entirely defined locally. Every community is part of a family of social systems that are regional, national, and finally global. Alan Fowler, development specialist and co-founder of the International NGO Training and Research Centre (INTRAC) in the UK, has developed a helpful diagram that shows how the micro-level of transformational development is located within an international social system (1997, 13). At the bottom of this diagram we find the transformational development that I have been describing: empowering communities, strengthening local institutions, and sustainable well-being. Fowler links this micro-level of development to the larger development environment of the national and international economic and political order. This is a critically important location of those who play god in the lives of the poor at a distance, those who seem particularly subject to Wink's "delusional assumptions."

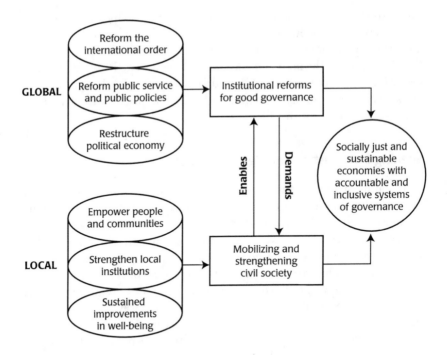

Figure 5-4: The micro- and macro-levels of development action.
(Adapted from Fowler 1997, 13)

Any understanding of transformational development that does not include concerns for reforming and restructuring at these higher levels is incomplete and somewhat naive. This is the point at which effective and discerning policy analysis and advocacy in all its forms must be included as part of the transformational development process. Fowler is right when he points out that the micro-level of development, where people are empowered and well-being is improved, must come together with the macro-level of development, where institutions are reformed for good governance, if we are to hope for "socially just and sustainable economies with accountable and inclusive systems of governance" (1997, 13).

One caution on the practice of policy analysis and advocacy. Too often agencies do the policy analysis with professionals and then presume to speak for those whom they claim have no voice. This implies that the poor are unable to diagnose their own situation and that they, in truth, have no voice. This does not have to be the case and, in ensuring that it is not the case, a transformational frontier can be crossed. The poor will be less poor when they learn to do their own analysis and find their own voice. This will require help and support, especially in addressing international structures, but this is no excuse for doing their advocacy work for them.[8]

Doing no harm

One of the recent discoveries working with the poor in situations called complex humanitarian emergencies[9] is that sometimes helping the poor can make things worse. We have always assumed that being humanitarian and being good were the same. We now know better. Hugo Slim has alerted us to the "dark side [of humanitarian action] that compromises as well as helps the people whose suffering it seeks to assuage" (Slim 1997, 1).

Mary B. Anderson, president of Collaborative Action for Development at Harvard University, has done a careful study of humanitarian and development aid in conflict situations (Anderson 1999). She has articulated a series of actions that may result in harm if we are not careful as to how and when we do things. Some of these warnings are more important when the context is violent, but we should keep all of them in mind in order that we meet the minimum standard for transformation: that we do no harm.

- Introducing resources into resource-scarce environments can increase competition and suspicion.
- Adding to the overall resources of an area frees local resources to be used for other things, such as further economic exploitation, violence, and war.
- Providing assistance can severely distort local economic activities and reduce incomes and employment opportunities.
- Working through existing political structures, formal or informal, in order to gain access or permission buttresses such structures and may prolong their malfeasance, corruption, or role in conflict.
- Adopting policies of solidarity with one group over against another contributes to their continuing separation and conflict.
- Targeting aid to specific groups within a community to the exclusion of others exacerbates tensions and competition.
- By setting up processes for determining who should receive assistance and who should not, groups are placed in competition and inter-group suspicion is increased.
- Hiring armed guards to protect aid programs means "buying in" to the existing conflict.
- Circulating pictures and stories of conflict and its impact can provide grist to the mill of accusation and counter-accusation which perpetuates conflict or alienation of groups (Anderson 1996b).

Expressing a bias toward peace

Doing no harm is important, but there is a positive counterpart that is equally important for those who follow the Prince of Peace. For example, Mary Anderson has developed a useful planning framework whose aim is to enhance local capacities for peace (Anderson 1999, 74).

When we choose our methods and set our goals for transformation, it is often possible to express a bias in favor of peace. This happens when we insist that community committees include men and women, poor and non-poor, or representatives from every tribal group or church and religious group in the village. Recent research into some of World Vision's area development programs in India, Ethiopia, and Uganda shows that insisting that local institutions involved with our development programming be inclusive of all groups in the community results in reconciliation and cooperative behavior (O'Reilly 1998).

In Bosnia, a community asked for help in rebuilding a water system destroyed during the war. The request was for three independent water systems, one for each ethnic group. A peace-building bias demands that this request be rejected in favor of developing an agreement to create a single water system designed and managed by people representing all three ethnic groups.

Affirming the role of the church

In many communities, living witnesses to God's larger story are already present in the form of the local church or churches.[10] The transformational development process that points toward the kingdom is already underway. We do not represent the arrival of God's people. Any Christian understanding of transformational development must take this fact seriously and accept that God has already put a living sign of God's kingdom in the community.

Too often Christian development professionals see the church as a distraction, or worse, an impediment to transformation. "They have separated themselves from the rest of the community." "They don't believe development is something the church should be doing." "The church is not professional enough; they don't know what they are doing." "The church has been validating the current political and economic system; they are part of the problem." We know the litany well. Yet we must face one fact squarely:

It is surely a fact of inexhaustible significance that what our Lord left behind him was not a book or a creed, nor a system of thought, nor a rule of life, but a visible community. . . . He committed the entire work of salvation to that community. . . . The church does not depend for its existence upon our understanding of it or faith in it (Newbigin 1954, 21).

Our goal must be to help the church be what it is intended to be, not to judge it or relegate it to the transformational development sidelines. Everyone is in need of transformation—ourselves, the poor, and the church. We are all on a journey. "Working toward a relationship of mutual spiritual accountability with local churches is part of what it means to be holistic in taking both the gospel and the context seriously" (Bediako 1996b, 187). If we are willing to love and accompany the poor toward transformation, why should we not be willing to love and accompany our brothers and sisters in Christ on their journey toward the same goal? Vinay Samuel provokes us:

> What would happen if we apply the same principles of community participation to the establishment and building of the church as we do for the agriculture, health and school projects? How does the idea of building people's capacity to plan and manage their own development relate to the establishment and sustainability of a local church and the believer's spiritual life? (1995, 145).

There are several critical contributions to transformational development that only the church can provide. First, the role of the church in transformational development is the same as ours: to be a servant and a source of encouragement, not a commander or a judge.

> The church can be the servant of its community, harnessing the wind and wood and water into technologies that make the world a little more habitable, or singing with the rest of creation the wonder of existence, or working side by side with all people of good will toward a better social order. If the church is to lead at all, it is in serving; in applying the creative energies released in Christ towards the stewardship of creation and the bringing of fallen structures closer to God's original purposes (Maggay 1994, 72).

Second, the church can and must be a source of value formation within the community. While not an exclusive source of values, people who are reading and living the word under the discipling of the Holy Spirit should be a significant source of inspiration and perspiration working for life and shalom. When the church is its best, it is a sign of the values of the kingdom and is contributing holistic disciples to the community for its well-being (see Figure 5-5). The church is more important as a source of people than as a source of instruction or prophetic word. Newbigin said it well:

> The major role of the church in relationship to the great issues of justice and peace will not be in its formal pronouncement, but in its continually nourishing and sustaining men and women who will act responsibly as believers in the course of their secular duties as citizens (Newbigin 1989, 139).

Finally, the church is the hermeneutical community that reads the biblical story as its story and applies this story to the concrete circumstances of its time, place, and culture. This is the community within the community from which the word of God is heard, lived, and revealed. This is the community that, because it knows the true story, can and must challenge the delusional assumptions and the web of lies.

SUSTAINABILITY

A great deal has been written in recent years about the need for development to be sustainable. There have been too many examples in the past of development programming that seemed to be making a difference as long as the staff and the money of the development agency were present. Program evaluations, performed after the money and staff were withdrawn, revealed that the entire development enterprise had proven more than the community could sustain on its own. Within a year or two, it was hard to find evidence that there had been a program at all. In some cases, things actually got worse because the community had become dependent on external resources and now suffered from diminished capacity.

We need to be careful how we think about the idea of sustainability. First of all, we must recognize that even the poorest community already has some level of sustainability. If the community were not sustainable before the development agency came, it could not exist. There is considerable evidence that poor communities are quite sophisticated in developing sustainable survival strategies (Jayakaran 1996, 8) in terms of food, water, housing, and living within the constraints of a marginal natural environment (Chambers 1997, 24).

The second caution is that the ultimate source of sustainable life is not ours to control. It is God through Christ who sustains life. Psalm 104 is a parable of this, describing God's active role in making springs, giving drink, causing grass to grow, and "bringing forth food from the earth: wine that gladdens the heart of man, oil to make his face shine, and bread that sustains his heart" (Ps 104:14-16). Most communities are already sustainable in some manner because God has been and is at work through them.

Third, we need to ask whether the idea of sustainability is enough. If sustainable simply means things are being maintained or that the project activities and impacts continue after we leave, is this a high enough goal? Don't we really seek sustainable growth, learning, and continuing transformation? I think we do, but we need to say so.

Finally, we need to define sustainability in two ways. First, we do not want the transformational development process to be dependent on us. This is a negative definition, but it is essential that the development agency keep such a definition clearly in mind. Defining sustainability this way, however, is less helpful to the community. Not being dependent on us does not mean that the community and its story are necessarily sustainable on their own.

The community needs a different understanding of sustainability. To do this, we have to return to the same categories we used to frame our understanding of poverty. The community's understanding of sustainability must include the physical, mental, social, and spiritual.

Physical sustainability

This dimension of sustainability includes all the basics that people need to live: food, water, health, economics, and a sustainable environment. Adequate food and nutrition require sustainable agriculture,[11] an approach to increasing agricultural production that is not dependent on chemicals that are costly or that damage the land and the water. Adequate water means sustainable water development that emphasizes more effectively managing rainfall run-off and ground water in ways that are sustainable (Serageldin 1995). As the examples of agriculture and water imply, physical sustainability implies enhancing the productivity and life-supporting capacity of the local environment in ways that ensure its future.

Physical sustainability also means people who are able to manage their own health care to the greatest extent possible. This means a community-based approach in which people are empowered to do what they can for themselves, utilizing local indigenous knowledge and traditional sources of health care, with minimal dependence on the high-cost, expensive health-care systems we are dependent upon in the West.[12]

Physical sustainability means enabling the poor to create wealth. Microenterprise development programs that promote capital formation in poor communities and that teach the poor to run small businesses and to save money form the economic foundation without which sustainability is impossible.[13]

Finally, we need to learn from the history of the so-called developed countries in their move toward material sustainability. They have developed the means to be sustainable (more or less) in terms of health, agriculture, water, and economics. However, this has often been done at the cost of environmental sustainability (Weaver et al. 1997, 233-58). We live in a robust and resilient world that has managed to contain several centuries of human creativity in the form of technological and economic development. We must thank God for both the creativity and the resilience of creation. It seems, however, that there are limits both locally and globally to this singular creation God has given to us.

As Christians working for transformation, we must learn what these limits are and respect them as good stewards would. Francis Bacon, a Christian philosopher of the sixteenth century and the father of natural philosophy (the breakthrough that opened the door to the development of science), said it well: "We can only command Nature by obeying her" (quoted in Urbach and Gibson 1994, 43).

Mental sustainability

I've already made the case that the deepest form of poverty is poverty of being, ontological poverty. Disempowering scars exist in the human and community consciousness of the poor. The web of lies is perceived to be the way things are—ordained, immutable, unchangeable. Transformational development that does not include restoring psychological and spiritual well-being is not sustainable. We must seek the healing of the marred identity of the poor. We must treat them as valuable human beings, made in the image of God, loved by God. We must listen to them as if they have something to contribute, because they do. They simply do not appreciate how much they know. We must encourage the belief that God is for them and that God has given everyone something to contribute.

The poor must come to believe in themselves—not in us, our development aid, or our development agency. If they believe we are the true instruments of development, then we have failed to create mental sustainability. Instead, we have created dependency and deepened their poverty.

Releasing people's capacity to learn is also a critical element of mental sustainability. Helping people discover that they can study and make sense out of their world, that they can identify their capabilities and vulnerabilities and plan based on what they learn, is part of a mental transformation that changes the people from the inside. Teaching people how to evaluate their efforts and to codify their experience is an empowering experience that sustains continuing transformation. At the end of the day, helping people learn how to learn is one of the most important parts of any transformative process.

Social sustainability

The need for sustainable systems takes us back to Korten and Friedman. Korten's alternative development (1990, 218) seeks to return some level of control over local resources—by which he means both natural resources and the information people need to make informed decisions—to the people who live in the community in hopes that this will lead to sustainable choices on the part of the community. Korten calls for the development of sustainable development systems that include local NGOs, the local private and public sector, and all the systemic links between the community and those whose decisions have an effect on the well-being of the community. This requires broadening local political participation, active mutual self-help, and empowerment. Because he believes that our environment can not sustain continuing economic growth and consumption, Korten argues against economics based on growth (1990, 132). His view of an alternative development seems to wish for a future that ignores or operates apart from economic globalization.

Friedman's empowerment approach also places emphasis on local deci-sion-making, local self-reliance, local participation in democratic processes, and social learning, but he accepts the inevitability of the constraints and influence of the "global economic forces, structures of unequal wealth, and hostile class alliances (1992, viii). Therefore, sustainability, for Friedman, requires sustainable social systems that are transformed into political power "to engage the struggle for emancipation on a larger—national and inter-national—terrain." Sustainable social systems and helping the poor have a political voice of their own are integral parts of social sustainability.

Alex de Waal, director of African Rights in London and a critic of relief aid, argues that humanitarian assistance must support the incipient sense of political engagement and instinct toward political accountability that true development must bring. Social sustainability must include establishing or supporting the development of local organizations with social agendas (de Waal 1997, 219). People need to develop a sense that, as part of a larger political community, they have rights on which they should insist—to de-velopment, to a sustainable livelihood, to respect for civil and political rights. They have the right to expect that humanitarian law applies to them (1997, 8). If this is ignored or not supported, then humanitarian aid simply creates support for oppressive political and economic structures and sustains their illegitimacy.

Recently, social sustainability has come to include a concern for building *civil society*, a term used to refer to nonprofit groups or voluntary associa-tions such as development agencies, environmental groups, service groups, sports clubs, church groups, peasant associations, self-help groups, and the like.[14] Civil society is the point at which micro-enterprise development, political empowerment, and nurturing social organizations come together. These groups are the social capital that, along with economic and human capital, constitute the productive capital of the community (Weaver et al 1997, 208). Civil society can also be the bridge between the micro- and macro-levels of development action, between the work of the community and the regional, national and global political and economic structures in which the community is embedded (see Figure 5-4 above).

Alan Whaites points out that this affirmation of civil society assumes a de Tocquevillian understanding of civil society in which civil society is a social good in that it acts as a defensive counter-balance against a strong (modern) state (Whaites 1996). The paradox is that most development NGOs operate in the context of a weak state where they must be concerned with not usurping the rightful role of the state. Some African governments feel that some international NGOs have stepped over this line.

A Christian view of social sustainability will require a theology of civil society that defines the roles and responsibility that individual Christians, voluntary Christian groups, and churches should play in order to add value to the societies in which they live. Jayakumar Christian and Walter Wink provide an important additional insight. Social systems, including civil society, are the domains of what Paul called the principalities and powers. As a result of their fallen nature, principalities and powers work within the social systems to devalue or degrade life. They deceive by working against any recognition of God being at work in social systems or even that social systems have a spirituality. The result is a materialistic view of social systems and a distortion of their mission.

No Christian view of building civil society can neglect the fact that social systems have a spiritual interiority. Working for civil society and for extending social power will bring us up against spiritual forces that do not want the poor empowered or a role for the church in the "secular" social order. Thus, in addition to community organizing, institution building, and political action, building civil society that supports social sustainability is a spiritual task requiring spiritual tools.

Finally, enhancing civil society presupposes the "freedom to develop" (Weaver et al. 1997, 220). Transformational development that does not include concerns for peace-building, human rights, and democratic participation is very limited indeed. Development in societies in conflict must be done in a way that decreases tensions and that nurtures local capacities for peace (Anderson 1996c). While some argue that human rights and democracy are somehow uniquely Western concepts, the fact that they square fully with the biblical tradition must move them onto the agenda for Christians involved in development. It is no accident that these concepts emerged in cultures that share the Judeo-Christian tradition. While one can discuss fruitfully the need to balance the rights of individuals with the rights of the community, it would be hard to imagine building civil society while ignoring the issues of freedom to assemble, freedom to speak, freedom to choose one's beliefs, and freedom to have a say in decisions affecting one's future.[15]

Spiritual sustainability

Spiritual sustainability begins with what seems to be a contradiction. While the community needs to believe that it is not dependent on the development agency, it must also believe passionately that it is dependent on God. No one is independent; we are all dependent on God, whether we acknowledge this fact or not. For centuries, contemplatives have opened their day with the prayer, "Thank you, O God, for waking me this morning, you didn't have to." Fortunately, most poor communities in the Third World believe this more deeply than most of us do in the West.

Another dimension of spiritual sustainability has to do with the contribution of faith-based organizations in the community. Churches, mosques, and temples are the location of value traditions without which human society cannot function. Decisions to include women in community decision-making, to stop killing girl children, to work cooperatively with those formerly demonized as "other," all require a value change that most often finds its roots in the transformative power of faith traditions (including, of course, civil religion or scientific materialism). At the heart of this kind of change is repentance and forgiveness, the twin foundations of reconciliation. At its best, this is the work of the religious community.

In spite of the uneven history of religions in terms of their contributions (or lack thereof) to human welfare, religious men and women, concerned for the spiritual welfare of the community, must play a role in the development of the community if it is to be transformational and sustainable. For Christians, this means surrendering a privileged place in the community and working alongside people who believe differently. This should not concern us. If our story is the true human story and if our God is the true God, then we need to become servants of all others and in faith believe that God is able to take care of himself.

Finally, as Christians, it is hard for us to believe in sustainable transformation in a community in which the church is not acting as the sign of the kingdom, of God's better future. The church plays this role by what it does even more effectively than by what it says. The church is not so much the Christians gathered, although it is this too, as it the place where Christians learn and are challenged to live the whole gospel in the fullness of the life of the larger community.

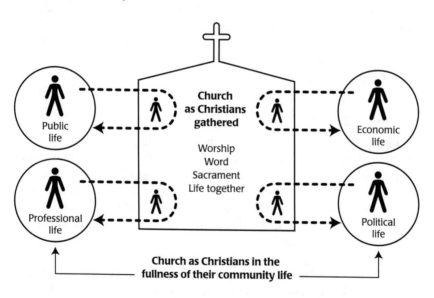

Figure 5-5: The church outside the building.

The presence of churches as both Christians gathered and Christians serving in the world is critical to genuine social transformation. Canadians Don Posterski and Gary Nelson studied churches that grow in the fullest sense of the word, in numbers, in depth and in social influence. These churches rate highly in "soul care" and "social care." Soul care is the development of personal faith, personal devotional life, day-to-day application of the faith, commitment to truth and teaching of the biblical command to love God and your neighbor as yourself. Social care is community service, importance of social action, helping the poor, and correcting injustices in society (Posterski and Nelson 1997, 225). It is hard to imagine sustainable transformation without churches committed to soul care and social care.

THINKING HOLISTICALLY

The need for this way of thinking about and viewing the world should now be clear. As we take on the challenge of working for human transformation, we will have to learn to think and act holistically in a variety of ways.

The whole story

We have to keep the whole story in mind and avoid the temptation to reduce it to the gospel story only. The biblical narrative is a whole story that spans creation, the call of Israel, the exile, Jesus and his death and resurrection, the church, and the end of history with the second coming. The biblical narrative is a story of a seamlessly related world of material and spiritual, of persons and social systems. If we truncate this story, we rob it of much of its life and meaning. The full story of Jesus begins at creation and ends with his second coming.

The whole gospel message

The gospel message is an inseparable mix of life, deed, word, and sign. We are to be with Jesus (life) so that we can preach the good news (word), heal the sick (deed), and cast out the demons (sign). This holistic gospel addresses all three of Hiebert's levels: the word of truth, the act of power, and the deed that works. Each dimension of the gospel message adds to the meaning of the others. Our life and deeds make our words intelligible; our words help people understand our life and deeds. Life, word, and deed are signs of the living presence of someone greater than ourselves.

While we should reveal the gospel message in whatever way best speaks to the immediate needs of our audience, over time all the dimensions of the gospel must be revealed for the good news of Jesus Christ to be understood in its fullness. Often the transformational development process begins with witness through good deeds. As relationships develop, the way we live our lives and treat people becomes a witness of life. Prayer, reminding people that God is the source of any good that is emerging in the community, and the occasional miracle are the witness of sign. When we answer the question "Why are you here?" or "Why are you making a sacrifice for the likes of us?" the answer is the gospel. This is the witness of word. Limiting our work of transformation to only one aspect of the gospel message impoverishes the message and obscures the person of Jesus.

A holistic view of people

Remember Figure 5-3 above? It illustrates a holistic understanding of a human being. There can be no meaningful understanding of a person apart from his or her relationships—with God, self, community, those he or she calls "other," and the environment. People as individuals are inseparable from the social systems in which they live.

A holistic view of time

We need to understand time holistically and not separate past, present, future, and eternity. People's past can be a barrier to transformation. Inability to imagine a future that is different from today is a transformational frontier. Separating the time of our story (past, present, and future) from the time of God's larger story (eternity) is also a mistake. Transformational plans for the next fifteen years must be made in light of all of human history and its ultimate destination.

A state of mind

One final word on holism. Holism is for the most part a state of mind or attitude. Holism must be in the mind of the practitioner as a habit—a way of living, thinking, and doing. Creating this mindset is very important since it is difficult to demand holism in the form of the program itself. No transformational development effort can do everything and work at every level of the problem. This means that the best test for holism is a negative test. If there is no work directed at spiritual or value change; no work involving the church; no mention of meaning, discovery, identity and vocation, then one should be concerned that the program is not holistic. The next step is to talk to the development promoter and the people. If they show no thinking that is holistic, then there is a problem.

A FRAMEWORK FOR TRANSFORMATION

Putting all of these ideas together, we have a framework for transformation that points us toward the best human future—the kingdom of God. This future is framed by the twin goals of transformation: changed people who have discovered their true identity and vocation, and changed relationship that are just and peaceful. These goals are sought with a process of change that is principle-centered. The development process belongs to the people; relationships are the critical factor for change; we need to keep the end of transformation in mind; we promote truth-telling, righteousness, and justice; and we are careful to do no harm. These principles are expressed through persons or groups of persons working in the community: God, the church, the holistic development practitioner, and the Evil One. Three of these are working in favor of a better human future, while the mission of the fourth is to distract, divide, and destroy. Finally, these transformational development principles and positive active agents seek to move a community toward the goals of transformation in a way that is sustainable physically, mentally, socially, and spiritually.

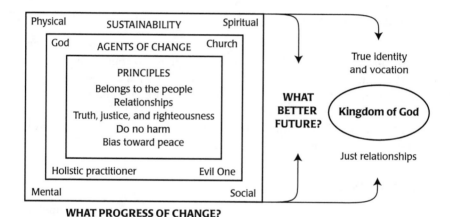

Figure 5-6: The framework for transformation.

6

Development Practice:
Principles and Practitioners

To this point we have developed an understanding of what poverty is and why people are poor. To this we have added an understanding of what transformational development is from a Christian perspective. The next question is, How do we work with the poor and the non-poor in order to help them articulate a vision for transformation and the means by which they can attempt to move toward this vision?

Answering this question takes some care. If we jump too quickly to development methodology, we can make some serious mistakes. There are some underlying assumptions that need clarification. Whose project is being planned? Who does the planning? What way of thinking about planning is best suited for development work? What requirements will we make of development-planning methodologies?

Finally, there are a whole series of considerations relating to the development practitioner. We need to address the mindset and characteristics of the holistic practitioner. What kind of formation and spirituality enables effective development promotion?

THE PRINCIPLES

Respecting the community's story

Earlier I described transformational development as taking place in the context of converging stories. The story of the development promoter and the agency of which he or she is a part is joining the story of the community and the individual stories of the people and groups in the community. Thus it is important to be very clear as to whose story the transformational development project belongs to. I also pointed out that everyone is quick to say that the story belongs to the people, and that it is a great deal harder to live this out in practice. Too often development workers unwittingly assume that their story is a better story; after all, they know how to do sustainable agriculture and understand maternal child health. It is a great and humbling challenge to lay down our own story and not pick it up again until the poor ask us to do so.

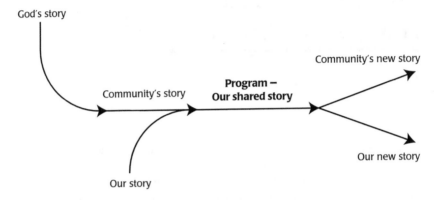

Figure 6-1: Convergence of stories.

At the same time, however, this convergence of stories means that the story of the community and the holistic practitioner will never be fully the same. Each story affects all the other stories. The poor will borrow from our story and, if we are not too proud, we will learn from theirs. There is no longer a single narrative in the community. This is why engaged, respectful relationships are so important to transformational development. Each story needs to engage all the other stories, and all need to engage the larger story of which all stories are part.

The history of the community

The community's story, up to the time the development practitioner arrives, is its history. The community comes from a past, and its memory of that past is the beginning of any new story. The community has been coping, adapting, and surviving. It has tried to innovate, sometimes with success and sometimes with failure. Good things have happened; the community has done things it is proud of. The positive elements of the past can be a source of vision and energy for the future.[1] Leszek Kolakowski has reminded us that we study history, not to find out what happened, but to discover who we are. Thus, helping the community tell its own story is critical to understanding its present and its identity as well as getting a glimpse of a possible future. Listening to its story also tells the community that we think its story is valuable.

There is also a need to help the community and ourselves recognize the activity of God in the story of the community. Whether Christian or not, whether religious or not, there is evidence of God's creative and redemptive work in the life of the community, if only we look for it. Wherever a disaster was averted or a blessing was unexpected, God was at work. Wherever things worked for life and against death, Christ's fingerprints can be seen—"All things were created by him and for him. He is before all things and in him all things hold together" (Col 1:17-18). Recognizing and naming God's part in the story of the community is an act of discernment, a spiritual act. It is also an act of healing. Asking the community to locate God in its history is a way of helping its members to discover that they are not god-forsaken.

However, there is also a dark side to recovering this history. This dark side takes two forms.

First, the history of the community is often told by those in positions of power, and usually they tell the history in a way that either supports their continuing claim to power or disempowers the community in terms of thinking about change (Christian 1998a, 15). Religious leaders sometimes reinforce fatalism by claiming that God wills what is or that the situation today is a just response to bad behavior in the past. Political or economic leaders may justify their positions of power on the basis of having been blessed or righteous or having served as the community's benefactors in the past. History is thereby distorted to serve an end. Illiteracy means the poor never have a chance to write their own history or read alternative views that subvert the stories of the powerful. But the poor do remember their history and can be helped to recover it and reread it. Any journey of transformation needs to begin by helping the community, and its various sub-groups, recover their own true stories.

Second, we need to be concerned about who made the community's history. Jayakumar Christian has pointed out that some people are freer to make history than others (1994, 201). Some have argued that if you are not a history maker, you become a tool in the hands of those who do make history. Thus, the very process of history-making can be a source of powerlessness and poverty. Knowing who participated in history-making in the past and why is critical to any effort to create a different kind of history-making in the future.

Listening to the whole story

We must also remember listen to their story in terms of both the seen and the unseen world. Hiebert, Shaw, and Tineou (1998) remind us that each level of worldview answers different questions. The top level of the unseen world is the domain of formal religion. Listening to people talk about this will reveal a community's understanding of the formal side of Islam, Christianity, or whatever belief system it accepts. This is where we will hear stories and propositions that answer questions about ultimate origins, about the purpose and identity of the universe, our community, and ourselves.

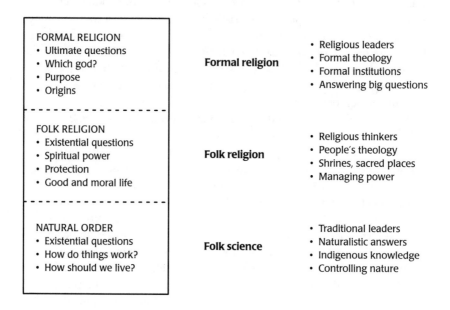

Figure 6-2: The three-tiered story of the community.
(Adapted from Hiebert, Shaw, and Tienou 1998)

The middle level of the worldview, while still spiritual and unseen, is the world of folk religion. There is a folk version of everything—folk Islam, folk Buddhism, and even folk Christianity. This level addresses questions about managing everyday life. Who has to power over this or that area of life? What do they demand of us? How do we live a full life? How can we be prosperous or avoid failure? What do we need to know about our past? How can we make the future more secure? What is the right moral order for us? The answers point to the interdependence of all things, to the sources of power and the management of power.

The lower level of worldview is the natural order, the material world. This is the world of science in both its modern and folk expressions. Nomadic people understand why and when to move their herds. Village healers have extensive knowledge of local herbs, barks, and leaves. The community has rules for how to live and work together. This is the world of hearing, seeing, touching, and feeling things.

The development practitioner is usually most interested, and most comfortable, working in the bottom level of the worldview. After all, this is the part of the world in which most development activities take place. This is where we dig wells, immunize children, improve agricultural practices, and carry out micro-enterprise activities. The problem arises when this is the only part of the community's story that we listen to or ask about. Its formal and folk religious views also have important information that we need to hear. Whether we agree or not, these domains of the unseen spiritual world are where the community will tend to locate the cause of its problems and the hope for their solutions. If we are unwilling to view the world from the community's perspective, and begin from there, then we are top-down development practitioners after all.

They know how to survive

The community already has a survival strategy. The community has well-established patterns for making sense out of its world and staying alive in it. Only in disaster situations will we find such severe dislocations that its people are unable to cope and survive. This already existing survival strategy is that part of the community's story that we call the present. Understanding this survival strategy is critical to any attempt to create a vision for a better future. There are two reasons why this is true.

First, we need to see the world the way the community sees it. Helping the community describe its survival strategy is also a way for us to see what the community considers important as well as the community's understanding of what causes things to happen or not happen. The community's survival strategy reveals its capabilities, resources, skills, and knowledge as well as its vulnerabilities, those areas of life over which the community feels it has little or no control. Capabilities are assets that can be invested in future development. Vulnerabilities are the things for which alternatives or mitigating strategies are needed.

Second, allowing a community to describe its survival strategy reinforces in the minds of the community members the idea that they have skills, local knowledge, and ways of working that are good and worth building on. Not everything in the community is wrong and ineffective. Enabling people to discover and declare their survival strategy is part of healing the marred identity of the poor.

Ravi Jayakaran has created a framework for reporting the community's description of its survival strategy. The part of the world the community feels it can control represents the seen or material world of nature where material cause and effect hold sway, the inside of the circle (Figure 6-3). They believe they can make things change, for good or ill, as a result of their own actions. This part of their survival strategy does not invoke religious or spiritual cause and effect.

The other part of their survival strategy, the part outside the circle in Figure 6-3, deals with what the community believes is outside its direct control. This is the world of spirits, gods, demons, and ancestors, the inhabitants of Hiebert's excluded middle.[2] Only spiritual explanations work in this part of their world. In search of some measure of influence in these areas of vulnerability, the community will assign gods or shrines or sacred places to these areas. The greater the lack of control, or the greater the perceived efficacy of the god, the larger the shrine.[3] The smaller gods that are invoked as the source of cause and effect in this unseen world represent a map of the community's vulnerability. To gain influence over this part of their life, the community also turns to shamans and diviners as those who have access to the unseen world and who can work for good or ill on behalf of individuals and the community. At this point the religious system and worldview can prove exploitative.

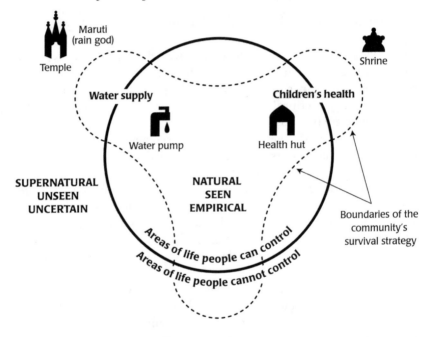

Figure 6-3: The survival strategy of a community.
(Adapted from Jayakaran 1997, 5)

This unseen world is a challenge for the development practitioner from the West. We must be able to accept talk about sacred places, shrines, and temples where people make offerings, doing the best they can to negotiate with the unpredictable and capricious unseen spirits who can change their lives for better or for worse. The map of its divinities is the way the community describes its vulnerabilities.

In Figure 6-3, for example, the health of children lies both within the domain the community can control and outside of it. This represents the uncertainty the community associates with the health of its children. Sometimes the cause of illness is germs or not having enough food. Since this is empirical and certain, people can take action to create change. Therefore, sick children are taken to the health hut or emergency feeding is sought. Other health problems are attributed by the community to the evil eye or an angry ancestor or spirit. For this, divining and sacrifices are the remedy. The survival strategy as the community describes it acknowledges power in both the seen and the unseen world.

This can get confusing. Both elements of the survival strategy are often described in religious language and involve religious institutions. We must be careful to discern the difference between religious language describing a physical process in contrast to religious language describing the unseen world of the spiritual. As an example of the former, the pre-modern water systems of Bali are marked by temples belonging to a large family of gods. The respective religious rituals associated with each temple serve to link all the temples in a way that results in a system of water management that ensures that even downstream users get their fair share of water (Lansing 1991, 59). This is an example of spiritual language and ritual providing the framework for a material distribution system.

For the part of the world the community cannot explain and control, such as bad weather, the coming of locusts, or failed businesses, the community invokes the unseen world of the spirits as the source of success or failure. The solution is sought in sacred places, shrines, and temples. Being able to untangle these accounts of cause and effect is important to development planning that begins where people are.

Bruce Bradshaw (1997) has developed a framework for describing survival systems. He suggests that any survival strategy must describe the sources the community looks to for provision, peace, justice, healing, guidance, and salvation. The following diagram describes how three tribal groups in Kenya described the sources of these things within the context of their traditional worldview. It is interesting to note that some elements deal with the supernatural, while others connote the recent arrival of Western science and education. The holistic practitioner must work with the community in a way that allows both worlds to be described and understood. This survival strategy is the point of departure for the development journey. To enhance our own understanding of how the community understands cause and effect, we must understand the survival strategy in their categories. The community will work more willingly to participate and take ownership when development interventions resonate with the survival strategy and attempt to enhance it. Then we can ask the transformational questions, What are the barriers to the community growing in its ability to survive? and Whose interests are served by these barriers?

Figure 6-4: Elements of Kenyan survival systems.
(From Bradshaw 1997)

Respecting indigenous knowledge

One of the more recent discoveries among development professionals is how much local communities actually know that is true and valuable.[4] With a humility that comes from experience, more and more development practitioners are giving the local view of almost everything a more serious hearing. Traditional medicine is not all superstition and nonsense. In fact, Western pharmaceutical companies are abandoning the random search for drugs in the laboratory in favor of listening to traditional healers and their knowledge of barks, leaves, and grubs.

In Kenya, they still tell the story of Lord Delamare, who "discovered" the rich grasslands north of Nakuru and couldn't understand why the Masai didn't graze their cattle there. He spent a fortune importing English cattle only to discover that the grass in that part of the Rift Valley lacks a key nutrient that results in poor milk production, resulting in the death of most of the calves. This, of course, was something that every Masai boy knew but was never asked.

Olivia Muchena points out that the problem is in the eye of the beholder (Muchena 1996, 179). As long as the facilitator assumes that taboos, myths, and related ethnic values and concepts of the community have no value, they will have nothing to offer the development process. Muchena points out that these "superstitious" ideas are the way communities encode knowledge. If they are taken seriously, important local knowledge can emerge.

In rural India an old man watched a water specialist use a vertical electrical sounding device for seeking the best site for an open well. "You don't need that," the old man announced. "Dig under the highest termite mound.[5] Or dig under those big trees that stay green during the dry season. Everyone knows that is where the water is." And so it was.

Respecting and seeking indigenous knowledge "requires a different way of relating to the local community, for they must become partners in the ministry, helping to educate the 'ministers' to the realities from their perspective" (Muchena 1996, 178). We need to listen with an expectation that there are things we can learn.

There are two reasons that we need to seek and value local knowledge. First, as the foregoing illustrations suggest, local knowledge may add to Western knowledge, providing we have the humility to believe that our knowledge system is not complete. Within the African worldview, illness may be the result of material causes, but it may also be the result of broken relationships. The whole person is sick, not just the material body. This kind of thinking is slowly being taken up in the West and is making our approach to medicine both more humane and more relational.

The second reason for respecting indigenous knowledge is more serious. Koyama calls attention to it in an interesting way when he tells his own story as a missionary in rural Thailand, fresh from a seminary in Japan. He describes the angry response of a Thai woman to his conversation about the gospel:

> She was annoyed at me for looking at her *in my own terms*. She felt that she was only an object of my religious conquest. I had a message for her, but I did not think of the possibility that she might have a message for me (Koyama 1974, 90).

Do we believe that the poor have a message for us? When we fail to listen, to see what we can learn, we are in fact telling them that they are without useful information, without contribution. By dismissing what they know, we further mar the identity of the poor. Our good intentions deepen the poverty we seek to alleviate.

Even when indigenous knowledge seems to be wrong, we need to take care. In a village in Tanzania the local people told a development worker that no motor vehicle was allowed to approach their one-and-only spring. If this should happen, they said, the spirit who lived in the spring would cause the spring to go dry. Wishing to show the villagers that this was not true, the development worker drove his four-wheel-drive vehicle by the spring. The water promptly ceased to flow. While there was a natural explanation for this,[6] it is nonetheless true that the development worker created several barriers to any hope he may have had for change. On the one hand, he had shown no respect for the view of the community, and on the other hand, he had reinforced their traditional worldview, something that may hinder development in the future.

Learning our way toward transformation

We have to stop and ask, What kind of planning is best suited for transformational development? For a long time, there was only one kind of planning. Processes were assumed to be linear or sequential and, providing we understood them properly, we simply set objectives and created a sequential plan for achieving the objectives. Development planning for a long time was simply an adaptation of this approach. With the exception of purely mechanical tasks, like getting a well dug or building a building, everyone in the development business tells stories of development plans that did not work or that came out very differently than planned. Communities consistently failed to behave or change as planned, but we did not know why.

The problem is that social systems are not linear. There are so many feedback loops in social systems (communities) that the only thing we can safely predict about the future is that it will be counter-intuitive. Something will happen, even good things will happen, but they will seldom be what we originally intended. With the arrival of chaos theory[7] and our growing understanding of complex (or dynamical) systems (Gleick 1987), we now know why.[8] There is underlying order in complex systems (snowflakes always end up looking like snowflakes), but the future of such systems cannot be predicted (no one knows what an individual snowflake will look like until it is formed).

Since social systems are complex, they also contain order, an order that will in time find expression. But social order can be recognized only when one looks at what was and what is. The ordering of the social system cannot be predicted. Such is the nature of complex systems. Said another way, social systems, and this most certainly applies to transformational development,[9] are self-organizing and therefore cannot be programmed with any accuracy over the long term.

What does this mean to development planning? We need to do two things. First, we need to shift our planning framework from the traditional management-by-objectives approach with five- to ten-year plans to a vision-and-values approach (Myers 1992a). Second, we need to make evaluation more frequent. Since the future cannot be predicted, we have to evaluate often enough to "learn our way" into the future.

How does this work? With a vision of where we want to be (the better future), and having identified the values by which we do our work, we set a marker on the horizon. However much off course our short-term work ends up, regular evaluations allow us to know where we are in terms of where we want to go. With a clear vision and values, we can now work on short-term plans, stopping periodically to see if where we ended up is directed toward our vision. If it is, we plan another step and evaluate again. If it is not, then we redirect our plan, take another short-term step, and evaluate again.

This shift has other implications. Chambers has identified what happens when the planning framework changes from making things happen to a more people-centered approach (1997, 37).

Point of departure	Things	People
Mode	Blueprint	Process
Key word	Planning	Participation
Goals	Preset	Evolving
Decision-making	Centralized	Decentralized
Analytical assumptions	Reductionist	Whole systems
Professional mindset	Instructing	Enabling
	Motivating	Empowering
Local people as	Beneficiaries	Partners, actors

Figure 6-5: From things to people.

From participation to empowerment

If the development story belongs to the community, then local participation is demanded as an acknowledgment of this fact. If poverty is in part a reflection of the marred identity of the poor, then participation is essential to any effort to restore their identity. If we agree that there are already resources within the community, then participation is the logical means by which this knowledge can be discovered and can become part of the development process. If we have the humility to know that we do not know enough to do someone else's development for them, then seeking local participation is the only safeguard against our doing unwitting damage. By any measure, local participation is a critical success factor for transformational development.[10]

The quality of participation

The quality of participation matters, however. Norman Uphoff, a development practitioner and scholar at Cornell University, claims that "the value of participation depends upon what kind it is, under what circumstances it is taking place and by and for whom" (Uphoff et al. 1979, 281). Uphoff goes on to suggest that we should assess the quality of participation in three

ways: Who is participating? What kind of participation? How is the participation occurring?

If participation is limited to local leaders, government personnel, and
agency staff, then participation is limited to the non-poor and will necessarily be flawed because of their desire to sustain their privilege. They are
easily tempted to play god in the lives of the poor.

These are Chambers's "uppers," people whose place and circumstances
of birth, education, and professional training result in an unspoken (sometimes) sense of superiority that greatly interferes with their hearing and
seeing (1997, 58-60). Development with them will be "top-down" and will
almost always fail to change any social power relationships. Chambers quips
(1997, 101):

> All powerful uppers think they know
> What is right and real for those below.
> At least each upper so believes
> But all are wrong; all power deceives.

But even if community residents are involved, care needs to be taken
that the group includes all social groups, men and women, non-Christian
and Christian, young and old. If they do not, those involved tend to act like
the non-poor in relation to the others who are not included (D'Abreo 1989,
161). Leaving any group out sows seeds for future injustice and strife.

Participation can also be flawed in terms of the level of participation.
Having an opportunity to hear someone else present a plan for you is a very
limited form of participation. Participation is meaningful when it means
ownership of the process, all the process: research and analysis, planning,
implementing, and evaluating.

Finally, we need to be concerned with how participation is occurring.
For its impact to be significant, the basis of participation must be as genuine partners, even senior partners. The form of participation must be integral and central, not occasional and formalistic. The extent of participation
must be complete and without limit. Finally, the effect of participation must
be empowerment. Empowerment is, after all, one of the means of transformation.

Said another way, this kind of full and complete participation is a form of
making systematic local autonomy or self-direction real. Communities discover that it is indeed *their* development process that is underway and that
they are capable of exercising choice and becoming capable of managing
their own development. The following guidelines for effective participation are adapted from a set proposed by Sam Voorhies (1996, 129-35):

- Participation begins at the beginning, with the community's story and
  analysis.

- Start small, in a manner that the community can manage largely on its own.
- Use a process or learning approach, not a blueprint. Help them learn how to learn.
- Encourage the community to mobilize its own resources. Get community members to invest.
- Encourage community members to run the program and experience the joy of their successes and learn from their mistakes.
- Build capacity. Participation that empowers needs to be learned; help them succeed.
- Invest in organizing; help them find new ways of working together.
- Have a bias toward peace. Participation means power, and power tends to divide. Be very inclusive.
- Communicate, communicate, communicate.

Changing people changes history

There is a more important reason that authentic participation is critical, more important than enhancing dignity or acting out our egalitarian values, as good as these reasons are. It can be argued that empowering participation is the single most critical element of transformation.

James Rosenau, in his analysis of change and continuity in the twentieth century, argues that, of the five basic forces at work at the end of the century, the most powerful one is that people have changed.[11] Ordinary people in the West now have a set of analytical skills that allows them to understand why things are happening to them and an orientation toward authority that is more self-conscious. "Today's persons on the street are no longer as uninvolved, ignorant and manipulable with respect to world affairs as their forebears" (1990, 13). If this kind of change—the ability to understand why things are as they are and the conviction that we can exert some level of influence over what happens to us—is one of the keys to social change in the West, then empowering participation must be at the core of transformational development among the poor. Only changed people can change history. If people do not change, little else changes in the long term.

Building community

As we bring our story to the story of the community, we face a challenge. How do we merge these stories so that they enhance each other and everyone learns and grows? The key is becoming community to each other. This is one of the reasons we respect all the elements of their story, that we take a social-learning approach to working together, and that we encourage genuine participation. Building community is what good neighbors do.

One of Kosuke Koyama's endearing contributions to missiology is what he calls "neighborology" (1974, 89ff.). Koyama reminds us that people need good neighbors much more than they need good theology or good development theory. Our work is about people before it is about ideas, about relationships before teaching or programs. Development workers who use being good neighbors as their metaphor for working alongside the poor will do better than those who see themselves as problem-solvers or answer-givers.

By listening to the stories of the poor, our new neighbors, and by sharing our stories with them, we become neighbors to each other. To have community we must have good neighboring. This takes time. Loving neighbors is not something that can rushed. Something gets lost when we hurry.

Taking our neighbor's questions into account is so time consuming that it is better to forget about time. It is better to learn to be patient. We must learn to speak our neighbor's language and understand our neighbor's memberships in overlapping communities. We must come to know what makes our neighbor laugh and cry. Once we come to love our neighbor, we realize that our love is rooted in the pain of God, the pain God feels when our neighbor is not loved (Erickson 1996, 154).

If we cannot genuinely love our neighbor, where can development begin?

THE PRACTITIONERS

Ultimately, the effectiveness of transformational development comes down, not to theory, principles, or tools, but to people. Transformation is about transforming relationships, and relationships are transformed by people. Techniques and programs only fulfill their promise when holistic practitioners use them with the right attitude, the right mindset, and professionalism. When development promoters have made the theory and values of transformational development their own, when they live them out in the real world of development practice, then good things can happen.

"Holistic practitioners"[12] is how I describe the Christian men and women who strive to carry out the transformational development described in this book. This section explores the attitude to which holistic practitioners must aspire, the profile of those who tend to be effective practitioners, and a few words on the formation of holistic practitioners. The chapter closes with an appendix describing the profile of a holistic practitioner. It was developed at a consultation on holistic ministry in Latin America that took place in Ecuador in 1996.

The attitude of the holistic practitioner

The profile of the holistic practitioner is deduced from our understanding of the goals of transformation (pages 115ff.) and the ten principles of transformation already described (pages 120ff.). With this framework of theory, we can ask what the attributes of a Christian development promoter should be. What kind of attitudes of mind and heart might a holistic practitioner aspire to?

Be a good neighbor. The requirement that we have the attitude of a good neighbor has its roots in the commandment that we are to love God and our neighbor. Chambers puts it simply, "The bottom line is be nice to people" (1997, 233). But being nice is only the beginning. We have to do more to be a true neighbor. Miraslav Volf, in his struggle to create a Christian understanding of reconciliation in the context of modern Croatia and the Bosnian War of the early 1990s, says that "we must have the will to give ourselves to others and 'welcome' them by readjusting our identities to make space for them" (1996, 29). Being a good neighbor requires our willingness to change who we are.

Be patient. Take as much time as it takes. Development does not work on a time table. Getting activities done on time may make donors happy, but it is unlikely to enhance transformation or sustainability. Remember that God is willing to walk at three miles an hour because that's the best that human beings can do (Koyama 1979).

Be humble before the facts. We don't know as much as we wish we did. The other person always knows more than we expect. Besides, we are both going to have to change our minds on things, anyway, as soon as new facts emerge.

Everyone is learning. It is obvious that without learning no transformation is taking place. Sometimes we forget, however, that if *everyone*—the poor, the non-poor, and the holistic practitioner—is not learning, then only limited transformation is taking place.

Everywhere is holy. We need to show respect for the poor. After all, God was in the community before us, working there since the beginning of time.

Every moment and every action is potentially transforming. We will never know what God uses for change until he does it. Everything we do carries a message. The only question is what that message is. Every action can heal or harm. In this sense, every action is a silent offering to God, a potentially transforming moment.

An example might help. Ravi Jayakaran reports carrying out a participatory evaluation in a village in India.[13] When he arrived with a colleague, the village brought out chairs for the visitors, while the villagers sat on mats. Ravi and his friend respectfully set the chairs aside and sat alongside the villagers on the dusty mats. They listened to the stories about the well and the school and the other things the project had accomplished. Finally, at the end of the conversation, Ravi asked them: What was the most important change? An older man said, "You are sitting on the same mat, looking me in the eye, and talking to us as equals. That's the biggest change." Sharing the same mat had more transformative power than digging the well or repairing the school.

Love the people, not the program. We always need to remember why we are in the development "business," who our "customer" is. We are here to serve people, not programs. Donors sometimes create environments in which we forget this basic fact.

Love the churches too. In many cases we have brothers and sisters already present in the community. They are a product of what God has already done before we came. These people are our family there. We need to be sure to stop by and introduce ourselves. They are there for our well-being as well as for the well-being of the community. Even if the churches are not all they might be, we need to remember that they are the single most critical element of any eventual spiritual sustainability. God has put gifts in these local communities of faith that are for the whole community, and they need to be identified and developed.

Cultivate a repentant spirit. We will make mistakes. We will do things we will regret. Part of loving our neighbors includes the willingness to go to them and repent of our mistakes and seek their forgiveness. Nothing removes the mystery surrounding our professionalism as well as a repentant spirit that shows that we are accountable to God and to those whom we seek to serve.

Act like dependent people. We need to show daily that we are a people who are dependent on God and not on our professional skills, our development technology, or our financial resources. People will see for themselves in whom we most truly place our trust. We need to be sure that our actions and our lives communicate that our trust is in the God of the Bible and nowhere else.

Whose reality counts? We must guard daily against the power of our education and experience. There is always a temptation to assume our view of reality is correct in a way that adds to the poverty of the poor. Chambers poses the critical questions (1997, 101):

Whose knowledge counts?
Whose values?
Whose criteria and preferences?
Whose appraisal, analysis and planning?
Whose action?
Whose monitoring and evaluation?
Whose learning?
Whose empowerment?
Whose reality counts?
Ours or theirs?

The characteristics of a holistic practitioner

The characteristics of a holistic practitioner are drawn from the framework for transformational development (Chapter 4) and the understanding of Christian witness in the context of transformational development (Chapter 7). This framework views the world as a seamless spiritual-physical whole. The goals of transformation for the development worker and for the community are recovery of true identity and discovery of true vocation. These goals are material and spiritual at the same time. This adds up to an absolute demand for holism in the programming, and there is no way to create holism without holistic practitioners. After all, holism is first and foremost in the development promoter or community organizer, not in the program. For this reason, we must pay special attention to the characteristics of the holistic practitioner.

Being Christian

We cannot witness to something that we are not. Holistic practitioners must be committed Christians. This is obvious, but it is not enough. Holistic practitioners also must be holistic disciples. We must love God with all our heart, mind, soul, and spirit, and we must love our neighbors as they love themselves. We must understand that God's rule extends to all of life—our relationship with God, ourselves, our neighbors, and our environment. We must be committed to being obedient to God's call to live out that rule in all areas of life. We must understand the bias of the gospel in favor of the lost, the poor, the forgotten, the ignored, and the exploited. We must live lives that announce the best news that we have—that living transformation is made possible by belief in Jesus Christ.

Being Christian means even more. Holistic practitioners must have a passion for developing a truly biblical worldview, in themselves and in others.[14] This means becoming increasingly aware of the modern (or sometimes traditional) worldview to which their education and socialization makes them captive. This means understanding how this nonbiblical worldview influences our understanding of poverty and our view of the better future we desire for ourselves and the communities with whom we work. This means working hard to re-create a genuinely biblical worldview that is truly holistic, including the supernatural and all that is good in modern science.

Being Christian means maintaining a clarity of mission at the same time that we love people as they are and appreciate their culture. We need to be able to begin where people are without forgetting who we are and our purpose for being there. Shenk reminds us that

the ministry of Jesus is notable for its clarity of focus and flexibility of response. Jesus responds to people in that way, Jesus allowed people to set the agenda. But, Jesus always responded out of who he was and what he represented. We know that Jesus both announced the Kingdom of God and embodied that reality, God's new order (1993).

Finally, being Christian means being part of the body of Christ by being a living part of a local fellowship of believers. A Christian apart from a church is ultimately a contradiction in terms. Christians are by definition a people, made in the image of a God, who is a relationship of three-in-one. No matter how comfortable the fellowship of a Christian charitable institution may be, an NGO is not and cannot be a church in the biblical sense of the word. We must guard against becoming a sanctuary for those Christians whose pain or disappointment with the church tempts them to try to approximate the church through their work in a parachurch agency. Though Christian relief and development agencies do devotions, study the Bible, and worship together, the church is the only community that God has chosen to be the home and family for God's people. A local church is God's choice for the community of the Word, the place where the sacraments and local accountability are to be found.

A word of caution. While it is true that holistic practitioners must be Christian, there is need for some humility. There are agents of transformation within and outside the community whose gifts and skills should be sought out and encouraged. Everyone has a contribution to make, Christian or not. To ignore or devalue such gifts is to devalue what God has created and is offering to us and to the community.

Having Christian character

Holistic practitioners need a strong Christian character, one that causes us to think more highly of others than ourselves. We must have a love for the poor and a call to serve those on society's margin. We must be able to see the image of God in even the most desperate or despicable of human beings and believe that this image is the truth about this person. We must believe that God has given gifts to the poor that can be called out and used by the poor for their own transformation. We must have a passion for helping people, both poor and non-poor, recover their true identity and discover their true vocation. We must believe that the poor are entitled to the same voice and dignity the holistic practitioner wishes for himself or herself. Holistic practitioners must believe that, when all is said and done, poor people have as much potential and can be as effective as any other human beings.

Holistic practitioners must live like Christians. We must be reliable and honest, demonstrating the fruit of the Spirit. We must believe in the transformative power of good relationships and seek to become friends with those we serve. We must be transparent, ever willing to speak of our strengths and our weaknesses, always bearing witness to God as the source of our strengths and the means by which our weaknesses are forgiven and overcome. We must live simply,[15] openly and invitingly, creating no barriers to being a good neighbor or living an eloquent life.

Holistic practitioners must act like Christians, having that genuine humility that being in Christ allows. We need the balanced humility that affirms the worth and gifts that God has given us and also claims the weaknesses and sin that work to undermine our Christian life. We need a humility that allows us to set aside all we know, save our knowledge of Christ, so that in our weakness the poor may find strength (1 Cor 2:1-3). We must understand ourselves as stewards, stewards of the gifts God has given us, stewards of our relationship with the poor, stewards of the resources we bring to the community and that the community already has.

Being professional

When God finished creating this world, God applied only one standard: it was good. God likes good work, and so must we. We should never believe or act as if being a Christian is an excuse to be amateurish in our work. There should be no dichotomy between being Christian and being professional.

The starting point for being professional is the challenge to become truly holistic. I've said before that holism is much more in the mind and heart of the practitioner than it is in the program. Without a profound commitment to developing a holistic worldview based on the Bible, the very work of becoming a professional can turn the Christian development worker into a functional atheist when he or she is doing professional work. The social sciences and, sadly, even much mission theology reflect the modern scientific worldview in which the spiritual and the material are unrelated realms, each with its own discipline. It would be a great pity if, in the name of becoming professional, we became less Christian.

Holistic practitioners need to develop a deep understanding of the complexity of poverty and its many dimensions and expressions. They need to be able to use the lessons of the social sciences and of Scripture to understand the causes of poverty—material, spiritual, cultural, and sociopolitical. They need to be able to develop sophisticated understandings of the local socio-political-economic-religious context and how this context works for and against the well-being of the poor. All of this needs to be done with the profound understanding that the community understands its reality in ways that are often deeper and more accurate than those of any outsider. Balancing the need to learn from the community and to take its indigenous knowledge seriously with the equally true fact that the holistic practitioner brings information and knowledge the community needs is a serious and continuing challenge. This is where a truly Christian character is so important. We come with gifts God gave us to add to the gifts God has already placed in the community; there is no room for superiority or pride.

Holistic practitioners need to develop skills for working with communities in ways that empower and liberate. They need to learn how to learn what the community already knows. They need to understand the basics of community-based health care, sustainable agriculture, water management, micro-enterprise development. They need to understand and be able to develop sustainable development systems linking families and communities with local government, business, and religious institutions so that life-enhancing relationships are formed. They need to understand the principles and skills of popular education that enable learning to take place at the direction and pace of the community.

Holistic practitioners need to understand and appreciate the importance of worldview and its impact on development. They need to understand values and how values are formed and changed. They must understand how the community understands cause and effect and how to help the community move from its traditional and/or modern worldview toward a more biblical one. This is very difficult work because the worldview of the holistic practitioner is itself often not biblical. Trying to help people move from their traditional worldview while suffering from a modern scientific one helps neither the community nor the practitioner. Both the practitioner and the community are in need of a worldview that has the God of the Bible at its center. This implies that each has something to learn from the other, and that both need to change.

To be professional, holistic practitioners need more than a good understanding of theology and social science. They also need to be "street smart." The Evil One is at work, and there are people who act in evil ways. Part of professionalism is being able to read the socio-economic-political-religious context and figure out who is doing what to whom. The price for our naivete in this regard will be paid by the poor. We need to be sophisticated enough to know that even aid is not neutral and that we are responsible for doing no harm.[16] There are hard ethical choices that will need to be made, and we must be equipped and prepared to make these moral choices "on the fly."

Yet the call to professionalism is not a call to pride. Everything we have, we have been given. Every transformation is an act of God, especially our own transformation. We must always remember that we are the servants of the master. John V. Taylor's admonition to missionaries is just as relevant to development professionals:

> We need to come off our religious high horse and get our feet on the lowly, earthy ground of God's primary activity as creator and sustainer of life. We must relinquish our missionary presuppositions and begin in the beginning with the Holy Spirit. This means humbly watching

in any situation in which we find ourselves in order to learn what God is trying to do here, and then doing it with him (1972, 39).

Chambers suggests that development professionals need to develop an attitude of seeking reversals as an antidote for professionalism becoming an impediment to the poor finding their identity, voice, and place.

	Normal tendencies	Needed reversals
Behavior	Dominating Lecturing Extracting	Facilitating Listening Empowering
Professionalism	Things first Men before women Professionals set priorities Transfers of technology Simplify	People first Women and men Poor people set priorities Choice of technology Complicate
Organizational style	Centralize Standardize Control	Decentralize Diversify Enable
Modes of learning	From above Rural development tourism	From below Relaxed, participatory appraisal
Analysis and action by	Professionals, outsiders	Local people, insiders

Figure 6-6: Seeking reversals.
(Adapted from Chambers 1997, 204)

Always learning

Holistic practitioners must know that they don't know all they need to know. They must be learners who are always seeking new insights from Scripture and from the community. They must be people who document, who ask questions, who listen to the stories of the people, and who spend time with the people in reflection. There must be a passion for discovering meaning. What have we learned? What worked? What did not? What did we miss? What is God saying to us in all this?

The formation of a holistic practitioner

Now we have to get real for a moment. Where does one find these paragons of virtue? Who can meet these standards? No one, of course. The holistic practitioner just described is a composite of the best that we can imagine based on what our experience and Scripture teach us. No individual will be what we describe. This is why formation is so important.

Formation begins with developing a clear understanding of what is desired in a holistic practitioner. Our description of the holistic practitioner earlier in this chapter suggests that formation needs to be thought of as a kind of disciple-making—developing mature Christians with the best professional skills possible. Only holistic disciples can participate in holistic transformation. With this in mind, we need to define the attitudes, behaviors, and skills that are needed. Then two things must be done.

First, we must be very careful to select people with the right gifts and character. We cannot make something out of nothing. The fruits of the Spirit—love, joy, peace, patience, kindness, goodness, faithfulness, gentleness, and self-control (Gal 5:22)—are a pretty good summary of the attitudes we seek in the holistic practitioner. Use them as part of the screening criteria, alongside the criteria for technical knowledge and experience.

Second, we have to provide intentionally and systematically for training and formation through formal training, hands-on experience, and mentoring, both within the agency and, if at all possible, through the churches agency staff attend.

In designing this approach to continuing formation, care must be taken to avoid the temptation to think of spiritual formation and professional training as two unrelated activities. Both are inseparable parts of developing the holistic practitioner. This means that spiritual formation, learning the spiritual disciplines, becoming competent in popular education, and doing PLAs (Participatory Learning and Action) and Appreciative Inquiry are all part of the formation of the holistic practitioner. We need to integrate being Christian with being professional.

Knowing who we are

In the chapter on poverty we discovered the importance of being ruthlessly self-aware. All practitioners come with "baggage" that can hurt or help them as practitioners. We need to become conscious of our assumptions about the poor and about poverty and why poverty exists. We need to become aware of these assumptions and seek out every manifestation that reflects the modern flaw of separating the material and the spiritual.

We need to discover what we are working for. What is our goal? Are we ourselves seeking what we wish the poor to seek? Are we on the same journey, or are we really imposing our story on others? Kwame Bediako, when speaking about the importance of holism in the practitioner, reminds us of the importance of Paul's insight in 1 Corinthians 15:1-11. Bediako writes: "Part of every genuinely pure motivation in Christian service is also the

Christian worker's own sense of need for the same gospel he or she seeks to incarnate and to impart to others" (1996b, 189).

Even our professionalism can be a liability if we do not ruthlessly explore its underpinnings. Vinay Samuel reminds us that every holistic practitioner is shaped by some particular understanding of progress, health, family life, participation, decision-making, market reality, economic principles, ethics, and spirituality (1995, 153). All inform the practitioner's understanding of the process and desired outcomes of transformational development. These assumptions and presuppositions about how the world works and how the world can be changed need to be made explicit and subjected to dialogue with the community and with the Bible.

Finally we need to examine our deepest motivations. Why are we in the development business? Whose needs are we serving when we serve the poor? There is undoubtedly more than one answer to these difficult questions. Yet we need to discipline ourselves to struggle for self-understanding lest we succumb to the temptation to play god in the lives of the poor, thus adding to their captivity to the god-complexes of the non-poor.

Becoming holistic disciples

Holistic practitioners must be holistic disciples themselves. Part of formation is being discipled, discipled in a holistic sense. The goal of discipling is to discover in God our own true identity and our own true vocation.

Holistic discipling must address all three levels of Hiebert's worldview framework. We must know the truth of God and the truth contained in God's word. This is why biblical literacy and doing theology are important. We must also know the power of God, the power that is greater than our temptations and greater than the power of the many devils in this world, who are working against what we do. This is where fasting and prayer are important. Finally, we must know the love of God in the real world of space and time, including modern science, with God as part of the explanation, and the important work of ethics and moral choices. The truth of God must become the justice and peace of God in the real world of our relationships.

In seeking holistic discipling we must explore our assumptions about where discipling takes place. When discipling is treated solely as a spiritual activity, we tend to locate discipling in the church as a spiritual exercise. While it is this, it is also much more. Remember that Jesus confirmed his true identity at his baptism in the Jordan Valley and clarified his true vocation in the wilderness arguing with the devil. Discipleship often happens on the periphery, the most frequent location of the risen Christ. A great number of my Christian friends testify to the fact that they learned far more about the true meaning of their faith and their Scripture working in dusty villages and squalid slums among the poor than they did in their comfortable churches.

In forming holistic disciples we will be helped if we overcome the traditional view of the whole "armor of God" (Eph 6:13-18) as being solely spiritual resources that are needed for the protection of our souls. They are also quite useful in the real world of doing transformational development. Paul's encouragement concerning the armor of God immediately follows his description of our struggle, "not against flesh and blood, but against the rulers, against the authorities, against the powers of this dark world" (Eph 6:12). Walter Wink and Jayakumar Christian make the case that Paul is referring in part to the structures and systems of power and oppression that play such a deadly, godlike role in the lives of the poor. Understanding spiritual warfare as relevant to the material world of social systems releases prayer and fasting to be tools for transformational development.

Since discipleship is about crossing our own transformational frontiers, we need to determine where these frontiers are. I found the work of Peter Kreef particularly helpful here. Kreef identifies our transformational frontiers by comparing the seven deadly sins with the qualities Jesus celebrates in the Sermon on the Mount:

Seven deadly sins		Sermon on the Mount	
Pride	Self-assertion	Poverty of Spirit	Self-giving
Avarice	To have	Mercy	To give
Envy	Resents another's happiness	Mourning	Shares another's happiness
Wrath	Destructive	Meekness and peacemaking	Saves and preserves
Sloth	Refuses to exert will toward good	Hunger and thirst for righteousness	Exerts will toward good
Lust	Dissipates and divides the soul	Purity of heart	Unifies the soul toward God
Gluttony	Consumes the world's things	Being persecuted	Accepts being deprived of the world's things

Figure 6-7: The transformational frontiers inside us.
(Based on Kreef 1986)

One final word on discipleship. Melba Maggay, a veteran of the Marcos era and the People Power movement in the Philippines, describes discipleship as a "dance of death" (1994, 79).[17] By this she means that, in the kingdom, dying is always productive. Maggay sees this kind of dying as productive in two ways. First, we cannot really love our neighbor and be in solidarity unless we are willing to die in some sense to ourselves. This is what Volf means when he says we need to change our identity to make space for the other. Self-emptying is the only way to genuine incarnation. Second, dying is the way to fertility. Each of us had to die to ourselves in order to be alive in Christ. Getting to Easter Sunday always requires living through Good Friday, at least in kingdom business. Technical power can come from good training and good experience. Spiritual power comes only this harder way.

Doing theology

Christians in mission have two sources of help that others do not have: the Holy Spirit, and the word of God. The Holy Spirit is the agent of discipleship, and the Bible is that unique and unusual book that reads us, even when we think we are reading it.[18] As soon as we make the claim that the Bible speaks to the whole of human life and is the most important source of a holistic Christian worldview, then holistic disciples have to be "doing theology" all the time. Teaching them how and how not to do theology is part of formation.

Everyone will agree that holistic disciples must be biblically literate, and of course, they must. They must be theologically literate as well, able to handle the grand themes of the Bible. Their theological and biblical literacy must begin in Genesis and end in Revelation. As shown in the second chapter of this book, understanding the whole biblical story and applying it to the theory and practice of transformational development are essential to professional practice that is truly holistic and Christian. But we need to go farther than this.

Holistic disciples also need to be taught to let the Bible handle them and to avoid spending all their time trying to handle the text. We need to give the living word of God the freedom to have the final say. We need to live with the expectation that the gospel will never be exhausted, that there is always more if we are humble enough to be silent before the text from time to time. This allows us to have a transformational hermeneutic, "a theological response that transforms us before we involve ourselves in mission in the world" (Bosch 1991, 189)

Doing theology also means being able to do theology ourselves at the same time that we are willing and able to assist others in doing their own theology. Holistic practitioners who are able to do theology will be more comfortable helping the community do its own theology, beginning with the truth of God that it already knows. This kind of theology takes special understanding on the part of the practitioner. Koyama, in his discussion of "neighborology," says that Christian workers are sandwiched between Christ's saving reality, which they have already experienced, and their experience of their neighbor as someone they love.

By submitting and committing himself to the Word of God, [the development worker] tries to communicate the message of the real Christ to his real neighbors. . . . He now moves on to see that his neighbor asks the questions and he seeks the answers in Christ" (Koyama 1974, 91).

Doing theology is also the key to solving the most serious problem that is part of the training of holistic practitioners. Most technical training, even in Christian institutions, is functionally atheistic. We seem to have forgotten that we were once "superstitious" people of traditional cultures, and we no longer remember how this changed. We in the West have largely forgotten the origins of our science and no longer ask how it is that the world is understandable to us (since we did not create it) or how it is that we have been able to keep figuring out how it works. The result is that our development technology too often carries a message that is not Christian. Unless holistic practitioners can do theology, there is little chance that they can provide the explanation for their effectiveness in finding water or saving children's lives in a way that points to the activity and character of a loving and concerned God. Once we begin to understand the words that must accompany our development technology, every technical professional will need help in becoming aware of his or her functional atheism and then receive training in how to rejoin word and deed so that credit is given to God, the only one to whom credit is due.

A spirituality that sustains

Holistic practitioners need a spirituality for the whole of life, a spirituality robust enough to keep them going in the very hard and dangerous times in which the poor live today. In the 1980s, a number of liberation theologians of Latin America made what may prove to be their most long-lasting contribution to the struggle for justice among the poor. They did so by turning their attention to the critical issue of what sustains holistic disciples for the long haul.[19]

The beginning is the realization that we cannot love our neighbor, or even ourselves, if we are not loving God with all our heart, soul, and mind. We've already noted that the disciples were called first to *be with* Jesus, and only then to preach the gospel, heal the sick, and cast out demons. Being comes before doing. We cannot share what we do not have. We cannot live eloquent lives that provoke questions to which the gospel is the answer unless our lives are made alive by the Spirit of the living God.

Protecting our inner self

Melba Maggay has given us a very helpful framework for protecting our inner life (1994, 92-95). She begins by noting something we all know yet too often ignore: "There is something about the daily exposure to poverty and other ills of society which tends to tear away faith and make agents of change some of the most cynical people around" (ibid., 92). The daily grind of poverty can mar our identity, too.

One of the keys, according to Maggay, is to keep a rein on our expectations. When we seek after transformation and justice with too much zeal, we can turn into fanatics who love the struggle so much that we forget to love God, our neighbors, and ourselves. When only total victory will do, we are always bitterly disappointed. The key is to teach ourselves and our people how to handle failure and to understand it as Christians. When Paul lists his failures and struggles, he talks about how this enables him to manifest the life of Jesus in his body (2 Cor 4). Maggay interprets this to mean that we need to be ready to "carry in our bodies, the marks of the cross, but also the hope and power of Jesus' risen life" (ibid., 93).

The other side of keeping a rein on our expectations is to release holistic practitioners from the demand, either from us or from within themselves, that they be successful. Following Jesus is about obedience, not success. Ultimately, transforming people and society is something only God can do. All we can do is discern what God is doing and obediently join in. This means that holistic practitioners who give up everything—themselves, their marriages, the well-being of their children—to be successful among the poor, are not doing the work of God. They are making idols of either their work or of the poor. We have a responsibility to help holistic practitioners free themselves in a way that allows them to make a gift of themselves, their character, and their skills, to all their relationships, beginning at home.

Searching for a balance between dedication and being driven is what Reinhold Niebuhr was trying to describe in his well-known Serenity Prayer, the prayer that every holistic practitioner must keep close to his or her heart:

> God,
> grant me serenity to accept the things I cannot change,
> courage to change the things I can,
> and the wisdom to know the difference:
> Living one day at a time,
> accepting hardship as the pathway to peace,
> taking, as Jesus did,
> this sinful world as it is,
> not as I would have it;
> trusting that you will make all things right,
> if I surrender to your will,
> so that,
> I may be reasonably happy in this life and
> supremely happy with you forever in the next.

Maggay also says that we can protect our inner lives if we practice a certain amount of detachment. She quotes a contemplative who said that "the best way to care about the world is not to care." By this she means that from time to time we need to check out mentally and psychologically, pursuing flights of fantasy, using our imaginations to visit a world that we can only hope for, the world where the dragon is slain and where there are no more tears. The visions of Isaiah 65 and John's Revelation are invitations to use our imaginations as a resource for renewal. Maggay says that such a "sanity escape" is actually the longing for a Sabbath. We need to withdraw from our work from time to time and sit back and look for what is good. Doing so allows us to see the seasons in our work, the times of success and the times of failure, the times of struggle and the times of breakthrough.

Eyes that see

There is another important contribution that only spirituality can make. Much of what I have described about the nature of poverty, its causes, and the way that leads toward restored identity and recovered vocation requires the spiritual gift of discernment. There is a reason that Jesus spent so much time in his work talking about the importance of "eyes that see and ears that hear."

A genuinely Christian spirituality alive and at work in the lives of holistic practitioners is the key to seeing what is true and what is not. We need a spirituality that enables us to see the world through the lens of the kingdom. It is only when we see as Jesus sees that we recognize marred identity and what is marring it, or detect god-complexes and their sources. Only through the lens of the kingdom can we see inadequacies in our worldview and the worldview of the people with whom we work. Only kingdom people view the world as a seamless material-spiritual whole. Only kingdom eyes can discern the presence and the deception of the powers in the institutions of this world. We need to help holistic practitioners develop a prophetic view of the world that accurately interprets current socio-economic-religious realities while still pointing to the future God is preparing for God's people (Bediako 1996b, 183).

Praying the kingdom

One of the consequences of healing the dichotomy between the physical and spiritual realms is that prayer can be released to be more than just a tool for personal piety. Prayer is now freed to be a tool for social action. And so it must be. We've already built the case for the causes of poverty being fundamentally spiritual. We have taken note of the role of pervasive evil and the deception of the principalities and powers as key elements in creating and sustaining poverty.

Charles Elliot, dean of Trinity Hall at Cambridge and co-founder of the Institute of Contemporary Spirituality, has devoted considerable effort to helping us understand this kind of prayer. His book *Praying the Kingdom* examines the role of prayer in the emergence of the kingdom of God in the world and then provides a series of meditation exercises from the Old and New Testaments that help the practitioner bring praying for the kingdom to the real world of working with the poor (Elliot 1985).

Praying for the kingdom means praying for restored identity and for recovered vocation, knowing that at the most fundamental level these are things that only God can do. Praying the kingdom means asking God's action in exposing the god-complexes of the non-poor, and for the even more difficult challenge of repentance by the non-poor for having assumed roles that only God should play. Praying the kingdom means remembering that bringing the kingdom is God's business and recalling that, at the end of the day, the kingdom comes down from heaven to earth when Jesus comes. We must not assume the burden for something we cannot do. When we do, we are suffering from a god-complex of our own, and it will crush us.

Caring for the holistic practitioner

Before concluding this section on the formation of the holistic practitioner, a word needs to be said about caring for holistic practitioners. Working for transformation among the poor and non-poor is very hard work, and it is very hard on the people who do it. Jesus did not send the disciples out in pairs by accident. He knew that he was sending them like lambs among the wolves.

The organization that sends people out onto the transformational development front lines needs to take responsibility for creating the environment in which holistic practitioners can thrive. Such institutions need to remember Christ's final admonition to Peter: "Feed my sheep." He did not say, "Manage my sheep," or "Train my sheep," or "Get the best out of my sheep." Jayakumar Christian (1998b) claims that, if a holistic practitioner cannot say of his or her ministry among the poor, "My love of Christ and my understanding of my faith has been deepened," then something is seriously amiss.

People who work on the front lines need time on the side lines. A day in the office once in a while is not what I mean. Holistic practitioners need time for physical and psychological rest and for spiritual retreat. They need to have the time and to be in a place where they can be reminded that God's world has beauty, quiet, and peace, not just ugliness, poverty, and conflict. They need to be able to hear the music and listen to the silence, to be able to pray and sit quietly before the Word.

People who work on the front lines need time on the sidelines for something else. They need a chance to learn from their experience. People need the time and the place to be able to sort out what has happened to them and to make sense of it. They need to figure out what more they need to know or to be, and have the opportunity to learn or develop. We have said repeatedly that holistic practitioners need to be learners all their lives, that their being is as important as their doing. Institutions that send holistic practitioners out need strategies and resources for their periodic rest and renewal.

One final word on caring for the holistic practitioner. A great deal has been learned in recent years about how people respond when faced with tragic events in their ministry—to the deaths of children, or people in whom they have invested, or other innocent victims. Such events—"critical incidents"—can mar the identity of the holistic practitioner in the same way that it mars the identity of the poor family. Specialized counseling techniques, many of which do not require advanced professional psychological training, are available. Institutions that send significant numbers of people to work in difficult places need to develop the strategies and resources to provide this kind of assistance to those who have made the sacrifice to go where things are very hard and harsh.[20]

APPENDIX 1:

THE PROFILE OF PRACTITIONERS OF HOLISTIC TRANSFORMATION

Knowledge	Character	Technical skills	Attitudes of the heart
Solid and broad biblical base	Reliable and honest	Administrative ability	Joyfulness
Vision for the kingdom of God	Fruits of the Spirit	Fundraising and networking	Humility
Culture of people with whom they work	Relational	Analyze politi-cal, economic, and social reality	Love of God and neighbor
Local, regional, national, and global context	Persevering	Community mobilizing and organizing	Self-emptying (incarnational)
Principles and techniques of social sciences	Submissive to God and superiors	Communication	Yearning for the kingdom
Development principles and practice	Servant spirit	Facilitator of learning (popular education)	Seeker of wisdom
	Ability to listen and learn	Teacher	Obedient and committed
	Christian	Reflection and documentation	Concerned for the dignity of others
	Transparent		Steward
	Flexible		
	Risk-taking		
	Disciplined		

7

Development Practice: The Tool Kit

With these principles for development practice always before us, it is time to turn to the various tools that enable communities to tell their story in a way that leads to a vision for a better future. While this book is not intended to be a "how to" manual for the development practitioner, it is important to review some of the major tools in use today in light of what we have learned about poverty, transformation, and holism.

The tools I describe are often referred to as development-planning tools, but I have already shown that the traditional understanding of planning is ill suited for changing social systems. It is better to think of these as learning tools. They help the community learn about itself. They help us learn. If used properly, they can lead to both of us learning our way toward a better future.

HELPING THE COMMUNITY TELL ITS STORY

From needs analysis to social analysis

Development practice traditionally began with identifying the community's needs or needs analysis. Rooted in a problem-solving approach, the task is to identify what is not working or is absent and plan to remedy the problem. This approach has some weaknesses.

First, it sees the poor community as a place full of problems, a negative point of departure. While this is understandable for those of us who tend to be a little messianic and see ourselves as God's problem solvers, it tends to obscure the importance of looking for what works and what brings life. I will return to this theme when I discuss Appreciative Inquiry, a recent development framework that seeks to begin work with a community from a more positive place.

Second, as we saw in Chapters 3 and 5, our understanding of the causes of poverty changes depending on the level at which we examine any given situation. As we dig deeper, both our understanding and the nature of our response changes. This also results in needs analysis developing into social analysis. We must use the tools of social science in addition to the tools of empirical observation. If we do not, we limit our response primarily to social welfare.

Problem	Level	Response
Hungry children	Need food	Social welfare
Nutrition knowledge Agricultural skills	Immediate causes	Community development
Land tenure Access to markets	Underlying causes	Advocacy
I have a right to the wealth I create	Worldview causes	Value change

Figure 7-1: Level of analysis tends to govern the form of the response.

If we employ the tools of social analysis, we need to do it in a way that empowers the community. Its members are the ones who need to develop the skills of social analysis if they are to become active participants in the transformational process. It is their history, and so they need to tell it. It is also their social structure, their context. Allow them to describe it. Finally, help them analyze and interpret it. They can learn to figure out how it works, who benefits, who's left out, who has the power and all the other things they need to understand in order to be able to work for sustainable change. Too often we do this analysis and thinking for them, assuming that this kind of work is too sophisticated for "uneducated" people. Such a decision is paternalistic and disempowering.

Helping people learn how to decode and demystify their social system is hard work because our own culture and worldview keep getting in the way. We are subtly tempted to help them see *our* view of their situation. This is how the spiritual side of their understanding of cause and effect often gets lost. We are trained to see the world in material terms and to locate causes solely in this material world. Our Western anthropology and sociology are loaded with assumptions that a non-Western community may not share.

This brings us back to the importance of knowing ourselves. We must be aware of our own cultural assumptions about how the world works and about what is good and bad. We must understand how our view of what is ethical is shaped by our culture.[1] We need to understand how our Christian tradition shapes our view of spirituality. We need to know what our own view of a better future is and what process of change we take for granted is best. We need to understand our own development needs. Without this self-understanding, our view of the world will seep into our efforts to help the poor do their own social analysis. We will also fail to recognize when we need to learn from them.

One last comment on social analysis and knowing ourselves. We need to be sure we have an adequate understanding of how systems fit together. What do I mean?

There are three ways to think about complex systems. The first is *stratiographic*. This view sees systems as parallel but not connected. There are multiple views of the world: yours, mine, theirs; the sociologist's, the evangelist's, and the economist's. But they don't touch or influence each other. This understanding of systems is inadequate when it comes to social systems because their dominant feature is the interaction and feedback between systems. This view also tends to reinforce the modern view that the spiritual and material are completely distinct from one another.

The second view of complex systems sees all social systems as part of a *comprehensive*, over-arching single system. This view assumes there is a grand unified view of all systems—God's view, if you will. This is what modernity posits: a unified theory for everything. The weakness of this view, many argue, is that if it exists at all, it can only exist for God and is inaccessible to human beings. Furthermore, if a flaw is found in one system, then the entire view fails with it. Too much depends on knowing everything about all the systems.

A third, more helpful view sees systems as *complementary*, such as the plumbing, electrical, and heating systems of a building. Each system is different, but they are interrelated. They must make sense when put together because they function in the same building. There are specialists for each system, but the critical view is that of the architect, who must be sure that the systems all fit together. When we help a community make sense of the social systems in which it is immersed, this view is more helpful than the first two.

A community needs to develop a family of social maps describing its social systems. If we do not understand the whole family of systems—social, personal/psychological, spiritual, and cultural—our assessment of cause and response is limited. A point of view is a view from a point.

Sub-System	Problem	Cause	Response
Biophysical	Illness	Germs	Immunization
Social	Marginalization	Ostracism	Reconciliation
Psychological	Crazy behavior	Unresolved past	Counseling
Spiritual	Possessed	Evil spirit	Exorcism
Cultural	Negative self-view	Worldview	Value change

Figure 7-2: Links among problem, cause, and response.

Vulnerabilities and capabilities

In the evolution of development practice, needs and social analysis turned to a more sophisticated way of describing the community. Struggling to find ways to work developmentally in the aftermath of disasters, Mary Anderson and Peter Woodrow, co-directors of the International Relief and Development Project at Harvard University, defined development as "the process by which vulnerabilities are reduced and capacities are increased" (1989, 12). They proposed a framework for analyzing these capabilities and vulnerabilities of communities (ibid., 7-9).

Vulnerabilities are long-term factors that affect how the community is able to respond to disasters or direct its development. We explore vulnerabilities to understand why the current situation exists and why it has affected those who are most affected. This helps us in two ways. First, it invites an understanding of why things are as they are, thus directing us to underlying causes. Second, it helps us be sure that our development plans do not actually increase vulnerabilities. Mud schoolhouses in earthquake zones provide schools, but they also create a risk to children's lives. Fertilizers increase agricultural production but also stress the soil and increase the vulnerability of farmers to moneylenders.

Capacities are long-term strengths within a society. Identifying them is one antidote to a purely problem-oriented approach to development and increases the confidence of the community to believe that it is capable of managing its own development. Understanding the survival strategy of a community is a way of displaying its capabilities.

Anderson and Woodrow divide the vulnerability-capacity analysis into three domains: physical and material, social and organizational, and motivational and attitudinal. The physical-material is where most of us tend to focus—no clean water, poor land use, and so forth. The social-organizational helps disclose the social organization, and identifies internal conflicts and how the community manages them. The motivational-attitudinal gets at issues like the marred identity of the poor, the god-complexes of the non-poor, and an inadequate worldview.

Anderson and Woodrow suggest that the analysis of vulnerabilities and capacities be done for men and women, and for the rich, middle-class, and poor. Analysis by gender and economic class reveals important things that are obscured by broad generalizations. Taking this next step forces us to get beyond the bias that often results in our analysis when we talk only to community leaders, who are often men and among the non-poor.

Community organizing

Community organizing emerged in the 1960s as Saul Alinsky searched for tools to empower people in the inner city to take a role in their own transformation. Community organizing is a process by which people in a particular area learn to take charge of their situation and develop a sense of the power they have as a group.[2] It helps poor communities organize in a way that allows them to challenge the political and economic structures that contribute to their poverty. The process of community organizing employs a continuous process of action-reflection-action. The community diagnoses its problems, seeks to understand those who are contributing to these problems, and organizes itself to confront those responsible.

The five steps of the community organizer include:

- *Networking:* Building relationships, identifying issues, and building trust.
- *Coalition building:* Gathering people and organizations together to address community needs identified by the people.
- *Action-reflection-action:* Using a dynamic, continuing learning process to examine why things are as they are and how earlier actions worked or did not work.
- *Leadership empowerment:* Forming locally led networks and coalitions. As local leaders emerge and gain the respect of the community, they must be trained.
- *Birth of a community:* Working together and experiencing success builds trust, and a sense of community emerges for those who share common issues (Linthicum 1991, 25-26).

While simple needs tend to be addressed in the earlier stages of community organizing, the continuous learning resulting from the reflection process tends to deepen the community's understanding of the causes of its poverty and the necessary steps toward solutions. More substantive issues tend to emerge, and systems and structures become the subject of examination and then action.

Community organizing has proven effective in creating community participation and ownership and has been particularly successful in dealing with inaction on the part of local government bodies. Community organization has also been helpful in urban settings with no community in a geographical or cultural sense. Organizing around a shared issue or concern creates a community of sorts for a period of time.

Community organizing also suffers from some important weaknesses. First, community organizing tends to focus on issues first and people second; the community tends to become those sharing a common concern. This can lead to divisions within the community. Second, community organizing tends to reduce the purpose of development to the creation of power. While power for the powerless is good and necessary, it cannot be the final end of development. Ultimately, all power belongs to God. Thus the slogan *Power to the people* is not a biblical concept, either for the poor or the non-poor (Christian 1994, 327). This focus on power leads to the most serious weakness of community organizing: Its effectiveness is derived from setting one group within a community over and against another group. This confrontational, win-lose approach, while often successful in the short term, can work against sustainability, reconciliation, and peace-building.

Participatory Learning and Action (PLA)

In the early 1990s a development-planning tool emerged that held great promise in terms of allowing the community to describe itself and interpret the workings of its social systems. The Rapid Rural Appraisal (RRA) methodology of the 1980s was shaped and reshaped by experience in participatory action-reflection research, agro-economic systems study, applied anthropology, and field research in farming. The result was called the Participatory Rural Appraisal (PRA). The PRA has gone through several name changes as it has found application in cities and refugee work. Today, many call it Participatory Learning and Action (PLA).[3] To show its growth and evolution, Chambers describes the difference between the Rapid Rural Assessment and the Participatory Learning and Action as follows:

	RRA	PLA
Mode	Finding out, extracting	Empowering, facilitating
Outsider's role	Investigator	Facilitator
Owner of process	Outsiders	Local people
Methods used	Secondary data	Handing over the stick
	Observing directly	Do-it-yourself research
	Interviews	Local analysis of secondary sources
	Seeking out experts	Mapping by the people
	Probing questions	Time lines by the people
	Case studies and stories	Trend analysis by the people
	Transect walks*	Causal linkage diagrams by the people
		Wealth and power rankings by the people
		Seasonal diagrams by the people

* A walk through a community noting everything and understanding its meaning.

Figure 7-3: Comparing the RRA and the PLA.
(Based on Chambers 1997, 115)

The evolution of the RRA into the PLA represents not so much a change in the tools as a change in the ways the tools are used. There has been a reversal in power and expertise. As outsiders help the local people to pose the questions and then find ways to answer their own questions, the local people are the ones who learn, who are empowered. This is in contrast to the development practice of the 1980s, when the people were more passive sources of information and the outsider tended to be the one who did most of the learning. Jayakumar Christian is harsh about this: "It is demonic to reduce the poor to a source of information."[4]

A wide variety of exercises has been developed as part of the tool kit for the PLA. Their common purpose is to allow the poor to declare what they already know in a way that invites them to assess and analyze what is working and what is not. The sum of all the information gathered will reveal the survival strategy for the community. (Common PLA exercises can be found in Appendix 1 at the end of this chapter.)

Done properly, the PLA is a helpful tool by which the poor can describe their social systems and survival strategy using their own categories. After watching and listening to the community as it carries out the various exercises, one can develop a fairly clear picture of the community's survival strategy, thus setting the stage for an analysis of capabilities and vulnerabilities. The goal will then be to build on capacities and reduce vulnerabilities.

But there is more, and it is as important as describing survival strategies and creating capability/vulnerability analyses. From the results of a properly done PLA exercise the poor can discover how much they really do know, what resources and skills they already have, and how resourceful they have been in the past. Helping the poor discover that what they know is valuable goes a long way toward helping them overcome their marred identity. A villager, upon hearing the result of a PLA exercise summarized by village leaders, remarked, "Hey! We're quite smart, aren't we?"

This sense of discovering what the community knows, and then encouraging its members to apply this information, can extend beyond development programming. Recent work shows that the PLA methodology can be used effectively to enable a community to complete its own policy analysis, thus empowering the community to become its own advocate in addressing the political and economic structures that are contributing to or sustaining its poverty (Holland and Blackburn 1998).

Appreciative Inquiry

Appreciative Inquiry (AI) is a postmodern entry in the field of action-research. It represents an attempt to move away from the rationalist, mechanistic, problem-solving frame that is characteristic of most research and seeks an alternative that better fits self-organizing social systems. If reality is socially constructed, as our postmodern friends tell us, then why not allow the community to construct its own reality and take ownership of it?

The starting point for Appreciative Inquiry is the belief that a community that is alive and functioning represents a miracle that can never be fully understood. There is always more to any social organization than we can discover by studying and analyzing its parts or its past. It follows, then, that we can never create or improve a social organization solely by pursuing rationally determined linear processes. David Cooperrider and Suresh Srivastva, the earliest champions of this innovation, describe it this way:

> The appreciative mode of inquiry is a way of living with, being with and directly participating in the varieties of social organization we are compelled to study. Serious consideration and reflection on the ultimate mystery of being engenders a reverence for life that draws the researcher to inquire beyond superficial appearances to deeper levels of the life-generating essentials and potentials for social existence. That is, the action-researcher is drawn to affirm, and thereby illuminate, the factors and forces involved in organizing that serve to nourish the human spirit (1987, 129).

The appreciative approach to social change posits that social organizations can be imagined and then made by beginning with what is already creating value. If we can determine what is for life and what is generating well-being, we can imagine its expansion. Having done so, the organization or the community will tend to move in this direction. "The more an organization experiments with the conscious evolution of positive imagery, the better it will become. There is an observable self-reinforcing, educative effect of affirmation. Affirmative competence is the key to the self-organizing system" (Cooperrider et al. 1995, 5).

In the development context, Appreciative Inquiry begins with the general goal of furthering an already existing, even if limited, life-giving, co-operative existence by asking the question: How did such a social phenomenon emerge in the first place?[5] Setting aside the metaphor of a machine as a complete way to answer to this question, Appreciative Inquiry begins not with analysis but with a holistic view of what already is and seeks answers to a new set of questions: What made social organization possible here? What allows the community to function at its best? What possibilities await the community that will allow it to reach for higher levels of health, vitality, and well-being? The focus of the appreciative approach is the discovery of what gives or enriches life.

In essence, Appreciative Inquiry is more than a method, it is a way of viewing the world. "It is an intentional posture of continuous affirmation of life, of joy, of beauty, of excellence, of innovation" (Johnson and Ludema 1997, 72). This should remind us of Paul's admonition in Philippians 4:8-9:

Finally, brothers, whatever is true, whatever is noble, whatever is right, whatever is pure, whatever is lovely, whatever is admirable—if anything is excellent or praiseworthy—think about such things. Whatever you have learned or received or heard from me, or seen in me— put it into practice. And the God of peace will be with you.

The underlying theological frame is that God has created a good and life-giving social world; wherever we find good in our world, we are seeing evidence of God's work and gifts. The biblical story is the account of God's project to restore the lives of individuals and communities, marred by sin, so that they can be good, just, and peaceful once again. An appreciative perspective encourages transformational development promoters to find God's redemptive work in the life of the community, and within themselves, and to seek to become more intentionally part of it. At a more personal level, the appreciative frame also fits the gospel account: in spite of our sin, God looks through our brokenness and, recognizing God's image in us, works to restore that image to its fullness.

AI stands in contrast to the problem-solving framework of most development research and planning methodologies. Instead of looking for what is wrong or missing and then developing problem-solving responses, it looks for what is working, successful, and life-giving, and attempts to see additional possibilities. The belief is that an organization's single-minded "commitment to a problem-solving view of the world acts as a primary constraint on its imagination and contribution to knowledge" (Cooperrider and Srivastva 1987, 129). The two frameworks can be contrasted in the following way.

	Problem solving	Appreciative Inquiry
Underlying assumption	Organizing is a problem to be solved	Organizing is a mystery to be embraced
Focus	Search for problems	Search for possibilities
Planning metaphor	A problem-solving tree	A possibility tree
Methods	Identify the problems	Valuing the best
	What are the felt needs?	What already is here that's good?
	Analysis of causes	
	Analysis of possible solutions	Envisioning what might be
	Action planning	Dialoguing about what should be
		Innovating what will be

Figure 7-4: Comparing problem-solving approach to Appreciative Inquiry.

The Appreciative Inquiry approach to linking research and planning is also different from the traditional development planning based on the problem-solving approach. It provides us with a different set of questions than the planning questions associated with problem solving: What's the nature of the problem? What is missing? What hinders? What helps? What is the solution?

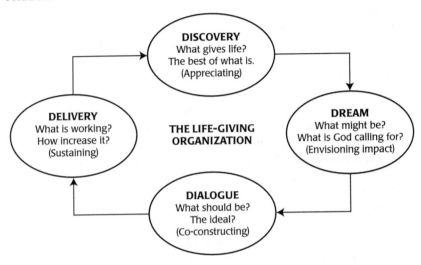

Figure 7-5: Visioning through Appreciative Inquiry.
(Johnson and Ludema 1997, 75)

Appreciative visioning begins with the discovery of what is working and creating life and value. This leads to dreaming about what might be if the good of today or the past were expanded or built upon. The next step is a dialogical one about what should be. What is best for us? This is the place where the view of the promoter comes in as he or she participates in this step of the co-construction of a vision. Asking about the ideal also opens the door to ethical considerations. Is this right for us? Is it fair? Will we be proud if we are successful? Finally, as a development vision is pursued, the evaluative step, often called *valuing*, inquires into what is working. What is surprising us that we like? How might we enhance these positive things?

This alternative mindset for development planning uses a very different kind of interviewing methodology. The key characteristics of the appreciative interview include the following (Cooperrider et al. 1995, 9):

- An assumption of health and vitality
- A desire to connect through empathy
- A sense of personal excitement, commitment, and concern
- An intense focus to listen with the right side of the brain
- Generative questioning, pointing toward clues, and guiding
- Belief in the community and its story (in contrast to doubt)

- Tolerance for ambiguity, generalization, and dreams
- A passion for dialogue and a dislike of monologue

This list makes clear the contrast between the appreciative approach and problem-solving, but we should also note that the distinction is not absolute. The last four characteristics of the appreciative interview are also typical of the mindset of many who use the Participatory Learning and Action methodology. I suggest that an Appreciative Inquiry mindset might prove entirely compatible with doing PLAs.

The appreciative bias can also be extended to evaluation. Rather than determining what went wrong and seeking solutions, the evaluation questions are different. What went right? What created energy and excitement? What emerged that people affirm as good? The response to such an evaluation exercise is to nurture and add energy to what is working. By focusing resources on what is working, we get an additional benefit. It helps us avoid the problem of retrying things that are not working, a favorite pastime of many social engineers in the West. Resources enhance what is working rather than what is not working.

Two notes of clarification. First, while the appreciative approach begins with the positive and the successful, it does not sweep the negative under the rug. In the light generated by Appreciative Inquiry, darkness no longer obscures identification of problems. Problems can be faced squarely, but within a psycho-social environment that allows them to be addressed with a maximum of energy and good will.

Second, while an appreciative frame will undoubtedly surface information that a problem-solving frame may not, and while it may also prove more helpful in allowing the community to recover its true identity and vocation, the problem-solving frame must not be discarded in the development practitioner's love of the most recent fad. The problem-solving framework has proven highly effective in the development of the West and suits certain kinds of developmental issues very well. Professional development practitioners will not force a choice that does not have to be made. They will do what can be done to incorporate the appreciative frame into existing development-planning tools and will continue to use both frames in a way that helps the community take control of its own development.

World Vision Tanzania has been very creative in adapting and using the appreciative approach.[6] Typically, a community welcomes a development NGO with hospitality and presents it with a list of things the community would like done. Getting the community to become its own agent of change is a challenge. Insisting on a discussion focusing on what has worked and on when and how the community has been successful in the past is very helpful in getting past the initial view of the NGO as the giver of good things. Through community meetings and focus groups, World Vision Tanzania works with the community using an appreciative framework to hear the community's answers to questions like the following:

- What life-giving, life-enhancing forces do you have in your community? What gives you the energy and power to change and to cope with adversity?
- Thinking back on the last one hundred years of your community, what has happened that you are proud of, that makes you feel you have been successful?
- What are your best religious and cultural practices? Those that make you feel good about your culture? That have helped you when times were tough?
- What do you value that makes you feel good about yourselves?
- What in your geographical area and in your local political and economic systems has helped you do things of which you are proud?
- What skills or resources have enabled you to do things your children will remember you for having done?
- How have your relationships, both within and without the community, worked for you and helped you do things that you believe were good for the community?

The net result of such an inquiry is often spectacular. The laundry list of problems the community would like the NGO to fix is lost in the enthusiasm of describing what is already working. The community comes to view its past and itself in a new light. We do know things. We do have resources. We have a lot to be proud of. We are already on the journey. God has been good to us. We can do something. We are not god-forsaken. This is a major step toward recovering the community's true identity and discovering its true vocation. With these discoveries a major transformational frontier has been crossed.

Norman Uphoff, in a study of an irrigation scheme in Sri Lanka that has proved to be sustainable seven years after the outsiders left to go back to their universities and NGOs, posed this question: Where does the social energy for sustainability come from? He points to three things: ideas, ideals, and friendship (1996, 375-78). Ideas have the power to shape how we view and respond to our world. Ideals tend to set our sights high and cause us to work together. Friendship means working together, valuing each other's well-being. Together, ideas, ideals, and friendships (relationships) release social energy, energy needed to overcome resistance to change that lives within the poor and non-poor alike. I believe this provides part of the explanation for the success of Appreciative Inquiry.

Logical Framework Analysis

The Logical Framework is an old tool with a new lease on life.[7] Developed in the 1970s, the Logical Framework is a classic expression of management by objectives. The Logical Framework is logical, linear, and comprehensive. It assists the development planner in setting program objectives, defining indicators of success, determining critical assumptions, establishing means of verification, and defining the resources necessary for implementation. The framework looks like this:

Objectives	Objectively verifiable indicators	Means of verification	Risks and assumptions
Goals:			
Purpose: 1. 2.			
Outputs: 1. 2.			
Inputs: 1. 2.			

Figure 7-6: Outline of the Logical Framework analysis.

The historical weaknesses in the Logical Framework had to do with who used it and how it was used. In the late 1970s it was the tool of the development planner, not the community. Information was gathered and analyzed by the planner and the work of thinking through the program plan was also the planner's. It was an attractive tool for top-down planners, many of whom assumed that good management meant good development. Its other major weaknesses were its devotion to the problem-solving approach and its assumption that social change was linear and manageable; these factors imposed a particular logic on the program and on the community. As these weaknesses became apparent, the usefulness of the tool was called into question by many practitioners, although donor groups, especially governments, continue to encourage its use.

Making the Logical Framework useful today takes us back to the question of when it is employed and who uses it. Once the development research and planning processes are truly owned by the community as a result of participatory processes such as the PLA and Appreciative Inquiry, the Logical Framework, suitably modified and simplified, can be a useful tool to help the community think through what it will take to work toward its dreams and to determine how its development process is doing.

In summary, there is a variety of tools for development planning, each reflecting a particular view of what needs to be done and how to go about doing it.

LEARNING FOR TRANSFORMATION

As I have pointed out earlier, evaluation is more important than planning when trying to change social systems. Social systems are counterintuitive and self-organizing. They usually resist the best efforts of the management-by-objectives folks. Regular, routine evaluation is the key to keeping the transformative journey moving in the right direction. We have to learn our way toward transformation. While this book is not the place to describe the broad and highly developed field of development evaluation,[8] there are some important questions that need to be answered, because they will change how we behave if we keep the answers in mind.

Whom is the evaluation for?

Too often it is for the donor. While accountability to donors is important, the kind of evaluation they seek may not be all that helpful to the community and its learning process. Sometimes, the evaluation is for the development agency, since it desires, quite correctly, to be professional, and professionals test the impact of their work rather than trust in their marketing stories. But the most important audience for continuous learning must be the community. It is the community's development, and anything that takes what is the community's and places it at the service of others mars the community's identity, making it poorer. Every development activity, from the simple to the complex, is an opportunity to learn. It is useful to contrast conventional evaluation and participatory evaluation (Narayan 1993).

	Conventional evaluation	Participatory evaluation
Who?	External experts	Community members, facilitator
What?	Predetermined indicators, often costs and outputs	Community-identified indicators, which may include process indicators
How?	Focus on objectivity, Distancing evaluator from people, Uniform and often complex procedures, Delayed report, not always accessible to people	Self-evaluation, Simple methods, Open-ended, Immediate sharing of results
When?	Usually at end of project	Frequently monitoring and evaluation blurred, Lots of small learning events
Why?	Accountability to donors	Empowerment enabling local people to learn, adapt, and control

Figure 7-7: Comparing conventional and participatory evaluation. (Narayan 1993)

What is evaluation for?

The traditional approach is to see if what was planned actually took place. Were goals and milestones achieved? Within budget? On time? The purpose is to locate problems so they can be solved or to assess progress so another phase can be planned. This is good and necessary. It is hard to talk about how to continue the journey to where you want to go if you do not know where you are.

But there are ways to enrich the evaluation process. Practitioners of Appreciative Inquiry ask what is working and what is creating energy. They seek the expressions of life-creation, growth, and change in order to enhance them by allocating money, time, and energy to furthering them. By shifting resources to what is working, they eliminate what is not working.

What changed?

Hopefully we answer this question at a whole series of levels and through a variety of lenses. At the simplest level, we evaluate how we did in terms of what was planned. But we must be just as interested in what happened that was not expected. Both failures and unanticipated successes can be opportunities to learn.

At another level—since we have said that transformation is more than things, knowledge, and power—evaluation needs to go beyond the number of wells dug, the number of classes held, or the number of confrontations with local officials. There are several dimensions of deeper change that need assessment.

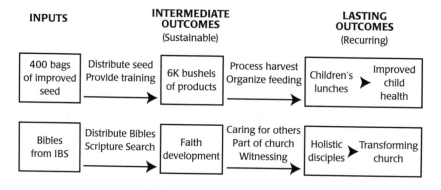

Figure 7-8: Changing the focus of evaluation to lasting outcomes.

Long-term impact

For too long, development practitioners have measured input and activity and called this evaluation. Many are now calling for the development

NGO community to take a harder look at the long-term impact of what they do. There are too many assumptions between inputs and impact to allow us to take for granted that good things will happen if we get the initial conditions right and proceed according to plan. Figure 7-8, above, shared with me by Frank Cookingham, is an example of inputs, intermediate outcomes and the lasting outcomes that we must learn to assess.

Identity, vocation, and relationships

Our conversation about the nature of poverty came to the conclusion that poverty was at its base relational. Flawed relationships—with self, others, the environment, and God—result in violence, conflict, greed, racism, and marginalization. This means that the key element of transformative evaluation is to assess relationships and how they are changing.

For the poor, this means recovering their true identity and discovering their true vocation. Has their marred identity shown signs of liberating recovery? Have they begun to discover the gifts that God has placed in their culture and in them as people? Are they beginning to act like stewards who have something to contribute? Are they seeking ways to make that contribution?

For the non-poor, the issue is also identity and vocation, but the questions are different. Have the non-poor begun to act like people who care and share? Are they less willing to play god in the lives of the poor? Are they becoming aware of the poor's true identity as children of God? Are they recognizing that the poor have been given gifts to use for their own development and to contribute to the development of their community?

Have they all—poor and non-poor—learned better to love God and love their neighbor?

Worldview and values

Relationships that don't work are reflected through the distortion of what are normally positive values. People may believe in values like loyalty and compassion, but in a distorted way that undermines their social good.[9] Examination of values and value change can thus be an important indicator of whether the community is moving toward the kingdom of God or not. The Evangelical Fellowship of India Committee on Relief (EFICOR) has described the process of value change as in Figure 7-9.

We have also said that the cause of poverty is fundamentally spiritual. Therefore, transformative evaluation must allow the community to assess the way its values and belief systems are changing. Are the elements of its worldview that are against life or that diminish life being changed? Has it encountered the true author of its story? Is there a new, transformative story at work in the community? Is fear of the spirit world diminishing? Are its social and religious practices doing more to release and empower people for growth and change? Are people better able to unmask the deceptions that diminish or reduce life? I will say more on the issue of worldview change in the next chapter.

Value	Today's distorted version	More kingdom-like version
Loyalty	Only to our family	To all in our community
View of person	Only powerful matter	All men, women, and children matter
Compassion	For those who can help us	For those who are in need
Repentance	Only if caught	Personal responsibility for wrong
Forgiveness	Only to our equals	To all who injure us
Sharing	Only with our family	With all who are in need
Equality	For those who own land	For all men and women
Justice	Only for the powerful	For all, even the weakest
Peacemaking	Within the family	Within the community and world

Figure 7-9: Values moving toward the kingdom.

Social institutions

If the god-complexes of the non-poor are expressed through systems and structures by those who inhabit the seats of power, then another test of sustainable change must be the degree to which the social systems and structures are changing. Do systems and structures point outside themselves or have they turned inward, concerned only with serving themselves? Have they begun to support and enhance life? Do they show evidence of turning aside from the lure of what Wink calls "delusional assumptions"? Is there evidence that the non-poor are allowing the poor to become actors and to define their own history and future? Is there evidence of repentance and a willingness to cease playing god in the lives of others?

Who changed?

In addition to what has changed, we need to pay attention to who has changed and in what way. This has two dimensions. The first has to do with the people and their view of who they truly are and what they believe they are here to do as human beings. This is the identity and vocation issue. I will say more on this in the next chapter.

The second dimension has to do with which groups within the community have changed and how. General evaluations describe the changes in the community as a whole. This often means change in terms of those who have a voice, usually the men and the non-poor. We need to expand our evaluative process so that we can hear from other actors, such as women and children. Furthermore, the kinds of questions we ask will change depending on which group we are listening to.

For the non-poor occupying structures of power, the set of questions is quite different, having to do with values and use of gifts. How do they perceive the poor? Who do they believe is the source of their wealth and position? What does it mean to be a productive steward of gifts and position? To whom does power belong and what is it for? How are they using their resources of money, position, and privilege?

If there is integrity in a transformative relationship, both parties must experience transformation. This means that we must find ways to assess how the development practitioner and the development agency are changing. What have we learned? What have we failed to learn that the community wishes we would learn? We need to give the people the responsibility for evaluating our performance. Did we do what we said we would do? Did we do it in ways that empowered or that created dependency? Imagine a meeting where we told the community members what we thought we were doing to be helpful to them and then were willing to let them tell us how well we had done? What would happen if we spelled out our understanding of transformation, our vision of a better future, our version of kingdom values and let the community tell us how well we lived up to all this and to what degree its members shared our vision and values?[10] I suspect a lot of learning would take place.

What do we assess?

What we assess is determined by what the community has set out to do. Assessment begins with the vision of the better future and the values to which the community aspires.[11] An example of how such a vision for a better future can translate into a set of development standards and measurable indicators is presented in Appendix 3 to this chapter, which contains the evaluative framework being used in North India by Jayakumar Christian.

Some NGOs have established organizational impact measures that they apply to all programming as a rough gauge of the overall effectiveness of their work. As an agency focused on the well-being of children in the context of a developmental approach, Christian Children's Fund is currently using a evaluative framework that assesses the following:

- Immunization coverage
- Malnutrition, with emphasis on moderate and severe
- Knowledge of oral rehydration therapy for management of diarrhea
- Acute respiratory illness management
- Access to safe water
- Safe sanitation practice
- Literacy, with an emphasis on female literacy
- Formal and non-formal education enrollment, with emphasis on pre-primary and primary education (CCF 1996)

World Vision is in the process of testing a framework for evaluating development impact that includes the well-being of children while also assessing the integrity and viability of the development process itself (Cookingham 1998). A number of the indices are experimental and will require testing. The framework consists of twelve elements. The corresponding standard and indicator information can be found in Appendix 4 to this chapter:

- Community participation
- Community organization
- Means to provide for basic needs
- Access to safe water
- Sanitation
- Nutrition
- Child immunization
- Child mortality
- Primary schooling
- Social relationships
- Emergence of hope
- Spiritual nurture

Will it last?

I addressed in Chapter 5 the four dimensions of sustainability: physical, mental, social, and spiritual. Continuous development learning must assess the issue of sustainability on all four fronts from time to time. Too often evidence of physical sustainability is taken as reassurance that everything is on track. This is naive. We need to know whether or not people are changing their view of themselves, of their worth, of their ability to make change permanent. We must find ways to test the emergence of a socially sustainable environment, including transformed power relationships, nurturing civil society, local institution building, emergent democratization, and the like.

Finally, the spiritual side of sustainability is often overlooked. Is the local worldview changing in ways that enhance life and turn aside from practices that diminish life or disempower people? Is a web of values emerging that will support ongoing, positive change? Is there a values-forming mechanism in the community that is working for the life and the good of the community?

Are we doing the right thing?

There must be an ethical side to evaluation. Contemporary work by people like Hugo Slim, Mary Anderson, and others have alerted us to the dark side of humanitarianism at the end of the twentieth century. We cannot assume that whatever we do is good and assume that we occupy the high moral ground as we work against poverty. This is particularly true for relief responses in complex humanitarian emergencies.

Hugo Slim has suggested an evaluative frame for ethics that is derived from Catholic social teaching.

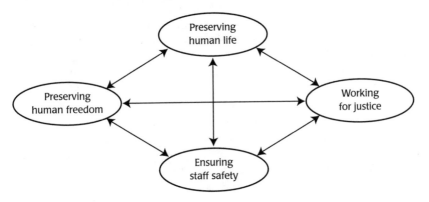

Figure 7-10: Competing values faced in the field
(After Slim 1997)

He begins by describing the competing values that create the sometimes difficult choices faced in the field: preserving human life, preserving human freedom, ensuring staff safety, and working for justice. Slim describes a moral responsibility framework focusing on the question: On what grounds will we be judged? There are five dimensions to this kind of moral inquiry:

1. *Intention and motivation:* What is our intention? What motivates us? Our intentions will most always be noble, but our motives may be mixed. We may wish to help and also want to be noticed and get credit.
2. *Capacity:* Did we have the capacity to do something we did not do?
3. *Knowledge and ignorance:* We will be judged on what we know. Do we know what we should know? There is vincible ignorance (ignorance we could have overcome) and invincible ignorance (things we could not have known). Did we do a political analysis? Or, were we legitimately surprised?

4. *Deliberation:* Did we think it through and seriously consider the full range of possible actions?

5. *Mitigation:* Did we take mitigating steps against the worst effects of our actions? Were we prepared for something we might have expected? (Slim 1997, 5-7).

Doing this kind of ethical analysis is essential for internal trust and morale, yet it takes time and is hard to do well on the run or under pressure. The challenge is to be able to make ethical snap judgments. This, in turn, means we need development practitioners with highly developed moral consciences. And this points us to demands for discipleship and values formation as part of staff training.

Learning holistically

Because we understand the cause of poverty to be fundamentally spiritual, we must make our evaluative work truly holistic. We need to go beyond assessing only the technical side of our work. We also need to look at the spiritual impact.[12]

What are the people learning about themselves? How has their view of themselves and their future changed? What changes can be seen in their understanding of who they are, where they have come from, and what they are here for? How has their worldview changed? What or whom do they fear? To whom do they pray? Has the way they explain cause and effect changed? To what or to whom do they attribute success? Is there any evidence that they are recomposing their story?

Because development technology carries a message, we need to ask what message the people are receiving. When a community health worker participates in an immunization campaign, we must not limit our inquiry to the extent of the immunization coverage. We must also ask how the local people understand immunizations and the cause of their effectiveness. If the answer is either powerful magic or modern medicine, then they have received effective protection against disease accompanied by an implicit message that is not Christian. This alerts us to the need to work harder on the message that accompanies our development intervention. This is how we can learn our way to better holism.

We also need to assess whether or not our transforming development has an impact in terms of how people view and respond to the gospel. Are the people more aware of the activity of God? How has their view of God changed? How has ours? Are people more open to the gospel and Christianity? Has their view of the Christian church changed? Are development practitioners prepared and willing to answer questions to which the gospel is the answer?

What is happening in the local churches? Are people coming to faith in Christ? If no one is interested in becoming a Christian, we ought to have the courage to take note of the fact and ask why this might be. While it may be true that it is not yet God's time for these people, it may also be true that no one is encouraging these people to become Christians or that the Christian message they are receiving is either unattractive or not understood.

This leads us to another critical question: What kind of Christians are emerging? Since part of the spiritual dimension of sustainability is the presence of a church (or group of churches) that loves God and loves its neighbors, we must be concerned with the quality of the new or revitalized Christians who are emerging within the community and, hopefully, within the development agency. The experience of the Christian church in the last part of the twentieth century provides ample illustrations of why this is an important question. In the United States, behavioral research indicates that the way regular church-going Christians live their Monday-to-Friday lives is indistinguishable from the way non-believers live. Christian leaders in Africa and the Balkans are struggling to make sense out of the violence and pain that Christians have done to each other and to others. Transformative evaluation needs to include attempts to assess the kind of Christians that are emerging.

What do people mean when they say they are saved? Is this a utilitarian statement indicating that the Christian God has proven to be more powerful, as evidenced by increasing wealth? African churches report stories of people who began to go to church because they believed that Jesus was a more powerful God than their traditional gods, only to lose interest when a son got sick or a business failed. Does being saved mean that we now have power over those who are not saved? Does being saved mean that our soul is saved, but our body and material life can still be lived out by the values of our cultural story? Is there evidence that our faith is transforming the whole of our life and our relationships?

Ultimately, the church is of value to the poor only if it tells them the truth that allows them to become less poor. The church has good news when it contributes to relationships being healed and to the emergence of truth, justice, peace, and righteousness. If Christians are not living and sharing the whole gospel for the whole person, then the message of the gospel is truncated and flawed. We need to know whether the Christians in the community are becoming truly holistic disciples: loving God and loving our neighbor, declaring a gospel of truth, power, and material transformation.

OTHER CRITICAL ISSUES

Research, planning, and evaluation have important contributions to make in helping the community tell its story, recover its true identity and vocation, and take another step in its pilgrimage of transformation. This is not enough, however. There are blind spots to which we must turn attention.

Listening to women

There are always voices that are not easily heard.[13] Among the most important is that of women. A great deal of gender research has been done in the last twenty years, and it is now understood that the roles of men and women in the life of a community are different. It is commonly agreed that women carry out a disproportionate share of the productive work relating to the family and community and are critically involved in areas that are key to development change. Women are vital providers of health care and are critical to the education of children, especially girl children. Women not only have information that needs to be part of the development process, but research shows that much positive social change is correlated with the education and involvement of women. Encouraging change only through men leaves enormous areas of community life untouched. If women are not involved and engaged, any development effort is limited.

Because many cultures insist that women be silent, especially in front of outsiders, their voice is hard to hear. Deliberate and creative efforts need to be made so that their view and their story emerges alongside that of the men.[14] This is why Anderson and Woodrow encourage the capabilities and vulnerabilities analysis be done separately for men and women. PLA and Appreciative Inquiry processes must also create mechanisms by which the voice of women can emerge (Williams and Mwau 1994, 250). Often women have knowledge that will not surface any other way.

There are additional reasons that women are important to the development process. Research suggests that women bring a different methodological bias to living life and hence to pursuing change. Women tend to be more relationally oriented and less oriented toward rules. When women talk about their experience of the gospel, they speak of a restored relationship, while men tend to talk about the price of their sin being paid in full. The incarnation is particularly attractive to women because they tend to see God at work in everyday activities such as getting food and washing clothes. Women tend to be more intuitive than men, and this may mean they will be more effective using the Appreciative Inquiry approach.

Dana Robert, in her seminal study of women in the American Protestant mission movement (1996), summarizes the role of women in an interesting way. Women did theology, Robert discovered, but in a decentralized, highly contextualized way, lived out more narratively than analytically. Women tended to ignore the church-centered theology of the formal mission structures and gravitated to the person-centered work of evangelism and kingdom-building. Women tended to be ministers of compassion, founding many of these ministries, and were instrumental in funding them and keeping them going. Robert determined that women were consistently interested in women and children, audiences that often proved to be the key to church growth, renewal, and positive social change. Finally, Robert noted that women were the first to embrace holism, an integrated view of body and soul. Women are too relational and incarnational to be willing to limit ministry only to caring for the soul.

Listening to children

If women do not always have a voice, children are usually only images of suffering and pain. Although much rhetoric has been invested in stating our concern for children and their well-being, our actions tell another story. "We deem children highly in emotional terms, but deem them 'useless' in any formal sense, excluding their contributions from measurements of work and production, and making them invisible in statistics, debate and policy-making" (Edwards 1996, 814).

Children tend to be seen as passive recipients of development aid. They are portrayed as sad, hungry, and desperately in need of assistance. This image dominates development planning and evaluation process as well. The result is that children are fed, educated, and not taken seriously. Chambers has posed the provocative question as to what entry point for change could be "more powerful in the long term than changing the way we treat children." He finds it odd that parents' treatment of children is not a "matter of massive global public concern, analysis, critical learning and sharing" (1997, 233). We should extend Chambers's concern to the way relief and development organizations sometimes treat children.

Why should children and their role be more important to us? First, as Michael Edwards of Save the Children UK points out, children are the future of the community. Childhood is where strength, stamina, health, and brain power are developed and when values are formed. In a sense, any better future begins with better children. Malnourished and poorly educated children are hardly a good harbinger of a better future (Edwards 1996, 820). Second, children and youth are important since there are so many of them in the developing world, making up as much as 40 percent of the population in the Third World. Third, most life-shaping decisions, including faith decisions, are made before the age of eighteen (Myers 1994).

Yet as Ravi Jayakaran told me, in Indian communities people often lose sight of the well-being of their children when times are hard. Responding to a crisis tends to shift the focus to saving adults. The future, and hence the children, are sacrificed in order for adults to survive the present circumstances. This leads Jayakaran to note that when the community shifts its attention to the well-being of the children, this is a sign of transformation. The community is healthy enough to invest in its children.

We need, however, to take our concern for children one step further. We need a change in thinking that allows us to see children as agents of transformation. Just as women in families are in a position to influence the other family members, so too are children. Nora Avarientos, a development practitioner in the Philippines, told me that "children can provide the message of hope in a poor community."

In a number of World Vision projects around the world, children have formed committees on issues that are important to them. Some help with the education of younger children through tutoring. Others work on children's rights, especially the right to be free from violence. Children suffering from family violence come to the children's committee for help. In a barrio of Barranquilla in Colombia, children painted a series of "posters" on the mud wall on the side of the road leading into the village, each illustrating one of the rights of the child. This was their way of educating their parents. In the Philippines, children's groups have organized to work against drinking and other addictions. Children sometimes say things adults cannot. In one case in the Philippines, a group of children stood up at a public meeting and told the local politicians, the honored guests of the meeting, that they needed to stop being corrupt.

Sarone Ole Sena, a friend and colleague of World Vision Tanzania, has began to include children in Appreciative Inquiry exercises. He helps them articulate their dreams as they begin to go to school for the first time. He insists that children see themselves as part of the community's dream. He has found that children's dreams for a community are often bigger, more stretching. In a remote area of Tanzania, the children in a village articulated a dream for 2020 in which every child was able to go to school; no children died because of diarrhea, measles, or the flu; men, women, and children worked together for the good of the community; and the community had healthy children for the next generation.[15]

Getting the pace right

The problem with plans is that every activity is accompanied by a date. This is a useful discipline, but it can lead to anti-development activity. Deadlines sometimes become more important than the event associated with the date. This is where an African view of time is more helpful than the Western view. In Africa, the time is marked when something is finished. Being "on time" is less important. Things are done when they are done. A view of time that measures the completion of an event rather than chronological time is better suited to sustainable development processes. Why?

We need to begin by asking whose development needs measuring. Too often projects are run on the time table of the development agency or the donor who provides the development funding. This makes no sense. It is the community that is on the transformational journey, and only God knows when the critical events will take place. This becomes even clearer when we remind ourselves what the goals of development are. If development performance is measured by when the wells are dug and when kids graduate from school, the Western chronology can be helpful. If the goals of development are the discovery of true identity and vocation, then these things are discovered when they are discovered. Chronology and deadlines are not very helpful here. For this reason many development agencies are seeking longer and longer time frames for their programming, although public funding sources are proving quite unhelpful in this regard.

There is a deeper reason for taking great care in getting the pace right. Koyama reminds us that straightness is not natural (1979, 30). Nature and social systems are made up of curves, of inefficiencies, of surprises. Only technology is straight and efficient. When Koyama says that "technological life makes us straight-minded," he is saying that technology can create a conflict between efficiency and meaning.

> The technologist has an inner drive to control and systematize. This is the point at which technology and the holy conflict. That which is controlled cannot be holy. The holy, in its dignity, rejects being controlled and scheduled. . . . How can we enjoy the fruits of technology yet retain the meaningful experience with the holy? (Koyama 1985, 135).

Empowering processes also resist the technological. They cannot be controlled or scheduled. Human development is not a straight line. As agents of transformation we must be willing to lay down our worship of the well-planned and the timely in favor of what is really important—the discoveries and insights that will come when they will come. Koyama concludes:

> Community building cannot be achieved by such efficient confrontation. It must be guided by the patient spirituality which is ready to accept inefficiency as it deals with a human being not as a "target." This sense of living with inefficiency opposes the spirit of imperialism (1985, 250).

Letting the spiritual come through

There is a tendency for development practitioners to tune out the spiritual.[16] Even those deeply committed to letting the poor speak for themselves tend to edit the spiritual out by dismissing it as superstition or ignorance. As a result we end up with large amounts of information about the material world and little or none about the spiritual realities of people's lives. Our information is about family size, incidence of disease, agricultural productivity, and water contamination. This material analysis tends to lead to material solutions: family planning, immunization, introduction of improved seeds, and bore holes.

Our lack of knowledge about values, religious practices, spiritual oppression, and the like limits our development response as Christians. If we truly understand the world as a seamless spiritual-material reality, then the scope of our development research must include both the fear of demons and the quality of drinking water, the impact of both witchcraft and of poor soil.

For example, few PLAs or Logical Frameworks contain descriptions of the spiritual side of the community's life, even though most third-world communities have a deeply religious worldview and describe the life of their community in spiritual and religious terms. How many causal diagrams refer to spirits, demons, curses, ancestors, and gods? How many transect-walk diagrams show shrines, sacred trees, and places no one will go to at night?

Sometimes this information is missing because the community thought-fully edits it out of its story. The members may have learned that educated outsiders are not interested or are critical of such information. Other times, it is missing because we never ask.

When we allow this side of community life to emerge, we learn some interesting and important things.[17] Using a typical PLA ranking exercise, a tribal group in India identified eight areas in which it hoped to see social change. The members were then asked to divide ten seeds among three possible sources of power and control over those eight areas: (1) the tribal group itself; (2) others (meaning outsiders like the government, people from neighboring towns, and NGOs); and (3) gods and spirits. As we can see in Figure 7-10, this tribal group sees itself with limited power. This is empirical evidence of its marred identity and forgotten vocation.

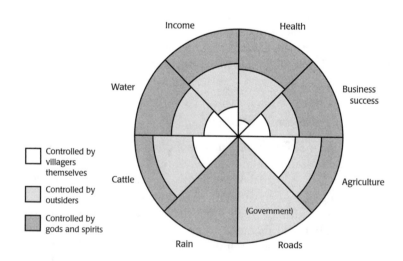

Figure 7-11: Who has control?
(Adapted from Jayakaran 1999)

The community believes that outsiders have considerable power. In the case of improving roads, the government is perceived to have *all* the power; not even the gods can help. This perceived power of outsiders is a window into the community's social, economic, and political systems. Helping the village residents explore, map, and name this outside reality can be helpful to them in recapturing some of this external control for themselves, pushing out the boundary of what they believe they can control. (This is related to Friedman's understanding of development as extending the boundaries of social power.)

The part of the conversation that tends to go unsaid by the community or ignored by the development promoter is the amount of control the tribal group ascribes to the unseen world of the gods and spirits. Yet the gods and spirits have significant levels of control, according to the villagers, in seven of the eight areas of their life in which they would like to see improvement.

This perceived power of the gods, spirits, and ancestors explains why technical development interventions are sometimes rejected; the community cannot afford to risk offending the true power behind what to us is a material reality. What we see as a simple material intervention—perhaps a well or micro-enterprise development—is perceived by the villagers as a spiritual challenge to the gods and spirits they believe are responsible for these areas of life. Since the daily life of traditional cultures is devoted to managing the power and control of the unseen spirit world, they are quite sensibly weighing the cost of innovation.

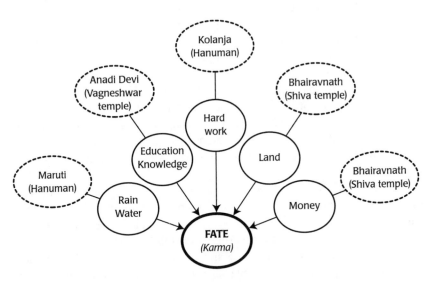

Figure 7-12: What influences fate? Material and spiritual causes.
(Adapted from World Vision India 1995)

Similar examples of the importance of the religious side of the story also show up in village causal diagrams developed as part of PLAs.[18] For example, when inhabitants of an Indian village were asked to brainstorm together on the things they would most like to change, they kept coming back to the importance of *karma* or fate. When asked what kinds of things influenced fate, they mentioned water, education, hard work, land, and money. Normally, a PLA exercise would stop at this point and the conversation would shift to helping the community decide how it wanted to improve these areas of material life. Considering the holistic nature of the local worldview, however, another question was asked: What influences these areas of your life? The answer came back in the forms of the names of local gods and their association with various temples. In the villagers' worldview there are spiritual forces behind the material changes that change one's *karma*. If the development practitioner does not share and seek this view, the PLA exercise too often ends before the full story is told.

Understanding the local view of cause and effect by letting the spiritual come to light in our development learning processes is very important. This is the only way that our understanding of the community's survival strategy is complete. If we tune out the spiritual, we will only be able to describe those parts of the survival strategy that lie "inside the circle" (see Figure 6-3). By editing out the spiritual means we will have ignored a significant part of the community's story, imposing our modern, scientific worldview in its place.

A community's strong belief that some causes are located in the spiritual realm also influences how it participates in the program. If the development intervention addresses something community members believe is largely controlled by the spirits, then, in their eyes, we are doing spiritual work, even though we are oblivious to this, assuming we are working in the concrete, real world of science. This presents the community with a serious problem: Who is more powerful? The development facilitator or the spirit world? Not knowing the answer, they sensibly step back and watch to see what happens. When we experience high participation in research and planning and then low participation in implementation, this may be the explanation.

Letting the spiritual side come through is only the beginning, of course. If we are sensitive enough to let this part of the community's experience and belief surface, we learn important things, but it is far less clear what we should do about what we have learned. Our modern selves tell us that the antidote to superstition is a dose of modern education. Indeed, education tends to be our answer for every social ill, even when the social problem persists in the face of our education. Yet our postmodern selves say traditional views must be respected as equally valid ways to believe and should not be challenged, thus creating a dilemma. Our religious selves as Christians say that all of this is demonic and needs to be subjected to the transforming power of Christ. Our scientific selves are tempted to edit the whole thing out and deny that it is even there. I suffer from all the foregoing illnesses and thus have few answers to offer and am stuck only with the painful questions. One of the frontiers in transformational development done by Christians is going to be figuring out how to do responsible transforming development that takes seriously the worldview of people whose worldview is largely religious without (1) validating expressions of the local culture that are anti-life, (2) ignoring the benefits of modern science, or (3) surrendering the tenets and the power of our Christian faith.

Whatever our reservations, we must have the courage and discipline to let the whole story of the people emerge. If the key to development is allowing people to tell their own story and then to begin the process of directing its continuing development, we have no other choice. The development tools I have described—analysis of capacities and vulnerabilities, Participatory Learning and Action, and Appreciative Inquiry—are not the problem. They do not automatically exclude the spiritual or religious side of life. It is the people who use the tools who are the problem. As good professionals they suffer from a modern bias that takes for granted that the spiritual is not relevant to the material world and hence is not needed when doing development work. This blind spot results in people inadvertently using development learning tools in a way that imposes a Western, materialistic worldview on local people. This is wrong.

APPENDIX 1:
THE PLA TOOL KIT
(From Jayakaran 1996)

Tool	Purpose	Outcome
Time lines	Describe key events in the community history.	Help the community own its own history. What effected change in the past?
Family line	Describe things that have changed in key families.	Demonstrate past coping strategies.
Trends analysis	Describe trajectories of change in the community.	Create a sense of direction and possibility of change.
Seasons diagram	See community life in a seasonal perspective.	Create a climate of dialogue on a wide range of issues. Good for planning purposes.
Resource mapping	Describe social, economic, and demographic resources.	Good for needs analysis and resource allocation.
Transects	Cartoon-like map of community key points, problems, and resources.	Good as an inventory of resources. Good for needs analysis. Also shows resource distribution.
Matrix mapping	Determine community preferences.	Understand rationale for community choices and preferences.
Venn diagram (Chappati diagram)	Describe institutions or people who are important actors in the life of the community.	Understand perceptions of power and relationships among powerful people or institutions. Can identify institutions that need strengthening.
Wealth ranking	Describe local economic system and its players.	Identify the poorest of the poor. Help community think about why non-poor are non-poor.
Causal diagrams	Describe local view of causally related events and actors.	Identify major development opportunities or barriers. Disclose survival strategy.
A typical day	Describe pattern of a typical day.	Identify roles, especially for women and children. Helpful for planning activities.
Conflict analysis	Describe dynamics of conflict.	Reveal major players and causes of conflict. Basis for exploring reconciliation.
Ten-seed technique	Measuring attitudes, ranking things.	An easy way to get to comparative percentages.

APPENDIX 2:
STANDARDS AND INDICATORS FOR THE ISAIAH VISION
(Adapted from Avarientos 1994)

Standards	Indicators
Children live.	No abortion. Children are born healthy and whole. Enhanced maternal care. Improved prenatal and postnatal care. No street children.
Children are healthy.	Breast feeding encouraged. Proper intake of food. Oral rehydration is normative. Access to health services. Access to potable water. Proper drainage and waste disposal.
Children learn.	Primary and secondary education for all. Appropriate vocational or college opportunities.
Children no longer suffer violence.	Child rapes monitored. Homes free from drugs and alcohol. Access to child-abuse services.
Children are free of economic sexual exploitation.	No children act as breadwinners. No children work at the expense of going to school. No children are sexually abused.
Children are free to be children.	Children have time to rest and to play. Children use free time for productive activities.
Old people live full lives.	Minimized occurrence of common diseases. Opportunity to develop potential. Engagement in productive endeavors. Engagement in wholesome recreation. Older people are respected and cared for. Older people serve as models and inspiration for young.
People enjoy the fruits of their labors.	Sustained livelihood and income meet basic needs. People share what they have. Maximized use of local resources without exploitation. Freedom from bondage to usury and tenancy. Everyone has access to economic opportunities.

Standards	Indicators
	People build and live in their own houses.
	No labor manipulation or exploitation.
	People are able to deal with oppressive structures.
	People are able to diagnose social situations, create their own plans, evaluate, hold each other accountable.
	People are able to fund their own development by local fundraising and by accessing resources intended for them from government, NGOs, and the private sector.
	Leaders become more professional and servant-like.
People enjoy community with each other, their environment, and communion with God.	Restored self-image (recovered identity).
	Individuals believe in their capability.
	Husbands and wives are able to resolve conflicts.
	Non-poor and poor, educated and uneducated, men and women, and different religions are able to work together harmoniously.
	No more land grabbing.
	Community works together for better future.
	Respect for people's opinions and rights.
	Care for the land and the environment.
	No illegal fishing or logging.
	Control of air pollution.
	Continuing use of the Bible in life and worship.
	Values move toward kingdom values: less vice, violence, hoarding, disharmony, strife, etc.
	Christians and churches work together.
	Christians understand and live holistic vision.
	Churches are working for the good of the community.
	Churches are concerned and helping the poor.
	Growing numbers of holistic disciples.

APPENDIX 3:
HOLISTIC EVALUATION OF AREA DEVELOPMENT PROGRAMS
IN INDIA
(Adapted from Christian 1998b)

Do our area development programs show a conscious attempt to . . .

heal the marred image of the poor?
- Affirm consistently that the poor are made in the image of God?
- Clarify the identity of the poor as God's children with gifts and skills?
- Enable the poor to see God in their history?
- Initiate hope-based action for change?
- Enable the poor to deal with structures, systems, values, and interiorities?

deal with the god-complexes that ensnare poor and non-poor alike?
- Reverse the god-complexes that keep the poor in their poverty?
- Transform power relationships?
- Prophetically proclaim the truth that power is God's?
- Reorder the relationship between truth and power (power does not equal truth)?

counteract the deception by principalities and powers?
- Establish the rule of God; announce that Jesus is Lord?
- Declare the deceptions of the principalities and powers?
- Unmask the ultimate powerlessness of the principalities and powers in the face of God's rule?

change inadequacies in worldview?
- Analyze the worldview of the poor and non-poor?
- Challenge the various aspects of reality that perpetuate poverty?
- Enable the poor to imagine a different future?
- Create hope in the midst of despair?
- Redefine power?
- Teach from the word; link the word to the context; allow the word to critique worldview?

restore just and peaceful relationships?
- Proclaim the truth within poverty relationships?
- Establish the truth in public life?
- Build covenant communities?
- Develop win-win relationships?
- Promote reconciliation; heal broken relationships?

use Christian development practices?
- Highly professional?
- Use prayer and fasting as tools of social action?
- Use the gifts of the Spirit as tools for development action?
- Enable staff to wear the full armor of God?

APPENDIX 4:
AREA DEVELOPMENT PROGRAM (ADP)
STANDARDS AND INDICATORS
(Adapted from Cookingham 1998)

	Standard	Indicator information
Community participation	Ownership of the development process increases over time until the communities in the area accept full responsibility for managing their development.	Level of participation by different groups in development planning, implementation, and monitoring; evaluation based on ratings made during focus-group exercises.
Community organization	Communities in the area are organized to sustain appropriate development processes.	Level of participation in legally registered associations, presence of local development workers and trainers, ability to obtain resources. Committee in each community in the sample will answer ten questions, and the answers will be verified by ADP staff.
Means to provide for basic needs	The proportion of households above the local benchmark for poverty increases over time.	Ability to provide household members with schooling, nutrition, and health care; inventory of common assets. Information to be obtained during survey of households.
Access to safe water	The proportion of households within fifteen minutes of safe water increases over time.	Information about the type of water source and the time to reach it obtained during survey of households.
Sanitation	The proportion of households that use sanitary latrines increases over time.	Information about disposal of human excreta obtained during survey of households. Latrines will be inspected.
Nutrition	The proportion of households consuming	Information about foods consumed at the time of the

Standard	Indicator information
minimum daily food requirements per local standard during the most difficult three-month season increases over time.	survey and in the most recent difficult season obtained during survey of households.
Child immunization — In communities where World Vision works directly, 100 percent of the children are fully immunized. In the entire area, 85 percent are fully immunized.	Information from immunization cards or mother reports obtained during survey of households. Results validated by checking ministry of health records, if available.
Child mortality — The proportion of live births still alive at time of survey increases over time.	Information about child mortality obtained from mother during survey of households. Results validated by checking ministry of health records, if available.
Primary schooling — The proportion of boys and girls who successfully complete primary education per the ministry of education standard increases until it is above the national average.	Information about primary schooling obtained during survey of households. Results validated by checking school records.
Social relationships — The index across communities in the area becomes more positive over time.	Ratings during focus-group exercises by different groups on treating people in the community respectfully and fairly.
Emergence of hope — The index across communities in the area becomes more positive over time.	Ratings of self-esteem and attitudes toward the future in focus-group exercises.
Spiritual nurture — World Vision staff is willing and able to provide spiritual nurture to people within the ADP communities. The index for this standard increases over time.	Index based on ways staff nurture its members' own spiritual development and nurture spiritual development in others in the ADP. Information collected by questionnaire and interview.

8

Christian Witness
and Transformational Development

THE NECESSITY AND THE CHALLENGE OF CHRISTIAN WITNESS

Why we must witness

Being Christian means being a witness. By definition the Christian faith is a missionary faith. *Gospel* means "message" or "good news." Messages are not messages unless they are announced. The word *evangelism* means to "announce the news."

When Christians say that they accept Jesus as their Lord and Savior, they are also saying that they intend to announce this fact in every facet of their lives and by every means available to them: by life, deed, word, and sign. For Christians, being a witness is integral to who we are and what we believe. But there are other reasons why we must witness to Christ in the context of doing transformational development.

First, the need to proclaim the good news of Christ is directly related to a Christian understanding of transformation. For Christians, belief is the beginning of knowing. Athanasius said that the gospel provided a new *arche*, a new starting point for the way we understand and make sense of our world. Augustine of Hippo took the biblical story as the point of departure for his radical reconstruction of his former ways of thinking, following the dictum *Credo ut intelligam*—I believe in order to know (quoted in Newbigin 1995, 9).

In this sense, Christian witness is the beginning of transformation. Melba Maggay reminds us, "Social change is primarily what happens to people in that level of being where the Spirit alone has access" (1994, 72).

Newbigin explains this further by saying that by proclaiming Christ we offer people the possibility of understanding what God is doing in history.

By sharing God's good news with people, we offer the beginning of the process of recovering identity and vocation.

[They receive] a vision of the goal of human history . . . a vision which makes it possible to act hopefully when there is no earthly hope, to find the way when everything is dark and there are no earthly landmarks (1989, 129).

I have already said that every development program represents a convergence of stories: ours, the community's, and God's. God's story is the only one that has the power to redirect and make sense out of all our stories. The best human future is one that moves toward the kingdom of God. Thus witnessing to God's story is the beginning of hope and the promise of a new story.

Second, we need to bring the best that we have. In our best moments our development processes are empowering and our development technology can make short work of dirty water, parasites, malnutrition, and poor agricultural production. Yet as good as all these things are, they are not the best news that we have. Because our own experience tells us that Christ has the power to seek, to save, and to recompose our stories into stories of hope and purpose, we can hardly help sharing this very best of our good news with others.

Finally, Jesus gave us two simple commandments. We are to love God with all we have and to love our neighbors as ourselves. This is the motivation that takes us to the poor in the first place. How can we say we love our neighbors if we limit our work to improving their material lives in the here and now and never share the news that holds the promise of transforming their lives now and forever?

For Christians, therefore, our thinking and practice of transforming development must have an evangelistic intent, although this needs to be understood with some care. This is not a call for proselytism; neither is it a call to coercive, manipulative, or culturally insensitive evangelism. It is not even a call for all development practitioners to become evangelists. After all, no one knows the moment when someone is ready for faith, nor is God limited to the staff of a particular Christian development agency in bringing God's good news. Rather, it is a call to be sure we do our development with an attitude that prays and yearns for people to know Jesus Christ.

Understanding evangelism

It may be helpful for me to say a little about the meaning of the word *evangelism*. Evangelism is the verbal sharing of the good news of Jesus Christ and his offer to fallen human beings, but we need to work a little harder to be clear on what we mean by this. Too often the gospel message is presented as a set of propositional statements. While this is true, it is not enough—and it can be misleading.

Tim Dearborn points out that evangelism is good news about a person, not just a set of propositions. The gospel invitation is to a relationship, not just intellectual assent or agreement to a set of ideas. In this sense, the gospel is not against other religions; it is simply true (1997, 37).

William Abraham, a Methodist theologian, clarifies this further when he reminds us that evangelism is not simply speaking about something that we believe or that we feel compelled to share. Evangelism is announcing something that has happened in the world about which everyone has a right to know.

> What makes proclamation evangelism is not the proclamation *per se*, but the message being proclaimed: the coming rule of God. . . . Without this announcement, people will not know about its arrival, nor will they have a clear view of what it means for the kingdom of God to come now in the present or in the future (1989, 59).

Walter Brueggemann, the Presbyterian Old Testament scholar, defines evangelism as an invitation to choose a new story, employing the biblical story as the "definitional story of our life, and thereby authorizing people to give up, abandon and renounce other stories that have shaped their lives in false and distorting ways" (1993a, 10). Brueggemann describes the act of evangelism as drama, a story with a beginning, a middle, and an end. The first scene is about the conflict between two powerful forces who battle for control of the future. The second scene presents the witness who gives testimony, telling the outcome of the conflict that he or she has already experienced. In the third and final scene, the listener must make an appropriate response to this witness.

It also may be useful to say a few things about what evangelism is not. Evangelism is not about sales. The gospel must never be treated as a marketable product that we entice people to "buy." "We are not purveyors of a commodity . . . but facilitators of a people's own discovery of their heritage as the children of Abraham" (Bediako 1996b, 187). Nor is evangelism about sales effectiveness. Vinay Samuel is fond of saying that evangelism is a commitment to sharing, not an announcement of expected outcomes. Finally, the greatest danger to wrong-headed thinking about evangelism is that we will use evangelism as a way to play god in the lives of other people, believing we know the state of their soul, when they need to say Yes to God, or that we know something about their future that they do not.

We are witnessing anyway

Sometimes we don't think hard enough about this business of being witnesses. Sometimes we think there are two choices: being witnesses or not being witnesses. This is not true. We are always witnesses to something. The only question is to what or to whom?

In a well-drilling project on the edge of the Sahara, a community watched a soil scientist and a hydrologist converse in highly technical language as they did soil chemistry and studied a hydrological survey. When asked what these two men were doing, the community replied that they were witch doctors. One was consulting the spirit of the earth and asking it where the spirit of the water lived. The other was reading magic texts in the search of power, just as their marabouts did with the Qur'an. Asked if these witch doctors were any good, the villagers replied that they were very good, better than their own witch doctors. "After all, they always find the water."[1]

When confronted with this interpretation of their actions, the men decided to go back the next day and explain the science behind their work in simple terms the village could understand. Explaining the miracle of finding water in the desert as "just science," however, is a witness, only this time to the efficiency of modern science and technology.[2]

Development technology continually creates this problem in traditional cultures.[3] Whether water is found in the desert or children do not die who normally would die, an explanation is demanded. With no explanation, the traditional worldview provides an animist explanation. Or, if the modern development professional reduces the good news to "just science," the explanation is a secular one. Either way, a witness is made that is not Christian and an invitation to idolatry has been extended.

To make it harder, it is not even enough to announce that we are Christians, as if this will change how the community understands the success of our development interventions. In Vietnam, when villagers were asked why a Christian NGO was helping them reconstruct their dikes, they explained that Christians care about the poor. When asked why Christians care about the poor, they responded that Christians were earning merit for their next life, a Buddhist explanation. When Muslims in Mauritania were asked the same kind of question, two responses predominated. Either Christians were earning their way into paradise, a Muslim understanding of charity, or they were getting rich by working in the aid business, a secular understanding of why expatriates serve overseas.

Finally, to make things even more complicated, even announcing that the intervention is made possible because the Christian God is a powerful God is not enough. If this is all that is said, Hiebert estimates that within three generations the people will be secularized. It is a question of simple pragmatics. As soon as the people figure out, as we in the West have, that technology works without God as part of the explanation, in time God is dropped from the explanation.[4]

The bottom line is that we need to be concerned about who gets worshiped at the end of the development program. Jayakumar Christian reminds us that whatever we put at the center of the program during its lifetime will tend to be what the community worships in the end (1998b). As we have just seen, if development technology is the focus, technology will be worshiped as the source of transformation. If the development agency and its expertise and resources are the central feature of the program, the agency will become the object of worship. In one case in India it was discovered that World Vision had been added to a tribal community's list of gurus—those who have answers the community does not have—and prayers and sacrifices had been instituted to ensure that this new guru kept helping the community. If money is the focus, then money is perceived to be the key to transformation. What we put at the center of our program is also our witness. We must always ask if we are acting as a dependent people, looking to God for every good thing. We want people to observe us and say, "Theirs must be a living God!"

The twofold challenge of Christian witness and transformational development

Christian witness presents an interesting pair of challenges to the development worker. I've just described the first part of the challenge. Every development effort witnesses to something. The only question is, To what is it witnessing?

The second part of the challenge has to do with the traditional framework of Christian witness. Too often Christian witness is pursued in a way that is contradictory to the development framework proposed in this book. In the spiritual arena, the community is assumed to have a problem of which it is not aware. The evangelist assumes the role of answer-giver to those who are assumed not to know the answer. Finally, there is an assumption that the evangelist knows something about the future of the audience that the audience does not know, namely, their ultimate destination if they do not believe.

At the most fundamental level, these claims are true. Christians do have a truth that the non-Christians do not have, and there is an obligation for us to share this news, even if people are not aware they need it. And Christians do believe that eternal life is only possible by believing in Jesus Christ as Lord and Savior. Yet there is a fine line between being faithful to these beliefs and crossing over the line and assuming a smug arrogance, playing god in the lives of those who do not yet believe. There is always the danger that we may act, not as undeserving recipients of a gift, but as people with a sense of superiority, expressing the "teacher complex" that Koyama feels damages the attractiveness of the gospel.

I doubt strongly whether the idea that the "people over there are enemies of God" is central to the Spirit of Christ. The Spirit of Christ does not support the spirit of greed to conquer others and self-righteousness to demonstrate our superior piety (1993, 293).

If done sensitively and without arrogance, the "go and tell" frame for Christian witness may be appropriate for a church or traditional mission agency, but it is not a good fit for a development agency for the simple reason that it is anti-developmental. It cuts across the idea that the community is the owner of its own development. It works against the notion of beginning where the community is and helping it find answers to its own questions. The initiative is with the outsider; the position of power and control is external. Since we don't do "go and tell" development, we should do what we can to avoid "go and tell" evangelism.

The second challenge of Christian witness in the context of doing transformational development is whether or not an alternative framework for Christian witness can be found that allows Christians to be faithful to the nature of their belief that the gospel must be shared and, at the same time, allows the kind of transformative development process I described in the earlier chapters. Is there a developmental approach to Christian witness? I believe there is.

WHO WITNESSES? PROVOKING THE QUESTION

The book of Acts describes the growth of the early church. Examining these stories reveals an interesting pattern that proves helpful with the dilemma I have just posed. Evangelism, the saying of the gospel, is often the second act of the story. What do I mean?

When Peter gives his first public statement of the gospel, we are told that three thousand believers were added that day. Yet his sermon was spontaneous, unplanned. He begins his message by saying, "Let me explain this to you." What was the "this" that needed explaining? The people of Jerusalem had gathered and heard the disciples praising God. Incredibly, each observer heard this in his or her own language. This powerful act of the Holy Spirit made the people utterly amazed, and they created their own explanation: the disciples must be drunk. Peter's message was in response to this amazement and was intended to correct an inaccurate explanation. Peter's evangelistic sermon answered a question being asked by the crowd.

The second articulation of the gospel in Acts follows a similar pattern. After healing the crippled beggar at the temple gate, the crowd gathers, astonished at the sight of the former cripple walking around and praising God. Peter once again finds himself needing to clarify the situation. "Men of Israel, why does this surprise you? Why do you stare at us as if by our own power or godliness we have made this man to walk? The God of Abraham, Isaac and Jacob, the God of our fathers, has glorified his servant Jesus" (Acts 3:12-13). Peter's speech is in response to a question from the crowd, provoked by evidence of the activity of God.

The same pattern emerges in the story of Stephen. His opportunity to share the gospel's recomposition of the history of Israel took place, not by plan, but as a result of his being falsely accused because he "did great wonders and miraculous signs among the people" (Acts 6:8). As a result of Stephen's preaching in front of the Sanhedrin, a Pharisee named Saul heard the gospel for the first time.

Do you see the pattern? In each case, the gospel is proclaimed, not by intent or plan, but in response to a question provoked by the activity of God in the community. There is an action that demands an explanation, and the gospel was the explanation. "Something has happened which makes people aware of a new reality, and therefore the question arises: What is this reality? The communication of the gospel is the answering of that question" (Newbigin 1989, 132).

This framework suggests that, in addition to the "go and tell" framework, we can also think of evangelism as the work the Christian community does—or better, that God does through the Christian community—that provokes questions to which the good news of Jesus Christ is the answer (Newbigin 1989, 133; Myers 1992b).

My search for an alternative framework for Christian witness is provided by this framework of living and doing our development in a way that evokes questions to which the gospel is the answer. It addresses the second of the twin challenges for Christian witness in the context of transformational development. When water is found in the desert, when children no longer die, when water no longer makes people sick, something has happened that needs an explanation. When trained professionals live in poor villages, and everyone there knows they could be making more money and their children could go to better schools in the city, this odd behavior provokes a question. The explanation is the gospel. The answer to the question, Who witnesses?, is that development facilitators do through the life that they lead, how they treat the poor, and how they promote transformational development.

There is much to commend this framework for Christian witness in the context of doing transformational development. First, the questions are asked by the people when they witness something they do not expect or understand. The initiative lies with them. This avoids Tillich's complaint that "it is wrong to throw answers, like stones, at the heads of those who haven't even asked a question." Second, the burden for response is on the Christians, not the people. If the people do not ask questions to which the gospel is the answer, we can no longer just say, "Their hearts were hardened," and walk away feeling good that we have witnessed to the gospel. Instead, we need to get down on our knees and ask God why our life and our work are so unremarkable that they never result in a question relating to what we believe and whom we worship.

There is evidence that the framework of living in hopes that the Holy Spirit will provoke questions to which the gospel is the answer is a valid approach. After four years of sacrificially working alongside the poor in a village in India, adhering strictly to a promise not to do overt evangelism, local political leaders came to the humble house of the Christian development worker, asking him and his family to leave. When asked for the reason, the response was, "The way you live is disturbing our people, causing them to ask questions about your God." In an interview in 1997, Sarone Ole Sena commented that, as Appreciative Inquiry gives voice to how the local religious and spiritual views have given strength and life to the community, the question invariably comes back: "What do you believe? What gives you strength and life?" In Mali, a mullah watched every week when the Christian nurse came to hold a clinic. When she had offered to begin her work in his village, he had told her that he was aware that Christians used health care as a mask for doing evangelism. She promised him she would never abuse her profession in this way. After a year he told her that, in addition to keeping her word, he had observed that she truly loved his people and cared about them. He then asked her to tell him more about Issa (the Arabic name for Jesus).

TRANSFORMATIONAL WITNESS

As we develop our thinking about Christian witness in the context of transformational development, we must be sure that our understanding of witness is as transformational as our understanding of development. We must be clear as to the goals for transformational witness. We must understand the organic nature of the gospel message. We need to overcome the dichotomy between evangelism and discipleship. Finally, we must be sure that our Christian witness shares the whole biblical story.

The goals of Christian witness

The goals of Christian witness are the same as the goals of transformational development: changed people and changed relationships. We desire that all people—the poor, the non-poor, and ourselves—be able to experience the lifelong process of recovering our true identity as children of God and the restoration of our true vocation as productive stewards in God's creation. This comes about only by restoring the family of relationships of which we are a part.

The only difference between the goals for transformational development and the goals for Christian witness is that Christian witness focuses more, but not exclusively, on our relationship with God through Jesus Christ, while the goals of transformational development focus more, but not exclusively, on the other four critical relationships: with self, community, others, and our environment. Because the focus of Christian witness is more on our relationship with God, witness-by-word moves to center stage alongside witness-by-life and witness-by-deed. The fact that the goals for Christian witness and the goals for transformational development are the same, except for focus, should be reassuring. They can only be the same if we have overcome the dichotomy between the physical (development) and the spiritual (Christian witness), the modern problem with which this book has been struggling throughout.

One final word on the need to verbalize the good news of the gospel. The motive to invite people to faith is not a form of imperialism or a messianic desire to make everyone over in our image, although I must admit with sadness that some Christians have acted out of these motivations. In our best moments the motive is much less selfish. We want others to know the good news about the Lord. The gospel of Jesus Christ is the best news that we have, better than community mobilization or development technology. As Christians, we have experienced the most fundamental of discoveries: "Ultimately, any social transformation happens in our deepest level of being, that part where God alone can go" (Maggay 1994, 71).

Gospel as life, deed, word, and sign

In Chapter 1, I commented at length about how the modern worldview of the West has encouraged us to separate gospel-as-word, gospel-as-sign, and gospel-as-deed. Any holistic understanding of Christian witness must reunite these three aspects of what is really a single gospel message. But there is a fourth aspect of the message that must be included in this reunification. The gospel is not a disembodied message; it is carried and communicated in the life of Christian people. Therefore, a holistic understanding of the gospel begins with life, a life that is then lived out by deed and word and sign.

When Jesus selected the twelve disciples, they were appointed so that "they might be with him and that he might send them out to preach and to have the authority to drive out demons" (Mk 3:14-15). When they returned from being sent out for the first time, we are told that they "went out and preached that people should repent. They drove out demons and anointed many sick people with oil and healed them" (Mk 6:12-13). The activist is eager to get to the sending and acting part, gladly taking note of the three-fold nature of the gospel: preaching words, healing deeds, and demon-sending signs.

What activists too often miss, however, is the *reason* for the appointing of the disciples in the first place: so the disciples would *be with* Jesus. Being with Jesus is the beginning of any biblical ministry. Yet being with Jesus means more than simply being a Christian. As the disciples learned, it also means traveling with Jesus, listening and learning from Jesus, being rebuked by Jesus—truly being with Jesus all the time.

This is the key to Christian witness that provokes the question to which the gospel is the answer. We will live eloquent lives only if we are being with Jesus, following Jesus, and seeking, by his grace, to become more like Jesus. The leading edge of witnessing to the whole gospel is being with Jesus. Only then do gospel words, deeds, and signs follow. Transformation is fundamentally about relationships, remember? Our ability to facilitate transformation depends on our being transformed, and this depends on our life, our relationship with our Lord.

We must also remember that the gospel message is an organic whole. Life, deed, word, and sign must all find expression for us to encounter and comprehend the whole of the good news of Jesus Christ. Life alone is too solitary. Word, deed, and sign alone are all ambiguous. Words alone can be posturing or positioning. Deeds alone do not declare identity or indicate in whom one has placed his or her faith. Signs can be done by demons and spirits or by the Holy Spirit. It is only when life, deed, word, and sign are expressed in a consistent and coherent whole that the gospel of the Son of God is clear (see Figure 2-6).

This organic relationship of life, word, deed, and sign creates an interesting ability for Christian witness to be "customer centered." We can lead with whichever part of the gospel message most closely relates to the needs of those to whom we wish to witness.

> The ministry of Jesus is notable for its clarity of focus and the flexibility of its response. In that way, Jesus allowed the other person to set the agenda. But Jesus always responded out of who he was and what he represented (Shenk 1993, 73).

For those afraid of spirits, we pray for the Holy Spirit to do the signs that show that God is more powerful. For those who are seeking intellectual truth, we begin with words. For those who are empirically inclined or seeking evidence that God is concerned for the material world, we begin with gospel as deed. For those who seek meaning in their relationships, we begin with gospel as life.

While we can lead with any aspect of the gospel message, we must never stop there. Any Christian understanding of transformation must find expression for all elements of the gospel message—life, deed, word, and sign— each in God's time. Everyone needs to encounter and engage the gospel message in its wholeness. To stop short is to truncate the gospel.

One final clarification. Having asserted the inseparability of life, deed, word, and sign, we must not overlook the question, How do people come to faith? Romans 10 points to the unique role of gospel-as-word. Neither gospel-as-sign nor gospel-as-deed is sufficient. In other words, the gospel message points people in a direction and toward a decision. The direction is toward the kingdom of God, and the decision is whether or not to accept Jesus as Savior and Lord and thereby enter God's kingdom. So, while we must recover a gospel message that is inseparably word, deed, and sign, we must also understand that its purpose is to invite people to reconciliation with God and with each other through Jesus Christ.

Evangelism and discipleship

In carrying out holistic Christian witness, it is helpful to remember that evangelism is not different from or unrelated to discipleship. Another of the inadvertent and unhelpful impacts of modernity and its separation of the physical and spiritual is that discipleship is too often reduced to developing one's relationship with God, with little or no attention to developing one's relationship with the community and the environment. This mental separation results in reducing prayer, reading the Bible, and worship to spiritual activities, obscuring their relevance to work and act in the "real" world. This is also the explanation for how some Christians spiritualize and privatize the Bible, and thus have trouble believing it speaks to the physical realms of politics, economics, and issues of race and culture. If the "real" world of Christians is solely the spiritual world, then discipleship is necessarily limited solely to spiritual things. This is an artificial limitation with tragic consequences.

Cesar Molebatsi, a Christian leader in South Africa, wrote the following to me in 1991: "My deepest pain is that, in the very continent where the Christian church is growing the fastest and where so many countries are mostly inhabited by Christians, we see rampant racism, ethnic violence, AIDS, corruption and increasing poverty. What kind of Christians are we creating?" I must ask the same question of my American culture, which claims the label Christian in the midst of racism, gang warfare, deserted cities, pornography, abortion on demand, drug use, and rampant consumerism. When evangelism is separated from discipleship, we tend to move on once someone accepts Jesus as Savior; there is the real risk that he or she will never know him as Lord. Catholic theologian Avery Dulles reminds us that evangelism is not complete with the first proclamation of the gospel: "It is a lifelong process of letting the gospel permeate and transform all our ideas and attitudes" (1996, 28).

William Abraham has defined *evangelism* as the "set of intentional activities which is governed by the goal of initiating people into the kingdom of God for the first time" (1989, 95). Defining evangelism this way, he brings evangelism and discipleship into a unified whole. Using initiation as a metaphor for evangelism, Abraham goes beyond baptism, the traditional end-point of evangelism, and adds five elements to his understanding of the work of evangelism:

- Owning the intellectual claims of the Christian tradition, without which understanding the kingdom of God is impossible.
- Appropriating the very particular moral vision that serves as the bedrock of moral action in the Christian community and the world. At its heart, this vision is about loving God and loving one's neighbor as oneself.
- Experiencing in their inner lives the kind of assurance that only the Holy Spirit can give.
- Receiving and developing gifts that equip one to serve as an agent of God.
- Appropriating those spiritual disciplines that are essential for responsible obedience to the joys of the Kingdom (Abraham 1989, 95-103).

Abraham's frame does one other thing for us that is worth noting. Evangelism always involves proclamation, but, if done with intent, may now include working for peace and justice, prayer, acts of mercy, patient conversation, caring for the poor, and even stern rebuke. "What makes actions evangelism is that they are part of a process that is governed by the goal of initiating people into the kingdom of God" (ibid., 104).

Telling the whole story

Finally, a holistic view of Christian witness requires that we tell our whole story. We must not reduce the good news simply to the account of Jesus in the gospels. We must avoid the risk that the central part of the story will be unintelligible without hearing the biblical story as a whole. To link the gospel to the process of development, the people need to hear about the God who created the world and their culture; the God who wants human beings to worship God and love their neighbor; and the God who wants and will enable them to be productive stewards in creation. Furthermore, in many traditional cultures people find it easier to recognize themselves and make an identity link with the Old Testament stories. The Masai quickly identified with the Old Testament accounts of nomads, cattle, and God's dislike of sin and then responded eagerly to the unexpected good news that the God of the Old Testament is also a God who forgives. We need to tell the whole story so that the gospel account makes full sense.

There is a second sense in which we need to tell the whole story. Too often the gospel is reduced to a personal gospel that restores an individual's relationship with God. And this is true. Yet the whole gospel is more than this. More on the role of the Bible and the whole biblical story later.

HOW WE MUST WITNESS?

Living eloquent lives

The Christian witness framework of provoking the question depends on the life, the lifestyle, and the management style of the development facilitator. For the development practitioner, the challenge is serious indeed. We need to do our work and live our lives in a way that calls attention to the new Spirit that lives within us. We need to relate to people and promote our development technology in ways that create a sense of wonder. We must seek a spirituality that makes our lives eloquent. Dorothy Day is reported to have admonished us to "live a life so mysterious that the only adequate explanation is the presence of a living, loving God."

A crucified mind

Our attitude in Christian witness is worthy of attention. I've already alluded to the temptation to slip into an unspoken attitude of superiority. This temptation comes in a variety of subtle forms. Sometimes we are sure we know best because we are development professionals. Sometimes it is because we are educated or come from what we feel is a more sophisticated culture. Sometimes we fall into the trap of unknowingly judging another culture as not quite as good as our own because of its fear of the spirits and its belief in the unseen. Sometimes it is because we have gotten caught up in the fact that we are Christians and the others are not. Whatever the reason, this kind of attitude acts like a corrosive acid, eating away at our effectiveness in transformational development and Christian witness.

Koyama has called over the years for Christians to set aside their often crusading mind in favor of what he calls the crucified mind, the mind of Christ. If anyone had the right to feel superior, it was the Son of God. Yet we know from the second chapter of Philippians that Christ chose to set this prerogative aside, even to the point of death on a cross. And so must we. Whatever we have was given to us.

There is another reason for humility in our Christian witness. We are the carriers of the message, not the actor. When Paul preaches the gospel to Lydia in Philippi, Luke reports that "the Lord opened her heart to respond to Paul's message" (Acts 16:14). The evangelist was the Holy Spirit; Paul was merely the messenger. Newbigin reminds us that "the mission is not, first of all, an action of ours. It is the action of God" (1989, 135). He goes on to say, "The gospel has a sovereignty of its own and is never an instrument in the hands of the evangelist" (ibid., 153). The good news is not ours to feel superior about or to use as a tool or a weapon. It is not our story; it is God's story.

The beginning of the crucified mind is the unconditional embrace of the other, just as Jesus unconditionally embraced us. Without regard for history or ethnicity, wisdom or folly, sin or saintliness, Christ embraced us and showed us the way to life. And so we must embrace the poor, accepting them as God presents them to us. Our professionalism and our faith were gifts to us in order that we might share them with others. "This is how God loves every person, and the one who is a messenger about the good news of God's love cannot limit the gift of God. The embrace itself becomes the message" (Motte 1996, 81).

Recognizing the fingerprints of God

I've already made the case that we are witnessing all the time, in everything we say and do. The only question is to whom are we witnessing. We also need to remember that God has been witnessing as well: "He was in the world, and though the world was made through him, the world did not recognize him" (Jn 1:10). The problem is that we are not always good witnesses and human beings are not very good at recognizing God, even when God tries to reveal himself.

The key, then, is to work harder at recognizing God's fingerprints in daily life as part of our daily practice of Christian witness. We need to use every conversation, every program activity, as an opportunity to point to the work of God. This is a strength of Appreciative Inquiry and its link to the "excellent or praiseworthy" things we are told to focus on in Philippians 4:8. All of these good things are linked to "whatever you have learned or received or heard from me, or seen in me" (Phil 4:9). We need to get away from the idea that development is a process in which God periodically intervenes and realize that God has a development process already underway in which the community and the development agency periodically cooperate.

Loving people toward recognition

The way we do development can be a source of witness. The way we treat the poor can be a way of announcing that a different spirit is at work in the community. When we treat the poor as equals, having wisdom that we wish to hear, they have a chance to begin the recovery of their true identity and the discovery of their true vocation. Remember my earlier story, "The most important thing that is different is that you sit on the same mat I do and you look me in the eye." Every time hope and vision emerge, we can stop to give thanks to its true source. Appreciative Inquiry and PLAs can be used to celebrate the work of God in the past of the community. Every time we challenge the web of lies with the truth we can speak of one who is Truth and whose truth we proclaim. Even the very process of reflection and our ability to learn point us to God. Where does this ability come from other than from a gracious God who does not insist on determinism? (Leupp 1996, 85).

Recognizing God in history

God works in every community's history determining times set for them and the exact places where they should live. God did this so that men and women "would seek him and perhaps reach out for him and find him" (Acts 17:27). The history of a people is a sign pointing to God, if we have eyes to see.

This directly contradicts the way history is normally perceived by the poor. They see themselves as being on the sidelines of both history-making and the telling of history. Helping the poor to learn to read their own history and to find their place and that of God in it is a transformational frontier and an opportunity for Christian witness. We need to teach them "to re-read their history with God as the point of reference" (Christian 1998a, 9). Christian calls this "drawing the portrait of Christ in their history."

Thus we can use our development processes as a way to help people draw closer to God by recognizing God's work in their past. One of the results of tools like Appreciative Inquiry and PLAs is that people can come to recognize the successes and the life-creating occurrences in their history. It is a short step to connect these instances with the activity and character of a loving and involved God: "In the past God spoke to our forefathers through the prophets at many times and in various ways" (Heb 1:1).

Recognizing God in creation

Psalm 104 provides a magnificent metaphor for helping us recognize God's work in creation. All the verbs relating to God are active: he stretches out the heavens, makes the winds, and covers the earth with water, setting its boundaries. God speaks and directs while the creation responds. This activity results in an ecosystem in which water is provided to the beasts of the field and birds have habitation. And all of this is so that human beings may thrive:

> He makes grass grow for the cattle,
> and plants for man to cultivate—
> bringing forth food from the earth,
> wine that gladdens the heart of man,
> oil to make his face shine
> and bread that sustains his heart (Ps 104:14-15).

Sadly, much of the Western world—and most development professionals—does not use this kind of a lens when we read nature. We assign the creative part to evolution, the ecosystem to science, and take over the responsibility for the parts about being glad, having shining faces, and producing the bread. We no longer need God as part of the explanation.

It does not have to be this way. Christians could work to recover this kind of metaphor for making sense out of the world. We might get some help from traditional cultures if we had the humility to listen. Their worldview is very close to Psalm 104. The only issue of difference is the name of the God who is active in creation and whether or not he had a son who died on a hill in Palestine over two thousand years ago.

Recomposing the program

One way to enhance the range of our witness is to reexamine all those parts of development programming that we may have assumed were without spiritual character. Once we begin to look for biblical metaphors and values in the routine, we will be surprised at the opportunities that we have overlooked.

For example, most programs call for a program agreement, stating what the agency will do and what the community will do. A simple, normal part of development administration. One inspired program manager in Senegal realized there was potentially something more. He realized that both Muslims and Christians are familiar with the biblical concept of covenant. The program agreement was transformed into a covenant between the people, the agency, and God. Old Testament language was deliberately employed and a covenant was written to say that the village would bring what it had, the agency what it had, and, when and if the well drilling was successful, God would be thanked. A simple piece of paper had been transformed. It was not just culturally more appropriate. God's activity and an occasion for praising God had been uncovered. There was now space to recognize the glory of God active in the world.

There is a wide range of other possibilities. The Greek words for salvation and healing are the same. This creates opportunities to reinterpret health-care interventions. Creation theology, agricultural practices, and environmental friendliness make natural partners. The same is true of micro-enterprise development and the biblical idea of being productive stewards; the prophetic literature even adds the social responsibility element that the worshipers of the unfettered free market cannot provide.

Seeking meaning together

Why are things this way? How do we explain success? Failure? Unexpected outcomes? What does this means? These questions always take us to heart issues. They move us beyond the surface of PLA results and capability and vulnerability exercises and raise the truly transformational issues of meaning and purpose.

When the results were posted of the ten-seeds exercise I described in Chapter 7, the tribal people had shown how little power they felt they had over income, health, roads, and food. They felt that most of the control over these areas of their lives belonged to outsiders and the spirit world. While this was very helpful to know, the more important question was *why* they believe this is the way things are. What explanation could they give for why they had so little control over their world? They responded with the epic story of their origins as a people (Myers 1998a).

It seems that Krishna was undertaking a meditative process by which he hoped to surrender all desire. A rival god was concerned that, were Krishna successful, he would gain favor. So he sent a beautiful woman to distract Krishna. The ploy worked, and the result was a dark-skinned son with thick lips, the image of this tribal group. A reminder of a failed spiritual exercise, the son remained in Krishna's household. Then this unwanted son accidentally caused the death of Krishna's favorite bull. Furious, Krishna banished the child. This, the tribal group explained, was why they had left the Himalayas and moved into what is now India.

The tribal group understood itself as a cursed people. This was the story of their origins. They had always been cursed. This was why the gods and spirits were so unkind. This was why the government was not interested in them and would not rebuild the road. This was why they were poor, marginalized, and frequently oppressed. This was why the tribal group believed it was less than human. It had been ordained from the time of the first member of their race.

Once again we encounter poverty of being and the deception of a distorted view of history. The very mythic origins of the people, the core of their self-understanding and worldview, validates, even mandates, their continuing poverty. Even their successes are coopted by this story. When asked why good things happen, they explained that their sacrifices and prayers occasionally worked, but that the curse held sway most of the time.

This discovery—triggered by asking questions about meaning—changed the development conversation in a radical way. While wells, improved agriculture, immunizations, and schools were still needed, they were not enough. Why? Doing development without understanding this story would lead to development that is neither sustainable nor Christian. Every success will be interpreted as the result of effective prayers or sacrifices. Every setback will confirm the truth of the curse account. The fact that we are Christian is irrelevant to their explanation of the events. We are simply incorporated into the tribal group's view of how the world works.

This kind of discovery demands an engagement about stories. This tribal group will only be transformed if it is able or is enabled to recompose the story of its origins. How do stories get recomposed? It is the right question, but it is a hard one to answer.

We get a hint in the story of every personal conversion. My story was recomposed when I became a Christian. From the day Jesus became my Lord, I told my personal story in a different way. The facts did not change, of course. I was born on the same date, had the same parents, and went to the same schools. But the meaning I give to the events in my life was transformed by my encounter with the gospel. I now tell my story in a different way.

An encounter with the true author of everyone's story is the only answer I can think of for the tribal group. Only the transforming power of the God who created the tribal group can empower it by rewriting its story. Its story, as its members now understand it, has truth in it. But it is still fundamentally a lie. The tribal group has been deceived, and this deception is the most fundamental cause of the people's poverty. At this level the tribal group's material and spiritual poverty have the same foundational cause: deception, the work of the devil. The truth and power of the gospel are the only way to transformation.

This is easy to say and yet seems very hard to bring about. Too often evangelism and Christian discipleship result in the Christian story being laid on top of the traditional story of a culture. As long as it is possible to live the Christian story and the traditional story at the same time, everything is fine. The problem comes when the two stories come into conflict. Too often, it seems, the traditional story wins out.

The United States is a good example. The great majority of people identify themselves as Christian. Over 40 percent attend church regularly. Yet, research shows that in behavioral terms, Christians are indistinguishable from non-Christians. As long as the Christian story and the American story are consistent, people are good Christians (and good Americans). When they are in conflict, they tend to act like good Americans.

This hierarchy of stories is reflected widely. African Christian leaders have complained that their congregations go to doctors (the modern story) and ask for prayers of healing (the Christian story), and, if these are not effective, consult traditional shamans (the African story) at night. In Bosnia the ethnic story is more powerful than the religious story of the Orthodox, Catholics, and Muslims. In Rwanda the tribal story won out over the Christian story, when the ethnic card was callously played by those seeking power.

Interpreting technology with God in the picture

Development technology carries a message. When children cease to die or agricultural production doubles, these "miracles" demand an explanation. The explanation usually comes either from the traditional worldview of the people or from the scientific worldview of the development facilitator. Neither points to the God of the Bible.

This is not a new problem. Acts 14 recounts that while preaching, Paul sees a man who had been lame from birth. Paul directs the man to stand up, and the man is healed. There are no words from Paul to explain how the healing took place. So the people provide their own explanation and announce that "the gods have come down to us in human form" (Acts 14:11). The people then, quite appropriately, set out to organize the required sacrifices and worship. Only then does Paul realize the mistake he has made and scrambles to explain that "we too are only men, human like you" (Acts 14:15), going on to explain whose miracle it really is.

Lesslie Newbigin has alerted us to an interesting pattern in the gospels. In the long sections of teaching in the gospel of John, most of his teaching is explanatory of something Jesus has done: healing the paralytic, feeding the multitude, giving sight to the blind man, raising a man from the dead. This link between words and deeds is also evident in the sending of the twelve in Matthew. The disciples were sent to cast out demons and heal every disease, and only then, Jesus said, were they to say that the kingdom of heaven is at hand. The preaching of the good news is an explanation of the healings. Newbigin observes that, as marvelous as they were, healings do not explain themselves. They could be misinterpreted—as in fact they were by Jesus' enemies, who attributed his works to Satanic power. "Healings, even the most wonderful, do not call this present world radically into question; the gospel does, and this has to be made explicit" (Newbigin 1989, 132).

The critical question is how to interpret development technology so that it is understood as evidence of the work and character of a loving, engaged God rather than setting itself up as the explanation of its own success. To answer this question, we need to understand what technology is for and whence it comes.[5]

Technology is good, but a limited good. While technology has made things efficient and has greatly sped up the rate of change in the material world, there are too many things that technology cannot do. Wolterstorff, in his discussion of shalom, points out that technology does help us toward shalom in terms of our relationship with nature, but it cannot help us create shalom within ourselves, with God, or between ourselves and our neighbors. Even when technology works in our relationship with nature, technology is a double-edged sword; it can make life easier or it can be used to kill our neighbor (Wolterstorff 1983, 71). Science cannot create and does not operate within a vision of what ought to be (Shenk 1993, 67).

So what is technology for? Lynn White points out that in the twelfth century Hugh of St. Victor described tools as a search for a remedy, a kind of penitential activity, to make the effects of sin a little less unpleasant by reducing cold, hunger, and weakness (White 1978, 13). By the end of the Middle Ages this understanding of technology found its full expression:

> The chief glory of the later Middle Ages was not its cathedrals or its epics or its scholasticism: it was the building for the first time in hu-

man history of a complex civilization which rested not on the backs of sweating slaves and coolies but primarily on non-human power (ibid., 22).

Francis Bacon, the catalyst of the end of Scholasticism and the beginning of the era of the natural sciences, criticized any philosophical endeavor that did not directly lead to the improvement of the life of human beings. In their origins, science and technology were human-centered and life enhancing, characteristics of the grace of God in human history.

It is only in more recent times that this understanding of technology has become distorted and has begun deceiving us. Technology has become self-justifying and an end in itself. Today, technology speaks only of power, of offering convenience, efficiency, and prosperity. Yet technology is a jealous god. Those who follow it must "shape their needs and aspirations to the possibilities of technology" (Postman 1997, 31). Worshiping any other god or any other good means slowing down or frustrating the benefits of technology. This modern technological god is a false god and worshiping it is idolatry. "Idolatry defrauds God, denying him of his proper honors and conferring them upon others" (Koyama 1985, 48). And this is precisely what we have seen happen when development technology works its "magic" in poor communities. Therefore, when we share development technology with poor communities, we must insist on asking if we are inadvertently promoting idolatry. Are we guilty of helping people exchange "their Glory [God] for an image of a bull, which eats grass" (Ps 106:20)?

The Christian interpretative words for explaining technology's good deeds begins with the obvious: "What do you have that you did not receive? And if you did receive it, why do you boast as though you did not?" (1 Cor 4:7). The human discovery of tools and technology is a direct result of an order-making God, who made a universe that operates within a framework of physical and moral laws. Furthermore, this God made human beings in God's own image, thus enabling them to discover how the world works. God granted us the ability to be creative, just as God was and is.

The issue of explaining God at work in nature has proven to be a difficult one. The intellectual challenge is to balance the need to acknowledge God's sovereignty with the fact that an object must fall to the ground every time, unless something prevents it. God must be God, and gravity must be gravity. Both must be true at the same time.

This creates two dilemmas. First, if the laws of science are laws, then God must keep them, and this seems to limit God's sovereignty and preclude miracles. This places God outside God's creation, with no room to act within created processes. Second, and equally serious, we cannot postulate that God is in control of every outcome since this (a) denies the possibility of human freedom, (b) provides no explanation for randomness, and (c) makes God responsible for evil, pain, and injustice.

Nancey Murphy has struggled with the issue of creating an account of divine action in nature that is consistent with Christian doctrines and yet also consistent with what we know about science (Murphy 1995). God sustains creation, governs nature, and cooperates with nature. Yet, based on our understanding of Jesus, God does this non-coercively, granting human freedom even if it means rejecting God or ignoring science.

Murphy accounts for this by noting the difference between physics at the human level in contrast to physics at the quantum level. Physics at the macro-level is governed by deterministic laws. If one drops a ball, it will fall to the earth every time. At the quantum level, however, physics works differently; probabilities rule. This upset Einstein so much that he fought quantum physics for years: "God does not play dice," he asserted. Einstein was right—and wrong.

The absence of determinism at the quantum level does not mean complete randomness or that nature is not governed by mathematical equations. The way out of this seeming dilemma arose with the emergence of the mathematics of dynamical systems, popularly referred to as chaos theory, that demonstrates that we can have deep order without determinism.[6] It is at the quantum level that Murphy postulates that we are free to make the claim that "all events are a result of God's causal influence" without having to set aside the determinism of the macro-physical world (1995, 354). At the quantum level, divine will and natural causation are no longer opposing acts.

By analogy we can apply this to the real world of human beings. Joseph acknowledges God's intentions when he recomposes his story on the occasion of confessing his identity to his brothers. He gives the historical account—the choice his brothers made to get rid of him—and the divine account—God sent me here to save lives (Gn 50:19).

Say what you believe

In his captivating account of his work among the Masai, Vincent Donovan tells the story of the Catholic mission strategy in Tanzania, with its school, mission hospital, and work to improve the Masai cattle. By caring for the Masai in concrete terms, mission by deed, some would come to faith in time, the argument went. The Masai were not to ready for direct verbal witness.

After several years of seeing no results, Donovan wrote to his bishop, announcing his intention to go out to Masai villages and do nothing but talk to them about his faith. A Masai elder asked Donovan his reason for wanting to talk to the elders. "You know us for our work among you in schools and the hospital. But I no longer want to talk about schools and hospitals, but about God in the life of the Masai." The response was immediate, "If this is why you came here, why did you wait so long to tell us about this?" (Donovan 1978, 22).

Sometimes Christians doing the work of transformational development are hesitant in talking about their Christian beliefs. Even people committed to Christian witness are reluctant witnesses for good reasons. Respecting the development process is important to them, and they do not want to witness in a way that undermines this important value. In addition, there is the danger of taking advantage of the implicit power relationship that invariably accompanies attempts to help the poor.

Sensitivity is a good thing, but making ourselves silent is not. In West Africa local Muslims criticized Christian facilitators for lacking spirituality because they were so reluctant to talk about their faith. In a personal interview in 1997 Nora Avarientos wisely counseled, "Don't put up your own ghosts. Speak what you believe!" This is a call for conversation, not monologues. The story of Jesus and the woman in John 4 suggests that treating people as equals and having provocative, stretching, engaging conversations about ultimate things are often valued and transformational.

THE BIBLE AND TRANSFORMATIONAL DEVELOPMENT

Why the Bible is important

I suggest that the narrative context of transformational development is the convergence of stories. The story of the community is joined by the story of the development facilitator and, for the duration of the program, they share a story. God has been and is at work in both stories and God is offering to both a better future story. This means that the biblical story must become an integral part of the transformational development process. Furthermore, the goals of transformation that I have suggested—recovering true identity and discovering true vocation—are derived from the biblical story and are the goals for both the community and the development facilitator. Seeking the truth from the biblical story is the beginning of transformation in our lives and our relationships. Therefore, engaging the biblical story must be central to the practice of transformational development done by Christians. This claim deserves a few clarifications.

First, as the word of God the Bible is the only true and unbiased source of guidance to the goals and means of human transformation. The Bible calls into account every other account of the human story—our account, the account of ideologies, of science and modernity, of every culture. The Bible is the one normative source that stands on its own and speaks for itself, as long as we let it. People do not have to believe Christians. God has spoken, and God's word is available to everyone.

Second, the Bible is not simply a book. It is a living word. An encounter with the Bible provides the possibility of an encounter with the One who knows us, the One who knows our past, our present, and our future. An engagement with the Bible sheds its own light, celebrating life and resisting anti-life, regardless of its location. Andrew Walls reminds us that the Bible is "a dynamic, developing, growing, creative factor in the mind; ever fresh, ever bringing out new things, never getting stuck in the past, never getting stale or out of date" (1996, 50).

The Bible is the only book that Christians believe stands in a privileged position over every human being. Hans-Ruedi Weber tells the story of a village woman in East Africa who walked around her village carrying a Bible. "Why always the Bible?" her neighbors asked teasingly. "There are lots of other books you could read." Speaking with authority, the woman replied, "Yes, of course, there are many books which I could read. But there is only one book which reads me" (Weber 1995, ix).

Third, the word of God is a creative word. God's word brought order to chaos, according to Genesis. Thus we must release God's creative word to bring order into our lives and the life of the community. Hope is found in the fact that the word of God is not constrained by the context in which it is heard.

Fourth, the word of God is the birthplace of our identity. We can be children of God "through the living and enduring word of God" (1 Pt 1:23). And the word of God gives us our place in our community (1 Pt 2:10).

Finally, for the Christian, the Bible is universal history (Newbigin 1989, 89). Unlike any other sacred book, the Bible speaks of human life in the context of cosmic history from creation to consummation. In spite of the particularity of Israel, and the even greater particularity of Jesus, the Bible is the account of everyone's past and everyone's future. To those who live within its story in faith, the Bible will create what Peter Berger calls a "plausibility structure," the biblical worldview, that provides a coherent and consistent framework for creating meaning in and providing explanation about the world in which we live.

How the Bible must be used

In order for the biblical story to be what I have just described, we must take note of some important conditions in terms of how the story is used. The challenge is the same as the one I described earlier in this chapter about matching our approach to Christian witness to the principles we've established for the transformational development process. "Go and tell" evangelism and participatory, grassroots-driven development simply are not consistent methodologies. This drove us to the "provoking the question" framework for Christian witness as a better fit.

The same is true for how we use the Bible. The "study, preach, and teach" frameworks of the expository preacher or the theological teacher are "outsider" methodologies in which experts provide the knowledge that the non-experts do not have.[7] Like "go and tell" Christian witness, this contradicts the principles of local ownership, local direction, and the idea that the responsibility for development, including spiritual development, belongs to the people and not to us. The challenge is to find ways of using the Bible in human and social transformation that place the responsibility for asking questions and seeking answers within the community itself.

There are two ways to think about using the Bible in a way that better suits the bottom-up framework of transformational development. The first is a product of what I have said about the ownership of the development process, and the second is a reaction to the way some Christians use (or misuse) the biblical story.

First, the issue of ownership. Since the development process must belong to and be controlled and directed by those who are seeking transformation, it follows that they are the ones who must engage and find their own answers and place in the biblical story. They need to discover for themselves that God has made them in God's image and that they have been given gifts and are expected to be productive stewards. They need to find for themselves the story that explains relationships that do not work for life and learn that God has provided a means for their restoration. After all, the Bible needs to be their story, not just ours.

Second, there is the issue of how some Christians use the Bible. We need to be aware of and work against some serious shortcomings. The first is the tendency of some Christians to assume that, since the Bible is about spiritual things, then the domain to which the Bible speaks is only the spiritual realm. This results in the Bible being used solely for personal discipleship, worship, and nurture of the soul. While this is good and proper, it unwittingly precludes the Bible from speaking to the material world of science and development. The Bible lies trapped in Sunday Schools, churches, and Bible study groups, where Christians use it for spiritual development. Our first challenge is to free the Bible from its spiritual captivity and allow it to engage and speak to the whole of human life.

The second limitation in terms of how Christians use the Bible is our temptation to use it in a way that "handles" or domesticates the Bible, thus making it our word instead of God's word. Especially in this modern world, we tend to assume the vantage point of the evaluator, the one who always does the examining. We too often speak for the Bible rather than letting it speak for itself. We must always ask whether we are being the servants or the lords of Scripture.

The third limitation is our tendency to treat the Bible solely as a text of inestimable utilitarian value. Such a view objectifies the text and works against the idea of the Bible being the living word of a living God, a God who might like to have a word with us. Engaging God's word in the right way with the right spirit might lead to a personal encounter with the One whose word it is.[8]

Part of the answer to overcoming these limitations is to avoid understanding the biblical text as we would a textbook. We must learn to go beyond studying the Bible solely in order to report what we have learned to others, since this is speaking for the text. We need to be willing to go beyond studying the Bible in order to select what we think is useful for what we want to do, since this is using and almost certainly limiting the text. When we stand outside the text and look into it as a resource from which we pick and choose, we are putting ourselves above the text. This stance is exemplified both by historical criticism and by those who favor proof-texting as a tool of persuasion.

The East African village lady is right. We must live within the text, allowing it to read us, to examine us, to bring life to us, perhaps even to personally encounter us. We must learn, and the people with whom we work must learn, to use the biblical text as an interpretive lens and as a possible meeting place with God.

Newbigin talks of "indwelling" the biblical story. When we dwell within the story, the story has the final say and the storyteller has an opportunity to say hello to us. Indwelling the story means living with the text in such a way that we, and those with whom we work, come to experience the story as fundamentally about us, about the poor and the non-poor (Middleton and Walsh 1995, 175).

> *We* are the people whom God liberated from Egypt and led through the Red Sea; *we* are the people languishing in exile and crying out for release; *we* are the disciples whom Jesus rebuked for misunderstanding his mission and to whom he appeared after his resurrection; *we* are the newly formed church who received the outpouring of the Spirit at Pentecost.

This framework of living within the biblical story and letting it speak for itself is the key to releasing the transformative power of the Bible as the normative story, the story that makes sense out of all other stories.

This is a whole new kind of Bible for many of us. We have to learn to set aside our own understanding of Scripture and allow the living word of the living God to say what it will, to us as well as to the community. Brueggemann says that "our situation needs to be submitted to the text for fresh discernment. . . . In every generation, this text subverts all our old readings of reality and forces us to new, dangerous, obedient reading" (1993b, 18-25). It is in this sense of letting the word of God speak its own word of transformation that I believe that the Bible must be applied within a Christian understanding of transformational development.

Experiences with the Bible and transformational development

Using the Bible as a tool for transformation in the development process is a fairly recent experience for Protestants. Allowing lay leaders to lead open-ended inquiries into the biblical story as it applies to the whole of life is something new. We are often more comfortable with the experts telling us what the Bible says or means. Even the phrase "Bible study" is assumed often to mean that someone, who is trained, teaches us, who have not been trained. We have delegated the responsibility for our own learning to pastors and the theologically trained, becoming passive recipients of their view of what the Bible says.

This section describes two emerging experiences that are searching for a new way to allow God and the Bible to speak for themselves in the development process. The first is the Scripture Search methodology of World Vision Philippines. The second is the Seven Steps method of the Lumko Institute in South Africa, a method currently being tested in World Vision programs in Latin America. I will close with a brief description of the "storying the gospel" approach of New Tribes Mission, which has the potential, if made more holistic, to contribute to the use of the Bible in Christian witness in the context of transformational development.

Scripture Search

The Scripture Search use of the Bible in transformational development[9] assumes the Bible is less a source of rules or a conceptual foundation and more of a creative encounter with God and the story God has chosen to tell us. If we will let it, "Scripture breathes hope, life, dynamism and immense possibilities beyond human imagination" (Alvarez et al. 1999). The Scripture Search process extends the traditional Protestant use and scope of the Bible in the following ways:

Traditional Protestant use of the Bible	Scripture Search use of the Bible
Primarily addressed to the individual	Primarily addressed to the community
Primarily about spiritual things	About all spheres of life, including the spiritual
Primarily about the world to come	Primarily about this world, and by extension, the world to come
Primarily written from the divine point of view	Primarily written from the divine point of view, but includes the view of the "least of these"

Figure 8-1: Scripture Search use of the Bible.
(Developed from Alvarez et al. 1999)

This framework is intended to help get past the spiritual captivity of the Bible that I described earlier. It allows the Bible to speak to issues of private and public morality, to Monday through Saturday, as well as Sunday, and to the work of the church as well as the work of the NGO.

In using the Bible in the communities, World Vision Philippines operates under the following assumptions:

- God is already at work in the community.
- Members of the community have accumulated a great deal of wisdom about all areas of life, including spiritual perspectives on life.
- The community is solely responsible for its own spiritual pilgrimage.
- People in community are capable of making their own application of spiritual truth to their local situation.
- The local churches have the major responsibility for contributing to the spiritual nurture of the community and hence Scripture Search is non-proselytizing.[10]

Scripture Search is done as part of an action-reflection-action process by which the community guides its own development. It is done by the same community group that is organizing and carrying out the other development activities. Working within this learning cycle, the Bible is used to illumine the past and guide the future. The Bible is used as a resource for the community's ongoing dialogue regarding commitments, values, beliefs, and traditions of the community, all of which affect the possibilities of the development program in positive or negative ways. Used in this way, searching the Scripture is not something isolated and separate but part of the normal development processes.

The Scripture Search methodology is a simple two-step process. First, a facilitator comes to a community meeting prepared with a Scripture reading, usually a story or a parable, for use during the reflection period when experience-sharing is at a high point.[11] The selection is based on issues the community is facing. The story or verses are handled like a case study, with open-ended questions. Preaching or teaching from the text is discouraged.

Second, it is up to the people themselves to discover the relevance of the text in their lives in light of the issues with which the group is struggling. Facilitators use a variety of non-directive methods to encourage wide participation and to draw out insights. Three questions tend to be used in most settings:

- What are the similarities between what is happening in this text and your experience now? (This encourages contextualization.)
- What light does this text and the experience of the people in it shed on your experience today? (This leads to prayerful reflection.)
- What do you think you should do about these insights as a group and personally? (This leads to actualization and results in a contribution to new plans that trigger the next action-reflection-action process.)

In the decade that World Vision Philippines has been developing this tool, staff members have seen both personal and social change emerge as a result. People report that their relationship with God has deepened, that their relationships with their spouse and children have improved, and that they are more deeply committed to serving their community than before. Community leaders report gaining confidence in leading the community. Because this process is done in community by lay people, it has proven highly effective in allowing Protestants and Roman Catholics to develop relationships and work together. This has translated into formal cooperation between Protestant World Vision and a variety of Catholic institutions concerned for spiritual formation.

As a result of their experience with Scripture Search, World Vision Philippines and the communities with which it works report discovering the Bible in a whole new way. "We have rediscovered the Bible as a powerful story explaining the meaning and purpose of life, full of cases that model abundance, reconciliation, forgiveness, transformation of persons, communities, nations and nature itself" (Alvarez et al. 1999).

The Seven Steps

Scripture Search is a life-to-Bible approach for using the Bible in a community setting. The Seven Steps approach, on the other hand, has a Bible-to-life orientation.[12] Both have their roots in the creative work of the Lumko Institute in South Africa, a lay Catholic institute that has been developing tools for the pastoral use of the Bible since the 1960s. The Seven Steps method has recently begun to be tested in World Vision programming in parts of Latin America.[13]

The Seven Steps is more a method of Bible reading, and less one of Bible study (Alvarez et al. 1999). The emphasis is on group listening and receiving, not on the left-brain work of determining meaning. The focus is on what God is saying to me (or us)—on sharing and hearing, not discussing and deciding. While this may sound open-ended in the

---

The Seven Steps

1. Invite
We remind ourselves that the Risen Lord is with us. Would someone like to welcome Jesus in a prayer?

2. Read
Let us open our Bibles to . . .

3. View with wonder
We pick our word or short phrases, read them aloud prayerfully, allowing enough silence between them to say the words three times in our hearts.

4. Listen
We keep silence for ___ minutes and allow God to speak to us.

5. Share
Which word or phrase has touched us personally? (Do not discuss any contribution.)

6. Group tasks
Now we discuss any task or work our group is called to do and report back on our previous task What new task needs to be done? Who will do what and when?

7. Pray
Anyone who wishes may pray spontaneously. We close with a hymn, chorus, or prayer that everyone knows.

Figure 8-2: The Seven Steps.

extreme, the practice of patient listening can translate into increasing the capacity for people to address program concerns within a climate of peace and receptivity. Thus Seven Steps is a counterpoint to Scripture Search, not simply a variation.

Like Scripture Search, Seven Steps takes place in small groups, usually the groups that are part of the development process. Its effectiveness is enhanced when the same people are in each meeting. Because it is based on listening to the spoken word, it can be used with people who cannot read. The texts that seem to work best are taken from the gospels and the psalms.

The facilitator of the Seven Steps process follows the outline shown in Figure 8-2. Each of the steps is carried out in a particular way. When the text is *read* aloud, the facilitator waits until people have found the text, because participation of every person is important. *View with wonder* means letting the word or phrase come to us. We are listening for God's word to us. *Listen* means just that, silent listening, enjoying Christ's presence with us. This is not a time for active prayer. *Share* is when people may speak, saying the word or phrase that has come to them and briefly sharing how it has illumined their life. The group listens and does not respond. This is not a time for discussion, teaching, or preaching. During *group tasks* the group becomes more verbal, moving from the Bible to life. Any issue relating to the work of the group or the program may arise. This is the reflection step of an action-reflection-action cycle, reporting back and planning ahead. While the text read aloud most often will not be linked thematically to the work at hand, "the practice of careful listening in the previous steps characteristically influences the way the participants approach their tasks and their relationships with each other" (Alvarez et al. 1999).

The results have been encouraging. Better team work, more inclusive participation in project work, and reconciliation, especially between Catholics and Protestants, have been reported. Many report deepening of their relationships with God and increased participation in local churches.

There have been some challenges to using this method, largely because listening to the text rather than mining it for meaning is a significant change for many Protestants. In many contexts the normative way of using the Bible is authoritarian. Someone in authority, a pastor or the development facilitator, tells everyone else what the text says and means. This tends to cause the group to rush through to step 5, when the talking can begin, and to step 6, when the reporting and planning take place. But the effectiveness of this method comes down to the skill of the facilitator and the willingness of the group to open itself to something new. It is very hard to shift from a framework of how we can use Scripture to one that allows Scripture to use us.

Storying the gospel

Scripture Search and the Seven Steps are helpful tools for engaging the Bible in relationship to life issues, values, priorities, and ordering relationships. Because they focus on a single text, however, they are less helpful in communicating the biblical story as a whole. Yet, as I have attempted to make clear, engaging the whole biblical story is foundational to how the story of the community and our story come under the transforming power of God's only true story. Storying the gospel is an approach that, if modified to fit better the context of transformational development, holds promise in this regard.

Storying the gospel was developed by Trevor McIlwain of New Tribes Mission as an evangelism tool for preliterate people. McIlwain noted that traditional people had trouble understanding and relating to the gospel story. The problem was more than simply the unfamiliar geographical and cultural roots of the gospel story. Preliterate people rely on epic stories and poems to tell the story of their culture and pass on its values. They rely on their story as a people to create meaning for today. Hearing the Jesus story, disconnected from the whole story of the biblical people, was hard to understand. There was no foundation for understanding the Jesus story, when it was told without reference to its origins or its future. Without hearing the whole of the biblical story, the listener may not know that there is only one God or understand the character of the God about whom we are talking. Without the whole story, how can people understand what God intends, or how everything came to be as we experience it today? Obedience, sin, grace, and faith are hard to understand apart from the story that gives them their particular Christian meaning.

McIlwain decided to resequence the biblical account so that it could be told as an epic story, beginning with creation in Genesis and ending with the second coming of Christ in Revelation. The result is a chronological teaching outline that tells the whole salvation story so that it builds a foundation on which a person, who has never heard of Jesus or of Israel or been to a city, can say with understanding, "Yes, I believe." McIlwain understood that it is the whole of our story as Christians that reveals the character and activity of the God of the Bible in human history. "The story of Christ begins in the first verse in Genesis" (McIlwain 1991, 32). If telling the whole biblical story is foundational to understanding the Jesus story and making an informed faith decision, no one should be invited to make such a decision until he or she has heard the whole story. In this sense, discipleship begins before the evangelistic act itself.

This approach is attractive to the transformational development process. As techniques like PLA and Appreciative Inquiry give the community the opportunity to share its story and to articulate what gives it life and meaning, the question usually comes back: "And you? What do you believe? What gives you life?" McIlwain's framework suggests a different response than simply saying that we are Christian or followers of Jesus Christ. We could, instead, share the epic story of our people, the biblical story. Sharing the whole story puts us in the position of addressing many of the issues that are contributing to the poverty we wish to transform—marred identity, inadequate worldview, oppressive relationships, fear of the spirit world, god-complexes, and the like. By telling our whole story we can address the issues of all human beings: Who are we? What are we for?

As I introduced storying the gospel, I alluded to a need for modification. As presented in the training materials and books, this method focuses solely on the issue of personal salvation and the Bible as the story of God's salvific work in history. While this is certainly true, it is not enough. Part of the story is left out. After all, God's story is about more than saving souls. The biblical account has a more holistic view of salvation, seeking the restoration by grace alone of our relationships with God, with each other, and with God's creation. While personal salvation through faith in Christ is the center of God's concern, it is not the limit of God's concern. If the chronological story of the Bible were made less narrow, so that God's concern for people as productive stewards living in just and peaceful relationships could emerge alongside God's concern for people living in right relationship with God, then we would have the full story in play.

THE FOCUS AND EVALUATION OF CHRISTIAN WITNESS

As we think about Christian witness in the context of transformational development, we need to remind ourselves of what the scope of that witness entails. We need to keep our hopes for transformation clearly in mind so that the way we witness, the content of our witness, and the way we use the Bible address the important transformational frontiers. Jayakumar Christian's proposal for understanding the fundamental spiritual causes of poverty helps us here.

Getting the focus of our witness clear will also inform our approach to evaluation, making it more holistic. The scope of our witness to the good news of the gospel will add new questions to the evaluation frame proposed in the last chapter. As I develop the scope of Christian witness below, the evaluator of transformational development should be asking this question: How can this be assessed or measured?[14]

Recovering identity and vocation

Recovering identity and discovering vocation are the twin goals of transformation. Everything else follows. Therefore, our Christian witness must address the issues of identity and vocation. This is not always easy, since one of the outcomes of poverty is an identity so marred that believing one is a child of God is like being asked to believe that one can fly. The first step is to treat people as if we believe they are made in the image of God and are as worthy of respect as anyone. How we treat and listen to the poor can be the beginning of recovering identity.

Another non-directive way to encourage recovery of identity and discovery of vocation is to encourage people to pursue their own investigation of the biblical story. Allow them to find themselves in the story and to hear the good news that their current story is not wholly true and that there is an Evil One who wants them to believe that they are god-forsaken. In a small Assemblies of God school in Central America, a boy was asked what he liked best about the school schedule. "The Bible study," he replied. Surprised, the researcher asked about meals, sports, and leather craft. "No, the best is the Bible study." When asked why, the little boy replied, "I am no longer a thief or someone who begs in the street. I am a child of God" (Dyrness 1998, 39). Learning who we really are is good news!

We can also help people recover their history and tell their own story as a way of recovering identity. Using PLA and Appreciative Inquiry can help people name what has been successful and what has created value in their past. Reading this positive side of their history alongside the Bible can lead to people linking their story to the biblical story, seeing where their account is true and where it is false. This way their chronological past becomes their "ontological" past (Bediako 1992, 4). Remember the story of the tribal people who believe they have always been cursed by God? We can barely imagine the joy and release of energy they would experience if they were able to discover for themselves that their story is true, in the sense that all people live under the curse of sin, but false in that this curse does not have the final say. In Jesus, God has provided for the lifting of their curse. The statement that they are a cursed people is a lie.

We must also witness to the non-poor concerning identity and vocation. We need to help the non-poor explore and identify their own poverty, to get in touch with what happens when one confuses being with having, or serving with power and control. The non-poor also need to read their story against the story of the Bible. The Bible has good news for them, too, even though they tend to find this hard to believe. The problem for the non-poor is that the cost of being who they really are and doing what they were meant to do is too high. Surrendering god-complexes and using human skill, the power of position, and financial resources like a servant is very hard indeed. This is why the rich young man walked away (Mt 19:16-22).

Just and peaceful relationships

True transformation occurs when people know their identity and their vocation and live in just and peaceful relationships. I have already explained the fivefold nature of these relationships: relationship with God, self, community, "other," and the environment. Christian witness within the context of transformational development must witness to Christ's lordship over all of these relationships and to his intention that being part of his kingdom means seeking justice and peace.

For the poor, our witness will include helping them find their voice and place. Once the poor begin to discover their true identity and vocation, they need to give expression to each. This change takes place at several levels. First, within the household. In Latin America, it is well known that spiritually changed lives lead to the reduction of alcohol consumption, treating drug addicts, reestablishing released prisoners, and kindling the imagination of students (Maldonado 1993, 196). When women believe the gospel in Colombia, the way they act and witness leads to the erosion of the *machismo* culture of the men. This means less drinking and womanizing, which in turn means more surplus money. The women invest this surplus in micro-enterprise, and the household income increases (Brusco 1986). This is transformational development at its best; we cannot tell where the spiritual and material change begin and end.

The second level is the social system. People who have discovered that they are children of God, with value and voice, are less likely to be passive in the face of political structures that see the poor only as votes. Evidence from area development programs in Tanzania, India, and elsewhere suggests that such people begin to demand that services due them are delivered and that politicians take them and their views more seriously. When people change, everything else comes under pressure to change (Rosenau 1990). In these ways holistic Christian witness addresses social, political, economic, and cultural relationships, calling into account those that inhibit life or limit the participation of the poor.

For the non-poor, Christian witness must include an invitation to lay down their god-complexes and to turn over to God those roles that are rightfully God's. Christian witness means a call to exercise leadership as stewards who think more highly of others than themselves. Leaders with a biblical worldview know that all power belongs to God and that they exercise power only as stewards, not as owners or masters. Of those who have more, more is expected.

Changing worldview

One of the sources of the web of lies that disempowers the poor and entices the non-poor to play god in the lives of the poor is worldview. This is why changing worldview must be a focus of Christian witness. However, to say that changing worldview is hard is not to say enough. Allowing the biblical story to truly transform any cultural story is difficult in the extreme. Getting a tribal group that believes it is cursed to transform that belief and view itself as a group of people whom God wants to bless is the most difficult of transformational frontiers.

Changing worldview means more than changing behavior. It is even more than changing beliefs or values. Changing a worldview means changing a people's entire story so that the community adopts a new story. This can be only done by a people, not by individuals. While changing the worldview of a people must be a goal of discipleship, it is the work of the Holy Spirit of God.

Some have argued that no culture can evangelize or change its own story. The community cannot see its flat spots and idolatries, and neither can we. Both have the need to see and correct inadequacies in worldview; this is their common task. Another way of saying this is to note that there is no difference between the evangelist and the disciple when it comes to worldview. Both are learning the gospel at the foot of the cross (Koyama 1985, 245). This is why is it so important that the development facilitator be open to and undergoing transformation even as he or she works to help the community experience transformation.

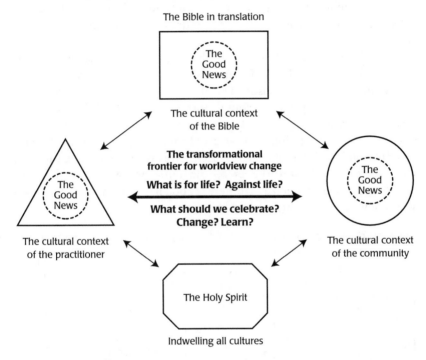

Figure 8-3: Helping each other change worldview.

Worldview change requires a two-way dialogue between the two cultures, with both open to the prompting and teaching of the Holy Spirit and the will to surrender themselves to the worldview contained in the Bible.[15] Each carrier of a culture brings to the table the ability to help the other culture see what needs changing. Each has things in its own culture that need changing.

Christian witness and changing worldview take us to the basic beliefs that create meaning and explain why things are as they are. This is where we address the issue of which God we are talking about. Who is being worshiped? This is an important question. The Bible is the account of God working on this question with God's people over the centuries (Hiebert 1998). Abraham began by worshiping El, the high god of traditional cultures. This God, who Abraham called El, then taught Abraham that God was also El Shaddai, El Elyon, and El Olam. In the following centuries this same God told Moses his name and taught Israel that theirs was a personal God, the God of the descendants of Abraham, Isaac, and Jacob. Today, God's people know that the Christian God is one God—Father, Son, and Holy Spirit. Changing worldview has to do with getting to know the name of the true God, becoming clear on whom we must worship to be truly human.[16]

Worldviews are also the source of answers to the question of who human beings are and what they are for. Because of the importance I have attached to the issue of identity and vocation in this book, it is obvious that this is another area of worldview that must be addressed with the goal of seeking a biblical view.

A third issue of importance when thinking about Christian witness and worldview is to consider what happens to traditional cultures when our Christian witness is not holistic. The effect of only witnessing to the spiritual truth of the gospel is a serious distortion of the gospel. In response to hearing the gospel only as word addressing spiritual need, people may experience only a conversion at the level of formal religion and begin to go to church, read their Bible, and identify themselves as Christians. Yet, the other two dimensions of their worldview remain untouched by the gospel. In fact, people may not even realize that there is good news for these parts of their worldview. The consequences can be serious.

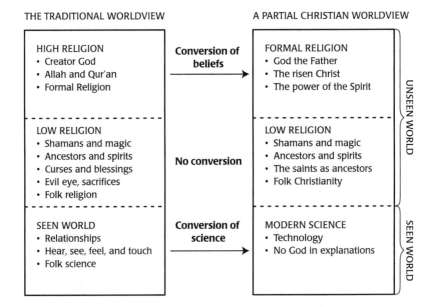

Figure 8-4: An incomplete conversion of worldview.

If the folk religion part of their worldview has not experienced conversion, animist beliefs continue to hold sway. Or they develop a kind of folk Christianity, marked by a Christianized view of magic. If the folk science part of their worldview has not been addressed by Christian witness, then the power of development may have converted this part of their worldview into a belief in modern science and technology, just as we in the West believe. This fragmentation of worldview, each part owing allegiance to a different story, creates psychological and intellectual incoherence and a kind of multiple personality. People try to live as Christians in their spiritual life and be like good moderns in their material life, while still being bound to their animism. This explains the actions of some Christians who go to the doctor for medical advice, ask the church to pray for healing, and visit the shaman at night. The bottom line is that our Christian witness must address and engage every level of worldview.

Another area of focus for Christian witness is the cultural system and its contribution to the web of lies that disempowers the poor and validates the god-complexes of the non-poor. Changing cultural systems is hard, but is too important a part of transformation to be ignored. Economic and political structures that are validated by the cultural system cannot be changed unless the undergirding validation is called into question. For example, the poverty-creating nature of caste cannot be adequately dealt with apart from the underlying religious beliefs that establish caste. Changing a dowry system that leads to children becoming bonded laborers, or altering the practice of saints or angel days that take away from productive time and require the poor to spend what little they have on alcohol and food cannot be done apart from changing worldview.

The how of changing worldview involves two points of action. First, as I pointed out earlier, the role of the biblical story must come into play. This is the normative story for all cultures and, as the living word of God, it is the source of possible worldview change. Andrew Walls explains the power of the living word to transform the worldview:

> The Word is to pass into all those distinctive ways of thought, those networks of kinship, those special ways of doing things, that give a nation its commonality, its coherence, its identity. It [the Word] has to travel through the shared mental and moral processes of a community, the way decisions are made in the community (1996, 50).

The second point of action centers in the Christian development facilitator. Working for worldview change requires sensitivity, skill, and openness to change on both sides. In one sense the work of worldview change is a form of spiritual discernment. Prayer and fasting are important tools as preparation. Changing worldview presupposes relationships of trust in which all parties believe the others are sharing in this process of discovery and are open to letting the Spirit speak a word of truth to any and all. The first step is an appreciative effort to identify local values that are kingdom values so that we celebrate what is already in the culture that enhances or supports life. At this point, in a spirit of dialogue, it is acceptable to ask prophetic questions about practices and beliefs that seem anti-life. Does this value make you proud? Does this value enable you to enhance life in your community? Even better, is this value something that you want your children to inherit?

An example might help. In a Tanzanian tribal context, one traditional belief held that to be the best, a true warrior, a person had to go to another tribe and bring back a head. Then the whole village celebrated. Challenging this anti-life practice began with a meeting at which men and women, young and old, attended. The starting point was trying to understand why this practice was celebrated. Why is it important? Why does it make the village proud? "It is our tradition," came the answer. Then the prophetic questions came. "How do you think the other community felt? What was its reaction?" "They prepare for war," came the response. The prophetic questions continued. "Does going to war make you feel exceptionally good about yourselves? Is this one of the 'prouds' that you would like your children to inherit?" At the end of long discussions, the answer came back that this is something they would like to change. They began to rethink their history in order to move toward a different future. The key was shifting the conversation from a past practice to the future they wish for their children.[17]

I want to emphasize the point that the beginning of worldview change must be listening and learning with no rush to judgment. Often an anti-life practice has a cause behind it that must be addressed before the people can even consider doing something different. In southern India a group of villages had a tradition of female infanticide. Instead of simply announcing the evil of this practice, the development facilitators began a quiet dialogue about how this cultural practice came into being. It turned out that these people were gypsies, a group with no standing in Hindu India. Because gypsies were associated with thievery, the police insisted that the men come to the police station to be locked up every evening. While the men were in jail, the police took advantage of the gypsy women. The village explained that its practice of killing girl children began with the fact that every girl child is a permanent memory of this humiliation.[18] Remember Jayakaran's limitations to growth? Behind every limitation, such as female infanticide, we must look for a stakeholder who has a vested interest in the limitation. Until the issue of the police and their abuse of women is addressed, changing the practice of female infanticide will be an uphill battle in the extreme.

Who changes?

Everyone

I have said several times that everyone who is part of the process must be open to transformational change. This is especially true in Christian witness. Even though we share the gospel, we must never assume we understand or express it fully. We must always be listening to the prompting of the Spirit, even in the voices of those to whom we witness.

Vincent Donovan tells a story that illustrates this wonderfully. After affirming the religious devotion of the Masai toward their high god, *Engai*, he challenged the Masai with the idea that unwittingly they had trapped or limited *Engai* when they made him their tribal god. He encouraged them to free *Engai*, thus allowing him to be the High God of all the tribes, even of the whole world. There was a prolonged silence and Donovan wondered if he had gone too far. Finally, the silence was broken by a question: "This story of Abraham's God, does it speak only to the Masai? Or does it speak to you? Has your tribe found this High God?"

Donovan admits that he almost gave a glib answer, until Joan of Arc inexplicably came to mind and he thought about the French and their tendency to associate God with France's quest for glory. Then he thought of the Americans and their belief that God blesses their side in wars. And then he thought of Hitler, who never failed to call on *Gott, der Allmachtige*, in his speeches. Vincent found himself silent with his thoughts for a long time. Finally, he said, "No, we have not found the High God. My tribe has not known him. For us, too, he is the unknown God. But we are searching for him. I have come a long, long distance to invite you to search for him with us. Let us search for him together. Maybe, together, we can find him" (Donovan 1978, 46).

Christian witness in the context of transformational development is a two-way conversation with the culture of the facilitator and the culture of the community both open to the word of God in the biblical account and to the activity of the Holy Spirit, who indwells both cultures. Christian witness is not negative campaigning. We do not have to speak positively about our faith by speaking negatively about theirs. We do not need the crusading mind that "exposes all their unclean spirits and promotes our own clean spirits" (Koyama 1993, 292).

John V. Taylor said it well:

> Ruthlessness has had a long run in Africa, and so long as the missionary encounter is conceived as a duologue one will have to "cede to the other." But may it not be truer to see it as a meeting of three, in which Christ has drawn together the witness who proclaims Him and the

other who does not know His name, so that in their slow discovery of one another, each may discern more of Him (Taylor 1963, 34-35).

Governments

There is one other often-unidentified area in which we must be willing to witness. Most Western governments are adamant that spiritual things and religion must not be part of the development process. This is more than a nonbiblical position. There is a deep irony here.

Governments in the West are worried about Christians being involved in development because they are afraid Christians will use their aid as a tool to encourage people to change their faith. To use aid to promote a particular religion is not appropriate, they say. And, of course, they are right. Any Christian would agree.

But Western governments go a step further and make a bad mistake. In the name of separation of church and state, a logical extension of the modern separation of the spiritual and the material, they require that the programming they fund can never include anything remotely religious in nature. This demand for purely materialistic programming is at complete odds with the holistic worldview of most of the people who are the recipients of development aid. Whether the poor are animists, Muslims, Buddhists, Christians, or Hindus, they believe in an integrated spiritual-physical universe. Western governments are guilty of the same sin they are concerned Christian agencies may commit: By the limitations they place on what is and is not appropriate in programs they pay for, they are using their money to promote a belief system, a faith, that is radically different from the people they are trying to help. Western governments are insisting on a particular worldview—secular liberal democratic—and imposing it, in the form of their funding choices and consultants, on people who do not accept this worldview. This is neo-imperialism.

The attitude of governments to religion in the context of development is flawed in another way as well. William van Geest (1993) has argued persuasively in a Canadian church and development dialogue that there is no such thing as development without value change, and that value change has to do with religion. The argument for this is unassailable. When a community is taught that clean water from pipes is better than muddy water from a stream, we are also challenging its belief that the water in the stream comes or does not come because of a water spirit who must be kept happy. When we challenge the acceptability of female circumcision or the insistence by village males that women have no place in the development dialogue, we are engaged in value change. I've already made the case that the cause of poverty is fundamentally spiritual. Development by definition is about changing culture and changing culture is about changing values and worldviews. By denying the role of religion in development, Western governments are setting aside one of the most critical factors to the success of any development initiative.

This is an area in which Christian NGOs need to make their witness in the public square. This stance by Western governments is wrong and harmful. We cannot be who we are and do what we do best unless we are willing to witness to this need for change.

SUMMARY

As I was finishing this chapter, an evaluation study arrived from an area development program in Agua Blanca, near Cali, Colombia. A sociologist and a development professional, both Christians, had spent an extended period of time allowing the women in the program to explain what had been most helpful and why in terms of spiritual nurture. Most of these women were Roman Catholic and had initially been more than a little suspicious of the work of an evangelical agency like World Vision in their area. As soon as their experience told them that the agenda was about deepening faith experience, not changing churches, the women became enthusiastic participants. Using open-ended interviews and a variety of group exercises derived from the popular education movement in Latin America, the study empirically developed the following indicators of impact in terms of spiritual nurture included (Atiencia and Guzman 1997, 12):

- A change in worldview, including a new view of life, death, poverty, and justice as well as of past, present, and future.
- The development of a devotional life, including prayer, a life based on the Bible and hope in the future.
- A vocation of service, including community leadership, community organization, and solidarity.
- A change in their understanding of God to one who is near, loving, and just.
- A new ethical dimension to life, both private and communal.
- A development that was holistic, including character formation, better self-image, and improved family and community relationships.

Also interesting in light of the framework for Christian witness I have presented in this chapter, the study concluded that the following were key elements of transformation in Agua Blanca:

- The lifestyle of the facilitators.
- The central role of the Bible in the lives of the facilitators and as a "training tool" for the community.
- The development of a devotional stance in daily institutional work. "Every intervention, every contact, provided a spirituality in which God is present and is the center of all activities. We can speak here of a spirituality as the basis for sustainable transformational development."
- The verbalization of the gospel.

Ultimately, the best of transformational development deeds are ambiguous. Good development is being done every day by Buddhists, Muslims, and atheists. The driving force for Christian witness in the context of transformational development is to be sure that credit is given where credit is due. We must take great care that we point, not to our own sacrifices or professionalism, and not to the effectiveness of our development technology, but to the fact that the good deeds that create and enhance life in the community are evidence of the character and activity of the God of the Bible, the God whose Son makes a continuing invitation to new life and whose Spirit is daily at work in our world.

APPENDIX 1:
SCRIPTURE SEARCH TEXTS FOR BIBLICAL REFLECTION
(Taken from Alvarez, Avarientos, and McAlpine 1999)

Jb 29:7-17	Advocacy
Eccl 11:1-6	Agriculture. Dealing with uncertainties
Ps 104	Agriculture. God's blessing
Ps 72	Agriculture. God's blessing, fertility, and justice
Jl 1	Agriculture. Land and desolation
1 Kgs 21:1-19	Agriculture. Land and justice
Gn 1:1-2:3	Agriculture. Land and life
Acts 2	Christian witness: Life, word, deed, sign
Acts 14:5-23	Christian witness: Life, word, deed, sign
Acts 16:11-40	Christian witness: Life, word, deed, sign
Mt 20:1-16	Development. Compare assistance received
Lk 6:1-5	Development. People and institutions
Lk 13:10-21	Development. People and institutions
Acts 16:11-24	Economics. Christian witness
Lk 12:13-21	Economics. Practices. Avarice
Prv 6:6-11	Economics. Practices. Diligence
Dt 15:12-18	Economics. Practices. Generosity
Lv 25	Economics. Practices. Justice. Jubilee
Gn 1	Economics. Practices. Justice. Stewardship, right, and responsibility
Dt 24:10-15	Economics. Practices. Justice. Treatment of weak
Am 8:4-8	Economics. Practices. Justice. Treatment of weak
Jas 5:1-6	Economics. Practices. Justice. Treatment of weak
1 Sm 17:34-37	Economics. Practices. Manual work
Acts 18:1-4	Economics. Practices. Manual work
Prv 1:8-19	Economics. Practices. Prudence
1 Thes 4:9-12	Economics. Practices. Self-sufficiency
2 Thes 3:6-15	Economics. Practices. Self-sufficiency
Mt 6:19-34	Economics. Practices. Trust in God
Mk 5:1-20	Economics. Practices. What is a human being worth?
Ex 31:1-11	Economics. Work. Expression of God-given gifts
Lk 3:21-22	Group. Foundations. Baptism
Jn 3:1-21	Group. Foundations. Conversion
Lk 22:15-34	Group. Foundations. Jesus
Jn 15	Group. Foundations. Jesus
Lk 1:39-56	Group. Foundations. Kingdom of God (personal/group)
Jn 4:1-42	Group. Practices. Transformation
Rom 12:1-8	Group. Practices. Transformation (ongoing)
Phlm 1	Group. Practices. Transformation of relationships
Lk 12:22-34	Group. Practices. Trust for physical needs

Mt 8:23-27	Group. Practices. Trust in crises
Gn 1:26-27	Group. Self-image
Lk 5:17-26	Health. Committee. Motivate, mobilize, and strengthen
Ps 127	Health. Family
Sg 4:1-5:1	Health. Family
Ex 15:22-27	Health. God's blessing
Ps 139	Health. God's blessing
Mk 2:1-12	Health. God's blessing
Rv 21:1-4	Health. God's blessing
Mt 10:5-15	Health. God's healing and prayer
Jas 5:13-18	Health. God's healing and prayer
2 Kgs 2:19-22	Health. Indigenous medicine
2 Kgs 4:38-41	Health. Indigenous medicine
2 Kgs 20:1-7	Health. Indigenous medicine
Jn 4:1-42	Health. Installation/monitoring of water pumps
Lk 13:10-17	Health. Justice
Lk 4:16-30	Holistic mission. Elements
Lk 24:36-53	Holistic mission. Elements
1 Cor 4:1-5	Management. Evaluation
Neh	Management. Evaluation and monitoring
Neh	Management. Implementation
Lk 9:10-17	Management. Implementation. Inadequate resources?
Neh	Management. Planning
Nm 13-14	Management. Planning. Baseline
Mt 13:31-32	Management. Planning. Membership expansion and why?
Gn 12:1-3	Management. Planning. Vision
Is 2:1-4	Management. Planning. Vision
Is 65:17-25	Management. Planning. Vision
Hos 2:14-23	Management. Planning. Vision
Gn 1:1-2.3	Management. Planning/Evaluation
Neh 5:1-13	Public awareness
Lv 20:1-5	Sponsorship. Importance of children
Lk 15:1-7	Sponsorship. Monitoring
1 Cor 12:12-31	Group. Identification of roles and responsibilities
Ex 18:13-27	Group. Leadership. Delegation of responsibility
Jn 4:1-42	Group. Leadership. Facilitating skills
Acts 18:1-4,24-28	Group. Leadership. Men and women
Gal 3:23-29	Group. Leadership. Men and women
Acts 8:14-24	Group. Leadership. Money
2 Sm 11-12	Group. Leadership. Power
Mt 6:1-18	Group. Leadership. Reality and appearances
Mt 23:1-12	Group. Leadership. Reality and appearances
Mk 9:33-37	Group. Leadership. Servant
Lk 22:15-34	Group. Leadership. Servant
Jn 13:1-17	Group. Leadership. Servant
Ex 3-4	Group. Leadership. Vocation
Mt 5:21-48	Group. Practices
Lk 10:25-42	Group. Practices
Lk 18:15-30	Group. Practices

Lk 19:1-10	Group. Practices. Behavior
Lk 8:40-56	Group. Practices. Choosing beneficiaries
Ex 1:8-22	Group. Practices. Civil disobedience
Gn 13:1-13	Group. Practices. Dealing with conflict
Acts 6:1-7	Group. Practices. Dealing with conflict
Mt 18:21-35	Group. Practices. Forgiveness
Lk 21:1-4	Group. Practices. Giving out of poverty
Lk 1:26-38	Group. Practices. Hearing and consenting
Mt 7:24-27	Group. Practices. Hearing and doing the Word
Lk 8:4-21	Group. Practices. Hearing and doing the Word
Lk 3:1-20	Group. Practices. Justice
Lk 12:13-21	Group. Practices. Money
1 Tim 6:3-10	Group. Practices. Money
Lk 4:1-13	Group. Practices. Power
Mk 11:20-25	Group. Practices. Prayer
Lk 18:1-14	Group. Practices. Prayer
Lk 10:25-37	Group. Practices. Responsiveness
Lk 15:11-32	Group. Practices. Rules and relationships
Lk 4:1-13	Group. Practices. Scripture
Lk 8:1-3	Group. Practices. Solidarity
Acts 11:27-30	Group. Practices. Solidarity
Jas 2:1-7	Group. Practices. Status
Mt 25:14-30	Group. Practices. Stewardship of gifts
Lk 10:1-12	Group. Practices. Strength and weakness
Jn 4:1-42	Sponsorship. Responding to real needs
Lk 19:1-10	Sponsorship. Treatment of families
Ez 47:1-12	Strategic initiatives
Col 1:15-23	Strategic initiatives. Church and world
1 Pt 2:11-25	Strategic initiatives. Church and world
Acts 2:37-47	Strategic initiatives. Models
Acts 4.32-35	Strategic initiatives. Models
Rv 2-3	Strategic initiatives. Models

APPENDIX 2:
BIBLICAL REFERENCES ON TRANSFORMATION
FOR REFLECTION AND LITURGY
(Hope and Timmel 1984)

Old Testament

Genesis 1:26-29	Creation and human beings as co-creators
4:9-10	Where is your brother Abel?
Exodus 3:1-15	God intervenes on the side of the oppressed
22:25-27	Do not keep the poor man's cloak
Leviticus 25:8-10	The Jubilee Year
25:35-28	Kindness to strangers
19:9-11	Sharing with the poor
19:13-15	Sharing with the poor
Deuteronomy 24:17-11	Leaving some of the harvest
Psalm 72:1-4	God's concern for justice
72:11-17	God's concern for justice
105:22-27	Celebration of the Exodus
Isaiah 1:11-17	I am sick of holocausts
3:13-15	The vineyard
11:1-9	They do not hurt or harm
58:1-12	Worship, poverty, and oppression
65:17-25	New heaven and new earth
Jeremiah 22:16	Is not that what it means to know me?
Amos 5:14-24	Woe to those who feel secure
6:1-6	Woe to those who feel secure
8:4-7	Woe to those who feel secure
Micah 2:1-2	Beat their swords into plowshares
4:1-4	Beat their swords into plowshares
Ruth 1-4	Love and faithfulness

New Testament

Luke 3:2-11	John the Baptist
4:16-21	He sent me to bring the good news to the poor

6:20-25	The beatitudes
19:1-10	Zacchaeus gives away his riches
10:25-37	The good Samaritan
16:19-31	Dives and Lazarus

Matthew 25:31-45	I was hungry and you gave me to eat

John 4:5-42	Woman at the well
8:3-11	Jesus stops the stoning of the woman
20:11-18	Jesus sends a woman to announce the resurrection

Acts 2:42-47	Sharing among the first Christians
4:32-35	Sharing among the first Christians

Galatians 3:26-28	Neither Jew nor Greek

Philippians 2:3-11	He emptied himself

James 2:14-17, 26	Faith without works

1 John 3:14-18	If anyone has the world's goods and sees his brother in need

Revelation 21:1-5	Behold I make all things new
13:1-17	The power of the beast

APPENDIX 3:
STANDARDS AND INDICATORS FOR CHRISTIAN WITNESS
(Developed by Bryant Myers and codified by Frank Cookingham)

Standards	Indicators
Cultural and religious change in project area	
Churches in the project area are active in the political, social, and cultural life of the area communities.	Examples of activities based on interviews with pastors and other church leaders. Descriptions of church activities by community members—examples of services provided to the communities.
Development technology is accompanied by an explanation which points to the activity of God.	Examples of explanations based on interviews of staff and project committee members.
The Bible is used in appropriate ways with people in communities as they plan activities, make decisions, and solve problems.	Descriptions of applications discussed during Bible studies in the community. Examples based on interviews of staff and project committee members.
Attitudes toward Christians and the gospel message	
Attitudes toward Christians become more positive over the life of the project.	Words used by community members to describe Christians.
People deepen their understanding of the nature of the God of the Bible.	Words used by community members to describe the character of the God of the Bible.
People become more open to listening to the gospel.	Number of people seeking or participating in discussions of spiritual things, attending Bible studies, or attending church services. Number of conversations about some aspect of the gospel between staff and community members.

Spiritual powers

	Descriptions of what controls individual lives, based on interviews of community members.
	Descriptions of what people do or whom they turn to when they are afraid of something, based on interviews of community members, pastors, and those who are sought for help.
	Descriptions by community people of who or what they believe controls the lives of World Vision staff.

Quality of witness

Staff learn the local language, are culturally sensitive and show interest in learning and understanding local customs.	Observations of language used as staff converses with community members. Comparison of appearance of staff dwelling with typical dwellings in the community. Knowledge of local religious beliefs and practices.
Staff members are perceived as caring people who love God and neighbor.	Words used by community members to describe staff.
Staff are perceived as a dependent people, who pray and act as a spiritual people.	Descriptions by community members of prayer experiences with staff. Observations of staff as they interact with community members—encouragement to pray, inclusion of prayer in conversations or meetings.

Notes

1. Charting the Course

[1] Having noted the holism in the biblical worldview and the fact that most traditional worldviews are holistic is not to say that the biblical worldview is animistic. The biblical and animistic worldviews are quite different, as a comparison of Figure 1-2 and Figure 1-3 makes clear. There is only one God in the biblical worldview and spiritual beings are both part of the created order and fallen, just like human beings.

2. The Biblical Story

[1] After all, God sent the Son to die for them so that they could become part of God's story.

[2] Not to be Trinitarian in our thinking is also dangerous. LaCugna reminds us, "A non-Trinitarian theology of God opens the door to every kind of ideology or idolatry, whether it comes in the form of a self-sufficient, masculine Father-God, or a plenipotentiary God who perversely wishes children to die, or an apathetic God who does not mind if people are always poor, or a violent, vengeful God who enjoys wars fought in his name" (1991, 395). Also, a non-Trinitarian view of God leads to a view of humankind "that is derogatory and detrimental because one human being is put forward as normative for another" (1991, 396).

[3] This should give us pause when we too quickly and uncritically blame poverty on population growth. New babies are not simply empty stomachs or economic sink holes. They are also creative human minds and spirits, endowed with creative and productive potential. They, too, can be fruitful. This myth is provocatively explored in Cromartie 1995.

[4] See the discussion of the god-complexes of the non-poor in Chapter 3.

[5] Robert Banks has addressed this in his helpful book *Redeeming the Routines: Bringing Theology to Life* (Wheaton, Ill.: Bridgepoint/Victor Books, 1993).

[6] Notice the holistic and relational framework for human growth: mind and body, in relationship with God and humankind.

[7] The relationship between the Holy Spirit, the kingdom of God, and the church was explored in an international consultation in March 1994 in Malaysia. The resulting booklet, *World, Kingdom and Spirit*, is worth reading and studying. It is available through the Oxford Centre for Mission Studies, St. Philip and St. James Church, Woodstock Road, Oxford. Tom McAlpine's book *By Word, Work and Wonder* (Monrovia, Calif.: MARC, 1995) also makes a helpful contribution.

[8] Note the diagram of Hiebert's framework, Figure 1-2 herein.

[9] This is the only answer to the postmodern self that believes that it is defined by someone else's will to power or by its instincts and drives, causing it to feel as if it is no longer an actor, since the points of its definition are outside its rational control.

[10] See the section on restored relationships as the goal of transformation in Chapter 5.

3. Poverty and the Poor

[1] With apologies to Christian, I have added the biophysical system for the sake of completeness. Chambers includes this. A weak mind and body, resulting from malnutrition, illness, and hard physical labor, are obvious contributing factors to the rest of Christian's system of disempowerment.

[2] The phrase "eternal yesterday" comes from Max Weber (cited in Curtis 1981, 427).

[3] "Delusional assumptions" is a term Wink uses to describe beliefs, taken for granted by the powerful, that create delusions that justify their power.

[4] Jayakumar Christian, personal interview, 1997.

[5] Jayakaran's framework for poverty as limitation echoes Friedman's observation that, while we do not know what a "flourishing human life" is, we "can know what inhibits it: hunger, poor health, poor education, a life of backbreaking labor, a constant fear of dispossession and chaotic social relations" (Friedman 1992, 12).

[6] It is interesting to note that this is consistent with the Hebraic worldview, in which relationships are the highest good, while alienation is the lowest.

4. Perspectives on Development

[1] This is the same question that Kwame Bediako (1992), Andrew Walls (1989), Augustine Musopole (1997), Cyril Okorocha (1994), and other African theologians and sociologists have been asking of African traditional religion, which, in spite of the significant inroads of Islam, Christianity, and modernity, persists as one of the most powerful forces at work on the African continent.

[2] The exceptions came largely from Latin America in the voices of Orlando Costos, René Padilla, and Samuel Escobar. In the United States, Ron Sider (Evangelicals for Social Action) and Jim Wallace (Sojourner Community) took the lead.

[3] This is why this book examined various understandings of who the poor are and why they are poor before considering approaches to transformational development.

[4] Korten's third generation addresses Friedman's idea of expanding domains of social power.

[5] In the late 1980s, World Vision began a move away from many small, community-based projects toward "area development programs," clusters of projects focused in some kind of meaningful micro-region. This move preceded a series of meetings with Friedman in which it was discovered that his concerns for the need to "scale up"—increasing access to social and political power—gave added emphasis to World Vision's new trajectory for development.

[6] This idea is well developed in Wright 1983.

[7] The United Nations Development Program (1995, 11-12) defined human development as "a process of enlarging people's choices and identified four essential

components that echo Chambers's: productivity, equity (access to opportunities), sustainability, and empowerment (ownership and participation)."

[8] It is interesting to compare this to Jayakaran's framework for poverty in Figure 3-9.

[9] This corresponds to Chambers's category "vulnerability" in his poverty trap.

[10] The time dimension of powerlessness as a transformational frontier is not part of either Chambers's or Friedman's accounts of powerlessness.

[11] This concern for establishing one's true identity is shared by Kwame Bediako (1992) and is further developed by Vinay Samuel's theology of dignity (Sugden 1997, 183-201). See the section on this in the next chapter.

[12] See Wink's delusional assumptions in Chapter 3.

5. Toward a Christian Understanding of Transformational Development

[1] World Vision in the Philippines, a Catholic country with a strong renewal movement emphasizing personal renewal and lay Bible reading, uses the biblical metaphor of Isaiah 65 to help poor communities visualize the future God intends:

- It is a place of joy; there is no weeping.
- Children do not die. People live full lives.
- People build homes and live in them.
- People enjoy the product of their own labor.
- The community is restored and harmonious.
- The unreconcilable live in peace.
- God is in their midst, answering them before they call.

[2] As I was finishing this manuscript, Tom Houston kindly sent me a Ph.D. thesis, completed in 1997 by Kenyan scholar Deborah Ajulu, in which she proposes a very similar frame for what she calls holistic empowerment. Posing four ethical questions, she argues that the sanction for empowerment is that every human being is made in the image of God (identity), that the purpose of empowerment is stewardship (vocation), that the how of empowerment is the establishment of biblical justice, and that the who of empowerment are both the poor and the non-poor (Ajulu 1997, 198-200). She also has an excellent section on the ways the non-poor are powerless (174).

[3] I will point out later that seeking true identity and vocation must also be the personal goal of development workers. We are just as susceptible to a web of lies as are either the non-poor or the poor. We are constantly tempted to play god in the lives of the poor, thus marring their identity and ours. An agent of transformation who is not also being transformed is capable of doing more harm than good.

[4] Helping people in this way is inherently a political and economic act. Not all governments, and certainly not the non-poor, who benefit from things as they are, will welcome this kind of transformation. Transforming things is acceptable; transforming people is less so. There are governments in the late 1990s who are attempting to curtail the role of development NGOs for this reason.

[5] Having said that discovering one's true identity and vocation has the potential to greatly enhance other kinds of transformative change, I must also say that identity and vocation are not enough. Newbigin reminds us, "No human project however splendid is free from the corrupting power of sin" (1989, 138). The continuing

deception, distortion, and distraction resulting from sin at work in us, in the non-poor, and in the community means that all development programming will be flawed and fallible. This is simple Christian realism.

[6] Volf would not have us be naive, however: "The initial suspicion against the perspective of the powerful is necessary. Not because the powerless are innocent, but because the powerful have the means to impose their own perspective by argument and propaganda . . . the groans of the powerless must disturb the serenity of their comforting ideologies" (1996, 219, 220).

[7] Care needs to be taken in how truth-telling takes place. People need to discover the truth about themselves and their reality. Working in ways that allow people to discover their own truth is itself a transformative action. After all, it is the truth that makes us free (Jn 8:32). Simply announcing the truth about others can be violent and counter-productive, and almost certainly robs them of a transformative movement. We must also have the humility to remember that we can never be sure we understand the truth about others or their situation.

[8] A description of this quiet revolution in policy analysis and advocacy work is available in Holland and Blackburn 1998.

[9] A complex humanitarian emergency combines civil conflict, large-scale displacement of people, mass famine, a failing economic system, and deteriorating government authority to the extent that public services fail and political control passes to warlords or regional centers of power (Natsios 1997, 7). Examples in the late 1990s include Rwanda, the Great Lakes region of Africa, Sierra Leone, and Bosnia.

[10] By "church" I mean the local body of believers who are doing their best to worship the God of the Bible, Father, Son, and Holy Spirit, and follow God's commands. Where there is more than one church, then I am referring to all churches. I have already commented on the flaws that are part of every church and have no illusions as to their perfection. Yet, with all their flaws, these are nonetheless God's people, called to be signs of the kingdom. As witnesses, they were there before we came and will be there long after the development intervention is over.

[11] Helpful sources on sustainable agriculture include Roland Bunch, *Two Ears of Corn: A Guide to People-Centered Agricultural Improvement* (New York: PACT, 1982); Ian Scoones and John Thompson, *Beyond Farmer First: Rural People's Knowledge, Agricultural Research and Extension Practice* (London: Intermediate Technology Publications, 1994); Jules N. Pretty, *Regenerating Agriculture* (London: Earthscan, 1995); and Miguel Altieri, *Agroecology: The Science of Sustainable Agriculture*, 2d ed. (Boulder, Colo.: Westview Press, 1995).

[12] Helpful sources on community-based health-care include *The Community Health Worker* (Geneva: World Health Organization, 1987); David Werner, *Helping Health Workers Learn* (Palo Alto, Calif.: Hespian Foundation, 1992); and *Helping Children Beat the Odds: Lessons Learned* (Ottawa, Canada: Canadian Public Health Association, 1997).

[13] Helpful sources on micro-enterprise development include Elaine Edgcomb and James Crawley, eds., *Institutional Guide for Enterprise Development Organizations* (New York: SEEP/PACT, 1993); Shirley Buzzard and Elaine Edgcomb, eds., *Monitoring Small Business Projects: A Step by Step Guide to Private Development* (New York: PACT, 1988); MEDA, *Small Business Development Program: Operations Manual*, 2d ed. (New York: Micro Enterprise Development Association [MEDA], 1993); and Charles

Waterfield and Ann Duval, *CARE Savings and Credit Sourcebook* (New York: PACT, 1996).

[14] Recall that Friedman claimed that social organizations and networks are the two primary means by which communities can expand social power (see Figure 4-4 herein; Friedman 1992, 68-69).

[15] This would argue against the universal and uncritical affirmation of all forms of civil society proposed by Jean-Francois Bayart (Whaites 1996, 242). Expressions of civil society that reinforce tribal, ethnic, or religious divisions within countries or communities would be hard to support in a Christian frame that assumes that every person is made in the image of God and that cultural diversity is a gift to the whole, not an excuse for division.

6. Development Practice: Principles and Practitioners

[1] See the later section on Appreciative Inquiry.

[2] We will not find the important gods of formal religion here. Vishnu, Krishna, Allah, Ngai, and the other high gods are not to be bothered with the mundane details of everyday life. The exception is the Christian view of God, which, because of the ongoing work of the Holy Spirit, the prayer of Christ on our behalf, and the Father's commitment to the culmination of history, remains engaged in our world.

[3] Ravi Jayakaran reports that each Indian village develops its own, usually unique, constellation of gods. The way a community does this is highly empirical. If community members suspect a god or spirit has some influence over an area of life, they make a small shrine out of stones and make a simple offering. If this god continues to produce, the shrine is upgraded by covering it and the offering is increased. If the god continues to be useful, the covered shrine is replaced by a small temple and walls are built around it. Gods and spirits can also be "demoted" for lack of performance. This is a different kind of empiricism than we are used to in the West (personal interview, 1997).

[4] One of the best summaries on indigenous knowledge is Warren et al. 1995. See also a related book on indigenous organizations, Blunt and Warren 1996.

[5] To live in a multilevel mound, termites have to have some kind of natural cooling system. Underground water close to the surface provides for this.

[6] Small physical disturbances in the soil can cause soil compaction that results in small springs drying up temporarily.

[7] In the last twenty years, a great deal has been learned from the study of complexity in nature. Chaos theory offers a way of seeing order and pattern where formerly only the random, erratic, and unpredictable had been observed. For a helpful, nontechnical introduction, see Gleick 1987.

[8] Additional reading on complexity should include Lewin 1992 and Kellert 1993.

[9] Uphoff has an intriguing chapter on complex systems theory and development as he found it expressed in an irrigation program in southeastern Sri Lanka (1996, 388). Chambers also mentions complexity theory briefly (1997, 194ff.).

[10] One helpful resource on participatory development designed to empower is Save the Children 1982.

[11] The other four are (1) changing technology; (2) cross-border threats like AIDS, pollution, and the drug trade; (3) the reduced capability of governments to solve

social issues; and (4) sub-groupism, that is, the tendency of people to resist globalism and seek identity in ethnic and religious groupings.

[12] I first heard this name for the Christians who promote holistic transformational development from Dr. Sam Kamaleson, formerly vice president for pastor's conferences at World Vision, now retired.

[13] Ravi Jayakaran, personal interview, 1997.

[14] While it is true that Christians have been struggling for two thousand years to develop a biblical worldview and still have a ways to go, we should not back away from this challenge. The fact that we see things only dimly is not an invitation to sit on the sidelines and withdraw from mission or theological reflection. A Christian worldview, however flawed, is essential to enabling the transformational development this book describes.

[15] There is more to a simple lifestyle than simple self-denial. Francis of Assisi understood that "he had to enter into the space of the poor of his day, because only in this space of the poor could he approach the condition God assumed in the Incarnation" (Motte 1996, 71).

[16] See the section "Doing no harm" in Chapter 4 herein; see also Anderson 1996b and Slim 1997.

[17] There is also an African resource that develops discipleship within the framework of dying to oneself: Bayo Famonure's *Training to Die: A Manual on Discipleship* (1989).

[18] We've already determined the importance of the whole biblical story to the task of transformational development. The use of the Bible in transformational development will be further developed in Chapter 8.

[19] Four helpful resources are Gutiérrez 1984; Galilea 1984; Beltrans 1986; and Green 1979.

[20] For some helpful resources, see Mitchell and Everly 1996; Figley 1995; and Parkinson 1997.

7. Development Practice: The Tool Kit

[1] Bernard T. Adeney's book *Strange Virtues: Ethics in a Multicultural World* is a very helpful assessment of this complex challenge (1995).

[2] A helpful summary of the application of community organizing in the context of churches and the city can be found in Linthicum 1991.

[3] For contacts and information on Participatory Learning and Action / Participatory Rural Appraisal (PLA/PRA), contact the Institute of Development Studies, University of Sussex, Brighton, BN1 9RE, UK. There is also a newsletter, *PLA Notes*, available from the Sustainable Agriculture Programme, International Institute for Environment and Development, 3 Endsleigh Street, London WC1H 0DD, UK. Two helpful manuals on PLA are Jayakaran 1996; and Pretty et al. 1995. Chambers also devotes several chapters to PLA/PRA in *Whose Reality Counts?* (1997).

[4] Jayakumar Christian, personal interview, 1997.

[5] The Christian Reformed World Relief Committee has applied Appreciative Inquiry to a study of best relief and development practices in its work partnering with NGOs around the world (see Johnson and Ludema 1997).

⁶ This work has been championed by Sarone Ole Sena and Dirk Booy within World Vision. An excellent summary of Appreciative Inquiry and its use in development programming and as an organizational development tool in the national agency office can be found in Booy and Sarone 1999.

⁷ For a recent assessment of the Logical Framework, see Crittenden and Lea 1992.

⁸ Helpful references on development evaluation include Marsden and Oakley 1990; Feuerstein 1986; and Stephens and Putman 1990.

⁹ Distorting values, robbing them of their social and personal good, is part of the job description of the one Jesus called the Father of Lies.

¹⁰ This is one reason that Korten's call for development agencies to make their views explicit is so important. The people have a right to know what is driving and shaping the way practitioners work with them (see Chapter 4 herein).

¹¹ World Vision in the Philippines has found that Isaiah 65 provides a useful framework in the context of working with the poor (see chap. 5 n.1 herein).

¹² See also Chapter 8 herein on Christian witness, especially Appendix 3, "Standards and Indicators for Christian Witness."

¹³ In addition to women and children, on which I comment, other groups are sometimes without a voice (see Anderson 1996a).

¹⁴ Helpful resources on gender and development include Wallace and March 1991; Macdonald 1994; and Williams and Mwau 1994.

¹⁵ For an introductory discussion of child-focused development, see Theis 1996.

¹⁶ See "Listening to the whole story" in Chapter 6 herein.

¹⁷ The following account of the Bhil is taken from Jayakaran 1999.

¹⁸ For pursuing holistic PLAs, see Jayakaran 1997.

8. Christian Witness and Transformational Development

¹ Augustine Musopole, the Malawian theologian, reports that the more successful the development intervention, the greater the reinforcement of traditional religion. "The more education, the better the job, the larger the house, the more you have to protect and the greater the temptation of witchcraft" (quoted in Myers 1997).

² Technology as the explanation will not do for reasons that go beyond the fact that this is not a Christian view. Shenk reminds us that "while science has given us unparalleled approaches and tools to identify and analyze problems, . . . science cannot create. Because science was assumed to be value-free, it did not operate within a vision of what ought to be. It could relentlessly and efficiently disassemble; it could not construct an alternative whole" (1993, 67).

³ See Bradshaw 1993 and Myers 1993.

⁴ Paul Hiebert, comment made at the World Vision consultation on "Changing the Story" (reported in Myers 1997).

⁵ Newbigin points us to Christopher Kaiser, who outlines the way the Cappadocian theological frame of the fourth century shaped, and in a sense permitted, the development of science. This framework provides strong hints for answering the question about how to interpret development technology in a way that includes God as part of the explanation. The four principles are (1) created by a rational God, it follows that the cosmos is comprehensible by the human mind; (2) as a free act of

God's will, the cosmos has relative autonomy; not everything that happens is the direct will of God; (3) because God created the spiritual and the material, they are of the same substance; and 4) because of the work of Christ in the incarnation, we may use material means for the advancement of salvation (Newbigin 1995, 7-8).

[6] Dynamical systems also provide the explanation for the behavior of social systems. Long known to be counter-intuitive, social systems behave as chaotic processes in which unpredictability is the norm. Yet mathematicians and scientists are discovering that such indeterminate systems do have deep order. The shape of a particular snowflake cannot be predicted, yet we know that every snowflake will invariably be recognizable as a snowflake. Every day in New York City, hundreds of thousands of people work with almost no knowledge of who is bringing tomatoes or flour or whatever, or how these foodstuffs are being delivered. Thousands of those involved in this logistical nightmare get sick, fail to make their delivery, or change their mind. Yet every day in New York, every restaurant and home has the food that it prefers on its table three times a day. This cannot be master planned, yet it happens. This is the deep order of a chaotic social system. By analogy, this is how God can be sovereign and yet allow free will and free choice.

[7] I am not implying that expository preachers or theological teachers are using inappropriate methods. In fact, exposition and formal teaching methods are ideal for church and classroom settings. I am only trying to say that community development is very different and thus makes different requirements of us when it comes to using the Bible.

[8] I am indebted to my wife, Lisa, for this insight. As a professional spiritual director, skilled in the practice of individual and group *lectio*, she has developed the language of "an encounter with Scripture" to signify this personal possibility and reserves the idea of "engaging with Scripture" for the act of seeking guidance and wisdom.

[9] The development of this process is largely the work of Rev. Malcolm Bradshaw, a long-time World Vision staff member in the Philippines, who came across a similar methodology in his personal encounter with the Catholic Renewal Movement in the Philippines and adapted it for use in the context of doing development.

[10] The distinction is nicely summarized by Malcolm Bradshaw: "World Vision's charism is probably more that of people discovering the King by gradual acquaintance of his ways through experiencing his reign in specific issues and problems of living, the experience being interpreted by their own search of an appropriate Scripture. Other charisms, such as evangelistic outreaches, are more fitting to overt 'church growth' than to the development process" (quoted in McAlpine 1995, 72).

[11] A listing of Scripture Search Bible passages and their related themes can be found in Appendix 1 at the end of this chapter. Another listing of biblical passages addressing the theme of transformation can be found in Appendix 2.

[12] The Seven Steps is an adaptation of an ancient approach to praying the Scriptures called *Lectio Divina*. In the first centuries of the Christian church the Bible was experienced as the spoken word in four movements: reading aloud, meditation (reflection), prayer, and contemplation (God's presence beyond words).

[13] This work is being led by Tom McAlpine of MARC.

[14] A list of standards and indicators used by World Vision for evaluating Christian witness can be found in Appendix 3 at the end of the chapter.

[15] The fact that the Bible is translated into both the language of the facilitator and the language of the community is significant. Translation of the Bible means that the word of God can find expression in all cultures. Sanneh points out that "translation relativizes culture by denying that there is only one normative expression of the gospel. . . . It opens culture up to the demand and need for change" (1987, 332). This opens the door to a conversation between our culture and that of the community on the goals and process of transformation.

[16] The issue of which God we are talking about is the point at which we need to take care with others who say they worship God. Without needing to make a judgment, we need to know if the God they worship has a Son named Jesus Christ and a Holy Spirit who is an active agent in human history.

[17] Personal interview with Sarone Ole Sena, 1997.

[18] Personal interview with Ravi Jayakaran, 1997.

Bibliography

Abraham, William J. 1989. *The Logic of Evangelism*. Grand Rapids, Mich: William B. Eerdmans.

Adeney, Bernard T. 1995. *Strange Virtues: Ethics in a Multicultural World*. Downers Grove, Ill.: InterVarsity Press.

Ajulu, Deborah. 1997. *Holistic Empowerment for Rural Development from a Biblical Perspective, With Special Reference to Sub-Saharan Africa*. Ph.D. thesis for the Department of Agricultural Extension and Rural Development, University of Reading, England.

Alvarez, Joy, Nora Avarientos, and Tom McAlpine. 1999. "Our Experience with the Bible and Transformational Development." In *Working with the Poor: New Insights and Learnings from Development Practitioners*, ed. Bryant Myers. Monrovia, Calif.: MARC (in production).

Anderson, Mary B. 1999. *Do No Harm: How Aid Can Support Peace—or War*. Boulder, Colo.: Lynne Rienner.

Anderson, Mary B., ed. 1996a. *Development and Social Diversity*. Oxford, UK: Oxfam.

———. 1996b. *Do No Harm: Supporting Local Capacities for Peace Through Aid*. Cambridge, Mass.: Collaborative Action for Development.

———. 1996c. "Understanding Difference and Building Solidarity." In *Development and Social Diversity*, ed. Mary B. Anderson. Oxford, UK: Oxfam.

Anderson, Mary B., and Peter J. Woodrow. 1989. *Rising From the Ashes: Development Strategies in Times of Disaster*. Boulder, Colo.: Westview Press.

Atiencia, Jorge, and Agelit Guzman. 1997. "The Impact of Christian Witness in the Agua Blanca ADP." Evaluation Report for World Vision Latin America Region.

Avarientos, Nora, 1994. "WV Philippines Development Standards and Indicators," personal communication (April 13).

Bamford, Christopher, and William Parker March. 1987. *Celtic Christianity: Ecology and Holiness*. Great Barrington, Mass.: Lindisfarne Press.

Banks, Robert. 1993. *Redeeming the Routines: Bringing Theology to Life*. Wheaton, Ill.: Bridgepoint/Victor Books.

Bediako, Kwame. 1996a. "Biblical Perspectives on Transformational Development: Some Reflections," an unpublished manuscript presented at the World Vision Development Training and Education Workshop, Lilongwe, Malawi (October 4-9).

———. 1996b. "Theological Reflections." In *Serving the Poor in Africa*, ed. Tetsunao Yamamori et al. Monrovia, Calif.: MARC.

———. 1994. "Jesus in African Culture." In *Emerging Voices in Global Christian Theology*, ed. William A. Dyrness. Grand Rapids, Mich.: Zondervan.

————. 1992. *Theology and Identity: The Impact of Culture of Christian Thought in the Second Century and in Modern Africa.* Oxford, UK: Regnum.

Beltrans, Benigno, S.V.D. 1986. *Journey into Solitude: A Manual for Retreats and Recollections.* Manila, Philippines: Arnoldus Press.

Blunt, Peter, and Michael D. Warren. 1996. *Indigenous Organizations and Development.* London: Intermediate Technology Publications.

Boff, Leonardo. 1988. *Trinity and Society*, trans. Paul Burns. Maryknoll, N.Y.: Orbis Books.

Booy, Dirk, and Sarone Ole Sena. 1999. "Capacity Building Using the Appreciative Inquiry Approach." In *Working with the Poor: New Insights and Learnings from Development Practitioners*, ed. Bryant Myers. Monrovia, Calif.: MARC (in production).

Bosch, David. 1991. *Transforming Mission: Paradigm Shifts in Theology of Mission.* Maryknoll, N.Y.: Orbis Books.

Bradshaw, Bruce. 1997. "Christian Witness and Transformational Development Workshop," developed for internal use by World Vision International.

————. 1993. *Bridging the Gap: Evangelism, Development, and Shalom.* Monrovia, Calif.: MARC.

Bragg, Wayne G. 1983/1987. "Beyond Development." In *The Church in Response to Human Need*, ed. Tom Sine. Monrovia, Calif.: MARC (1983). Also in Vinay Samuel et al. *The Church in Response to Human Need.* Grand Rapids, Mich.: William B. Eerdmans (1987).

Brueggemann, Walter. 1993a. *Biblical Perspectives on Evangelism: Living in a Three-Storied Universe.* Nashville, Tenn.: Abingdon Press.

————. 1993b. *Texts under Negotiation: The Bible and Post-Modern Imagination.* Minneapolis, Minn.: Fortress Press.

Brusco, Elizabeth. 1986. "The Household Basis of Evangelical Religion and the Transformation of Machismo in Colombia." Ph.D. thesis, City University of New York.

Center for International Development and Environment of the World Resources Institute. 1990. *Participatory Rural Appraisal Handbook: Conducting PRAs in Kenya.* Prepared jointly with the National Environment Secretariat of the Government of Kenya, Egerton University, and Clark University (February).

Chambers, Robert. 1997. *Whose Reality Counts? Putting the First Last.* London: Intermediate Technology Publications.

————. 1994. "The Poor and the Environment: Whose Reality Counts?" Working Paper 3. Brighton, UK: Institute of Development Studies, University of Sussex (May).

————. 1983. *Rural Development: Putting the Last First.* London: Longman Group.

Christian Children's Fund. 1996. "State of CCF's Children 1996: Annual Impact Monitoring and Evaluation Report." Richmond, Va.: Christian Children's Fund (July).

Christian, Jayakumar. 1998a. "A Different Way to Look at Poverty," *Body and Soul.* London: World Vision UK.

————. 1998b. "Reflections on Poverty and Transformation," lecture series for the WVI Board of Directors (March).

————. 1994. *Powerless of the Poor: Toward an Alternative Kingdom of God Based Paradigm of Response.* Ph.D. thesis. Fuller Theological Seminary, Pasadena, Calif.

Cookingham, Frank. 1998. "Ministry Standards Working Group: 1998 Guidelines for Field Testing." World Vision International internal working paper.

Cooperrider, David, Jim Ludema, Suresh Srivastva, and Craig Wishart. 1995. "Appreciative Inquiry: A Constructive Approach to Organizational Capacity Building." Workshop for World Vision Relief and Development. Department of Organizational Behavior, Wetherhead School of Management, Case Western Reserve, Cleveland, Ohio (May).

Cooperrider, David L., and Suresh Srivastva. 1987. "Appreciative Inquiry in Organizational Life," *Research in Organizational Change and Development* 1, 129-69.

Cray, Graham. 1997. "Communications Methods and the Contextualisation of the Gospel." Paper read at the Lausanne Contextualization Revisited Consultation, Haslev, Denmark (June).

Crittenden, R., and D. A. M. Lea. 1992. "The Logical Framework Approach: The Limitations of a Useful Tool in Project Planning and Management," *Yagl-Ambu Papua New Guinea Journal of the Social Sciences and Humanities* 16(4) (December).

Cromartie, Michael. 1995. *The 9 Lives of Population Control*. Grand Rapids, Mich.: William B. Eerdmans.

Curtis, Michael, ed. 1981. *The Great Political Theories*. New York: Avon Books.

D'Abreo, Desmond A. 1989. *From Development Worker to Activist: A Case Study in Participatory Training*. 2d edition. Mangalore, India: DEEDS.

Dearborn, Tim. 1997. *Beyond Duty: A Passion for Christ*. Monrovia, Calif.: MARC.

de Waal, Alex. 1997. *Famine Crisis: Politics and the Disaster Relief Industry in Africa*. Oxford, UK: James Curry.

Diamond, Jared. 1997. *Guns, Germs and Steel*. New York: Norton.

Dilulio, John, Jr. 1995. "The Coming of the Super-Predators," *The Weekly Standard* (November 27).

Donovan, Vincent J. 1978. *Christianity Rediscovered*. Chicago: Fides/Claretian.

Dulles, Avery. 1996. "Evangelizing Theology, *First Things* 61 (March): 27-32.

Dyrness, Andrea. 1998. "Seeds of Change: NGOs, The Church and Educational Reform in Central America." Report for the Strachan Foundation.

Dyrness, William A. 1997. *The Earth Is God's: A Theology of American Culture*. Maryknoll, N.Y.: Orbis Books.

Edwards, Michael. 1996. "New Approaches to Children and Development: Introduction and Overview," *Journal of International Development* 8(6): 813-27.

Elliot, Charles. 1987. *Comfortable Compassion? Poverty, Power and the Church*. London: Hodder and Stoughton.

———. 1985. *Praying the Kingdom: Towards a Political Spirituality*. London: Darton, Longman, and Todd.

Ellul, Jacques. 1967. *The Presence of the Kingdom*. New York: Seabury.

———. 1948. *The Presence of the Kingdom*, trans. Olive Wyon. New York: Seabury.

Erickson, Victoria Lee. 1996. "Neighborology: A Feminist Ethno-Missiological Celebration of Kosuke Koyama." In *The Agitated Mind of God*, ed. Dale T. Irvin and Akintude E. Akindade. Maryknoll, N.Y.: Orbis Books.

Famonure, Bayo. 1989. *Training to Die: A Manual on Discipleship*. Ibadan, Nigeria: Salem Media.

Feuerstein, Marie-Therese. 1986. *Partners in Evaluation: Evaluating Development Programming and Community Programmes with Participants*. London: Macmillan Publishers.

Figley, Charles, ed. 1995. *Compassion Fatigue: Coping with Secondary Traumatic Stress Disorder in Those Who Treat the Traumatized*. Philadelphia, Pa.: Brunner/Mazel.

Fowler, Alan. 1997. *Striking a Balance: A Guide to Enhancing the Effectiveness of Non-Governmental Organizations in International Development*. London: Earthscan Publications.

Friedman, John. 1992. *Empowerment: The Politics of Alternative Development*. Cambridge, Mass.: Blackwell.

Friere, Paulo. 1990. *Pedagogy of the Oppressed*. New York: Continuum Books.

Galilea, Segundo. 1984. *The Beatitudes: To Evangelize as Jesus Did*. Maryknoll, N.Y.: Orbis Books.

Gleick, James. 1987. *Chaos: Making a New Science*. New York: Viking.

Green, Thomas, S.J. 1979. *When the Well Runs Dry*. Notre Dame, Ind.: Ave Maria Press.

Gunton, Colin. 1997. "The Trinity, Natural Theology, and a Theology of Nature." In *The Trinity in a Pluralistic Society*, ed. Kevin J. Vanhoozer. Grand Rapids, Mich.: William B. Eerdmans.

Gutiérrez, Gustavo. 1984. *We Drink from Our Own Wells: The Spiritual Journey of a People*. Maryknoll, N.Y.: Orbis Books.

Hall, Douglas John. 1985. *The Stewardship of Life in the Kingdom of Death*. New York: Friendship Press.

Hiebert, Paul G. 1998. *Missiological Implications of Epistemological Shifts*. Valley Forge, Pa.: Trinity Press International.

———. 1982. "The Flaw of the Excluded Middle," *Missiology* 10(1): 35-47.

Hiebert, Paul G., Dan Shaw, and Tite Tienou. 1998. *Folk Religions: A Christian Response to Popular Religiosity*. Grand Rapids, Mich.: Baker Books.

Holland, Jeremy, with James Blackburn, eds. 1998. *Whose Voice? Participatory Research and Policy Change*. London: Intermediate Technology Publications.

Hope, Anne, and Sally Timmel. 1984. *Training for Transformation: A Handbook for Community Workers*. Harare, Zimbabwe: Mambo Press.

Jayakaran, Ravi. 1999. "Holistic Participatory Learning and Action: Seeing the Spiritual and Whose Reality Counts." In *Working with the Poor: New Insights and Learnings from Development Practitioners*, ed. Bryant Myers. Monrovia, Calif.: MARC (in production).

———. 1997. *Wholistic World View Analysis: Seeing Their World As They See It*. Madras, India: World Vision India.

———. 1996. *Participatory Learning and Action: User Guide and Manual*. Madras, India: World Vision India.

Jenson, Robert W. 1993. "How the World Lost Its Story," *First Things* (October).

Johnson, Richard Boyd. 1998. *World View and International Development: A Critical Study of the Idea of Progress in Development Work of World Vision Tanzania*. Ph.D. thesis, Oxford Centre for Mission Studies, Oxford, UK.

Johnson, Scott, and James D. Ludema. 1997. *Partnering to Build and Measure Organizational Capacity: Lessons from NGOs around the World*. Grand Rapids, Mich.: Christian Reformed World Relief Committee.

Jones, E. Stanley. 1972. *The Unchanging Person and the Unshakable Kingdom*. New York: Abingdon Press.

Kellert, Stephen H. 1993. *In the Wake of Chaos*. Chicago: University of Chicago Press.

Kleinman, Arthur, and Alex Cohen. 1997. "Psychiatry's Global Challenge," *Scientific American* (March).

Korten, David C. 1991. "Two Visions of Development." Overhead transparency from People-Centered Development Forum (April 23).

———. 1990. *Getting to the 21ˢᵗ Century: Voluntary Action and the Global Agenda*. West Hartford, Conn.: Kumarian Press.

Koyama, Kosuke. 1993. "'Extend Hospitality to Strangers'—A Missiology of Theologia Crucis," *International Review of Mission* 82, no. 327 (October).

———. 1985. *Mt. Fuji and Mt. Sinai: A Critique of Idols*. Maryknoll, N.Y.: Orbis Books.

———. 1979. *Three Mile An Hour God*. Maryknoll, N.Y.: Orbis Books.

———. 1974. *Waterbuffalo Theology*. London: SCM.

Kraybill, Donald B. 1978. *The Upside Down Kingdom*. Scottdale, Pa.: Herald Press.

Kreef, Peter. 1986. *Back to Virtue: Traditional Moral Wisdom for Modern Moral Confusion*. San Francisco, Calif.: Ignatius Press.

LaCugna, Catherine Mowry. 1991. *God for Us: The Trinity and Christian Life*. San Francisco: Harper Collins.

Lansing, J. Stephen. 1991. *Priests and Programmers: Technologies of Power in the Engineered Landscape of Bali*. Princeton, N.J.: Princeton University Press.

Leupp, Roderick T. 1996. *Knowing the Name of God*. Downers Grove, Ill.: InterVarsity Press.

Lewin, Roger. 1992. *Complexity: Life at the Edge of Chaos*. New York: Collier/MacMillan.

Linthicum, Robert C. 1991. *Empowering the Poor*. Monrovia, Calif.: MARC.

Luscombe, Ken. 1997. "Road to Hope Urban Project: Strategic Assessment." Evaluation report for World Vision Mauritania (August).

Macdonald, Mandy, ed. 1994. *Gender Planning in Development Agencies*. London: Oxfam.

Maggay, Melba. 1994. *Transforming Society*. London: Regnum.

Maldonado, Jorge E. 1993. "Evangelicalism and the Family in Latin America," *International Review of Mission* 82, no. 326 (April).

Marsden, David, and Peter Oakley, eds. 1990. *Evaluating Social Development Projects*. Oxford, UK: Oxfam.

McAlpine, Tom. 1995. *By Word, Work and Wonder*. Monrovia, Calif.: MARC.

McIlwain, Trevor. 1991. *Firm Foundations: Creation to Christ*. Sanford, Fla.: New Tribes Mission.

Middleton, J. Richard, and Brian J. Walsh. 1995. *Truth Is Stranger than It Used to Be*. London: SPCK.

Mills, C. Wright. 1993. "The Structure of Power in American Society." In *Power in Modern Societies*, ed. Marvin E. Olsen and Martin N. Marger. Boulder, Colo.: Westview Press.

Mitchell, J. T., and G. S. Everly. 1996. *Critical Incident Stress Debriefing: An Operations Manual for the Prevention of Stress among Emergency Services and Disaster Workers*. 2d edition, revised. Ellicot City, Md.: Chevron Publishing Company.

Motte, Mary. 1996. "In the Image of the Crucified God." In *The Agitated Mind of God*, ed. Dale T. Irvin and Akintude E. Akindade. Maryknoll, N.Y.: Orbis Books.

Mouw, Richard J. 1989. "Thinking about the Poor: What Evangelicals Can Learn from the Bishops." In *Prophetic Visions and Economic Realities: Protestants, Jews and Catholics Confront the Bishop's Letter on the Economy*, ed. Charles R. Strain. Grand Rapids, Mich.: William B. Eerdmans.

Muchena, Olivia. 1996. "Sociological and Anthropological Reflections." In *Serving the Poor in Africa*, ed. Tetsunao Yamamori et al. Monrovia, Calif.: MARC.

Murphy, Nancey. 1995. "Divine Action in the Natural Order: Buridian's Ass and Schroedinger's Cat." In *Chaos and Complexity: Scientific Perspectives on Divine Action*, ed. Robert Russell et al. Berkeley, Calif.: Center for Theology and the Natural Sciences.

Musopole, A. C. 1997. "African World View." Prepared for Changing the Story: Christian Witness and Transformational Development Consultation, World Vision, Pasadena, California (May 5-10).

Myers, Bryant L. 1998a. "We Are a Cursed People?" *MARC Newsletter* 98(1) (March).

———. 1998b. "What Makes Development Christian? Recovering from the Impact of Modernity," *Missiology* 26(2) (April): 143-53.

———. 1997. "Changing the Story: Christian Witness and Transformational Development." Notes from Changing the Story: Christian Witness and Transformational Development Consultation, World Vision, Pasadena, California (May 5-10).

———. 1994. "State of the World's Children," *International Bulletin of Missionary Research* 18(3) (July).

———. 1993. "What Message Did They Hear?" *MARC Newsletter* 93(4) (December).

———. 1992a. "Beyond Management by Objectives," *MARC Newsletter* 92(2) (June).

———. 1992b. "Provoking the Question," *MARC Newsletter* 92(1) (March).

Narayan, Deepa. 1993. "Participatory Evaluation: Tools for Managing Change in Water and Sanitation." World Bank Technical Paper, no. 207. Washington D.C.: The World Bank.

Natsios, Andrew S. 1997. *U.S Foreign Policy and the Four Horsemen of the Apocalypse*. Westport, Conn.: Praeger Publishers.

Newbigin, Lesslie. 1995. *Proper Confidence: Faith, Doubt and Certainty in Christian Discipleship*. Grand Rapids, Mich.: William B. Eerdmans.

———. 1989. *The Gospel in a Pluralist Society*. Geneva: WCC.

———. 1986. *Foolishness to the Greeks: The Gospel and Western Culture*. Grand Rapids, Mich.: William B. Eerdmans.

———. 1981. *Sign of the Kingdom*. Grand Rapids, Mich.: William B. Eerdmans.

———. 1954. *The Household of God*. New York: Friendship Press.

Oden, Thomas C. 1986. *Crisis Ministries*. New York: Crossroad.

Okorocha, Cyril. 1994. "The Meaning of Salvation: An African Perspective." In *Emerging Voices in Global Christian Theology*, ed. William A. Dyrness. Grand Rapids, Mich.: Zondervan.

O'Reilly, Siobhan. 1998. *The Contribution of Community Development to Peacebuilding: World Vision's Area Development Programs*. Milton Keynes, UK: World Vision UK.

Parker, Cristian. 1996. *Popular Religion and Modernization in Latin America: A Different Logic*. Maryknoll, N.Y.: Orbis Books.

Parkinson, F. 1997. *Critical Incident Debriefing: Understanding and Dealing with Trauma*. London: Souvenir Press Ltd.

Paz, Octavio. 1972. *The Other Mexico: Critique of the Pyramid*, trans. Lysander Kemp. New York: Grove Press.

Posterski, Don, and Gary Nelson. 1997. *Future Faith Churches: Reconnecting with the Power of the Gospel for the 21ˢᵗ Century*. Winfield, British Columbia: Wood Lake Books.

Postman, Neil. 1997. "Science and the Story that We Need," *First Things* (January).

Pretty, Jules N., Irene Guijt, John Thompson, and Ian Scoones. 1995. *Participatory Learning and Action: A Trainer's Guide*. London: International Institute for Environment and Development.

Robert, L. Dana. 1996. *American Women in Mission: A Social History of Their Thought and Practice*. Macon, Ga.: Macon University Press.

Rosenau, James N. 1990. *Turbulence and World Politics: A Theory of Change and Continuity*. Princeton, N.J.: Princeton University Press.

Samuel, Vinay. 1995. "A Theological Perspective." In *Serving the Poor in Asia*, ed. Tetsunao Yamamori et al. Monrovia, Calif.: MARC.

Sanneh, Lamin. 1987. "Christian Missions and the Western Guilt Complex," *The Christian Century* (April 8).

Save the Children. 1982. *Bridging the Gap: A Participatory Approach to Health and Nutrition Education*. Westport, Conn.: Save the Children.

Serageldin, Ismail. 1995. *Toward Sustainable Management of Water Resources*. Directions in Development series. Washington, D.C.: World Bank.

Shenk, Wilbert R. 1993. "The Whole Is Greater Than the Sum of the Parts: Moving beyond Word and Deed," *Missiology* 20 (January).

Slim, Hugo. 1997. "Doing the Right Thing: Relief Agencies, Moral Dilemma, and Moral Responsibility in Political Emergencies and War." *Studies on Emergencies and Disaster Relief*. Report no. 6. Uppsala: Nordiska Afrikainstitutet.

Stephens, Alexandra, and Kees Putman. 1990. *Participatory Monitoring and Evaluation: Handbook for Training Field Workers*. Bangkok, Thailand: Regional Office for Asia and the Pacific, RAPA, Food and Agriculture Organization of the United Nations.

Sugden, Christopher. 1997. *Seeking the Asian Face of Jesus: The Practice and Theology of Christian Social Witness in Indonesia and India 1974-1996*. Oxford, UK: Regnum.

Taylor, John V. 1972. *The Go-Between God: The Holy Spirit and Christian Mission*. London: SCM.

———. 1963. *The Primal Vision*. London: SCM.

Theis, Joachim. 1996. "Child-focused Development: An Introduction," SEAPRO Documentation Series. Save the Children (May). Westport, Conn.

Todd, Emmanuel. 1987. *The Causes of Progress: Culture, Authority, and Change*. Oxford, UK: Basil Blackwell.

UNDP. 1995. *Human Development Report 1995*. New York: Oxford University Press.

Uphoff, Norman. 1996. *Learning from Gal Oya: Possibilities for Participatory Development and Post-Newtonian Social Science*. London: Intermediate Technology Publications.

Uphoff, Norman T., J. M. Cohen, and A. A. Goldsmith. 1979. *Feasibility and Application of Rural Development Participation: A State of the Art Paper*. Ithaca, N.Y.: Cornell University, Rural Development Committee, Center for International Studies.

Urbach, Peter, and John Gibson, trans. and eds. 1994. *Francis Bacon: Novum Organum*. Chicago: Open Court Publishing.

van Geest, William. 1993. "The Relationship between Development and Other Religious Activities and Objectives." Presented at the Churches and Development Dialogue sponsored by Canadian International Development Assistance (CIDA). Toronto (June).

Volf, Miraslav. 1996. *Exclusion and Embrace: A Theological Exploration of Identity, Otherness, and Reconciliation*. Nashville, Tenn.: Abingdon Press.

Voorhies, Samuel J. 1996. "Community Participation and Holistic Development." In *Serving the Poor in Africa*, ed. Tetsunao Yamamori et al. Monrovia, Calif.: MARC.

Wallace, Tina, with Candida March, eds. 1991. *Changing Perceptions: Writings on Gender and Development*. Oxford, UK: Oxfam.

Walls, Andrew. 1996. *The Missionary Movement in Christian History: Studies in the Transmission of the Faith*. Maryknoll, N.Y.: Orbis Books.

———. 1989. "The Significance of Christianity in Africa," public lecture, St. Colm's Education Centre and College, May 21.

———. 1987. "The Old Age of the Missionary Movement," *International Review of Mission* 66 (January).

Warren, D. Michael, L. Jan Slikkerveer, and David Brokensha. 1995. *The Cultural Dimension of Development: Indigenous Knowledge Systems*. London: Intermediate Technology Publications.

Weaver, James H., Michael T. Rock, and Kenneth Kusterer. 1997. *Achieving Broad-Based Sustainable Development: Governance, Environment, and Growth with Equity*. West Hartford, Conn.: Kumarian Press.

Weber, Hans-Reudi. 1995. *The Book That Reads Me*. Geneva: WCC.

Whaites, Alan. 1996. "Let's Get Civil Society Straight: NGOs and Political Theory," *Development in Practice* 6(3) (August).

White, Lynn Jr. 1978. "The Medieval Roots of Modern Technology and Science." In *Medieval Religion and Technology: Collected Essays*. Berkeley, Calif.: Center for Medieval and Renaissance Studies.

Williams, Suzanne, and Adelina Mwau. 1994. *The Oxfam Gender Training Manual*. Oxford, UK: Oxfam.

Wink, Walter. 1992. *Engaging the Powers: Discernment and Resistance in a World of Domination*. Minneapolis, Minn.: Fortress Press.

Wolterstorff, Nicholas. 1983. *Until Justice and Peace Embrace*. Grand Rapids, Mich.: William B. Eerdmans.

World Vision India. 1995. "Record of PRA/PLA Walk through Exercise" (November).

Wright, Christopher J. H. 1983. *An Eye for an Eye: The Place of Old Testament Ethics Today*. Downers Grove, Ill.: InterVarsity Press.

Index